More Praise for *Leadership Conversations*

"*Leadership Conversations* is an excellent framework for executives to use worldwide in leadership training programs. It encourages grounded thinking around leadership and is a practical guide for developing leadership skills and discovering and forming one's authentic leadership style."

—Carol Roche Austin, head of human resources, Permira Advisors LLP

"*Leadership Conversations* is a practical and valuable book. The leadership and communication principles are presented in a clear manner that is relevant to leaders at all levels. The real-world insights will help readers be more effective leaders, driving high performance and success."

—Tom Mutryn, EVP and CFO, CACI International

"Cultivating leaders is key to the growth of any organization. *Leadership Conversations* translates years of experience into an easy-to-follow road map to help identify leaders and push them to reach their maximum potential."

—Ed Erhardt, president, global customer marketing and sales, ESPN

"Katerva's rapid rise to a world stage with its thought leadership in sustainability could not have happened without following the principles in this book. Leadership conversations are the key to creativity and can spur global innovation."

—Terry Waghorn, founder and CEO, Katerva

"With multi-national operational challenges, I need practical advice that I can implement quickly. *Leadership Conversations* delivers with examples and guidance on how to have effective conversations."

—Wesley J. Johnston, EVP and COO, Americas; Dimension Data

LEADERSHIP
CONVERSATIONS

LEADERSHIP
CONVERSATIONS

CHALLENGING HIGH-POTENTIAL
MANAGERS TO BECOME
GREAT LEADERS

ALAN S. BERSON
RICHARD G. STIEGLITZ

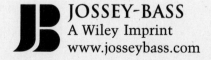

JOSSEY-BASS
A Wiley Imprint
www.josseybass.com

Published by Jossey-Bass

A Wiley Imprint

One Montgomery Street, Suite 1200, San Francisco, CA 94104–4594—www.josseybass.com

Jossey-Bass books and products are available through most bookstores. To contact Jossey-Bass directly call our Customer Care Department within the U.S. at 800–956–7739, outside the U.S. at 317–572–3986, or fax 317–572–4002.

Wiley publishes in a variety of print and electronic formats and by print-on-demand. Some material included with standard print versions of this book may not be included in e-books or in print-on-demand. If this book refers to media such as a CD or DVD that is not included in the version you purchased, you may download this material at **http://booksupport.wiley.com**. For more information about Wiley products, visit **www.wiley.com**.

Library of Congress Cataloging-in-Publication Data

Berson, Alan S.

Leadership conversations : challenging high-potential managers to become great leaders / Alan S. Berson, Richard G. Stieglitz. – 1st ed.

    p. cm.

Includes bibliographical references and index.

ISBN 978-1-118-37832-8 (cloth); ISBN 978-1-118-55188-2 (ebk.) – ISBN 978-1-118-55186-8 (ebk.) – ISBN 978-1-118-55187-5 (ebk.)

  1. Communication in management. 2. Leadership. 3. Executive ability.

I. Stieglitz, Richard G. II. Title.

  HD30.3.B476 2013

  658.4'092–dc23

  2012042025

Printed in the United States of America

FIRST EDITION

HB Printing 10 9 8 7 6 5 4 3 2 1

To all the teachers in our lives—family, friends, and colleagues

Contents

Preface
Are You Having Leadership Conversations?

Whether you are the high potential who receives the news or the executive who delivers it, everyone feels good when he hears or says, "Congratulations—we have an amazing new assignment for you. It's an opportunity to confirm that you are a rising star."

Exciting? Yes, but any new opportunity also entails new risks. Research consistently shows that nearly half of high-potential executives fail to reach their full potential. The fancy name for it is midcareer derailment. Considering that the derailment usually occurs within eighteen months of a major promotion, perhaps you should wait a while before uncorking the champagne. As the high potential who is being promoted or who is promoting others, you need to be prepared and clearheaded. But prepared for what? Armed with which skills and perspectives?

For starters, look at the subtle messages embedded in the typical statement that follows the promotion of a high-potential executive: "I have no doubt that you're up to this new challenge. But if you run into a problem, call my assistant, and he'll squeeze you into my calendar."

If you are on the delivery side of this conversation, your lack of active involvement is setting the high potential adrift to succeed or fail alone—you have not provided leadership. If you are on the listening side, we hope you realize that you should expect little assistance from your boss—which should scare you because, at a minimum, you need a conversation about expectations, your boss's and yours. If instead you take the statement as a sign of the boss's confidence that you can handle the new assignment simply by doing more of what you did in the past, then keep your resume up-to-date, because you may well find yourself among the half who are looking for another job within eighteen months.

HIGH POTENTIALS DON'T KNOW WHAT THEY DON'T KNOW

Most high potentials are derailed not by things they know they need to learn but rather by things they did not even realize had changed. What new challenges do you face when you climb the leadership ladder? How must you think differently? What new actions must you take? The answers to these questions are the difference between success and failure. What we want you to avoid hearing or saying is "Poor Dave, we thought he could handle more responsibility. But it looks like he just doesn't have what it takes to be a leader. His reputation may never recover from this disaster. That's unfortunate because we had high hopes for him."

As they rise in an organization, high-potential executives must integrate management and leadership skills in successively more accomplished ways. The new challenges require leadership conversation skills that few executives instinctively possess and that are only now beginning to be taught in the top MBA and executive training programs.

THE CHALLENGE OF MOVING UP

Each time a high potential is promoted, her job changes in fundamental ways; and if she fails, the hole into which she falls is deeper and the recovery more difficult. The hole is especially deep when she crosses the threshold from individual contributor to manager or from manager to leader, as she must basically change how she thinks and what she does to achieve the same success she enjoyed in the past. She also must accept that other people—her boss, role models, mentors, coaches, and team—are vital to her success.

High potentials who derail usually tell us they wish they could go back and do things the right way now that they have broader experience and deeper skills. This book is about succeeding the first time—helping you and the high potentials who work for you prepare for the future, rather than marching into it only partially equipped to succeed. Conversations that connect and align you with your people, your peers, and your bosses are the straightforward path to success.

LEADERSHIP CONVERSATIONS—THE BOOK

This book presents concepts and practical tools to show high potentials how to hold conversations that align followers with leaders. Most of the case studies we cite are taken from our business careers and our experiences in conducting executive education programs. All the case studies are real. However, we use fictitious names and alter or omit immaterial details because leadership conversations among rising high potentials are inherently sensitive, and we feel obligated to protect these individuals' identity and respect their privacy. So, except for publicly available information, we have not identified people or organizations by name in the case studies. Our intent is to focus on ideas and actions rather than on personalities and reputations.

The book is designed for high potentials who are looking to make the transition into top leadership roles, and for those looking to mentor and guide their rising stars. A high potential is any executive from first-line manager to CXO who has the desire and skill to advance. The book poses questions that

- Invite you to reflect on and enhance how you manage and lead today
- Challenge you to develop a vision for how you will manage and lead in the future
- Encourage you to assist other high potentials to do the same

The case studies in the book are about leaders in private industry, government, the military, nonprofits, and educational institutions. From a management and leadership viewpoint, these five sectors are becoming more and more alike. Executives frequently migrate among the sectors, and best management and leadership practices are freely exchanged via the Internet and social media.

When you receive a promotion or join a new organization, your direct reports, peers, and bosses will watch your every move. They will listen equally to what you say—and do not say—gleaning meaning from each interaction with you. Will they hear, feel, and do what you intend? How accurately and completely will you understand their goals and desires? How well will you stay in touch with the shifting demands of your market? The power of *Leadership Conversations* lies in showing you how to have conversations that answer these questions and inspire others to align with your vision and follow you as a leader. Achieving greatness will require you to conduct effective leadership conversations.

We have seen too many high potentials fail because they did not get the mentoring, coaching, and training necessary to succeed. We have also seen, as employees and consultants, organizations where executives defaulted to management activities when a leadership focus was appropriate—and not even recognize the difference. This book will prepare you to communicate effectively and think like a leader to produce results that propel you, your people, and your organization to greatness. Consciously engage in leadership conversations with those around you to incorporate this learning into your leadership persona.

MY LEADERSHIP CONVERSATIONS—THE WEBSITE

The companion website to this book, www.myleadershipconversations.com, enables you to personalize your reading experience and tailor it to specific situations and issues. On the website you will find a brief leadership assessment that will measure your leadership and management strengths and provide you with an individualized leadership profile. As you read this book, visit the website frequently to engage in conversations with leadership experts, with us, and with others who have high potential and are facing issues similar to yours. The website also provides social, community, coaching, mentoring, and implementation resources.

Consider sharing your leadership assessment results with a trusted adviser or some of your colleagues. They can assist you in interpreting your results relative to the specific needs of your industry and your unique professional growth path. Sharing your leadership journey with them will push you to continually reexamine how you show up as a leader, why you are getting your current results, and what your career goals might be, and to define your path to achieve them. In short, you will be pushed to engage in leadership conversations.

PART 1

THE HIGH-POTENTIAL CHALLENGES

Your challenge as a high-potential executive is to motivate people to pursue shared goals, even though their responsibilities vary widely. The image of an ideal leader has swung from the benevolent dictator in the Industrial Age to the servant leader in recent years. Yet those models merely flip-flop the dominant and supportive roles in the leader-follower relationship. When executives attempt to control rather than motivate people, or pander to them by abandoning their leadership prerogatives, they risk losing their people's respect and allegiance—if not actually losing them as employees.

The leadership conversations model shows you how to engage in effective conversations that create connection and alignment among leaders and followers. Everyone has valuable ideas and experiences that he or she is encouraged to contribute to the conversation. By expecting excellence from the mailroom to the executive suite, effective leaders tap into multiple viewpoints to achieve the organization's goals while concurrently assisting each person in progressing along his or her own professional path.

Part 1 describes the attributes of great leaders and asks you to consider if you really want to be a leader (Chapter 1); portrays differences between the management mindset and the leadership mindset and explains how to blend the two for maximum effectiveness (Chapter 2); introduces the four types and three perspectives of leadership conversations (Chapter 3); and defines the steps on the leadership ladder that we use to discuss the challenges inherent in rising from one organizational level to the next (Chapter 4).

CHAPTER 1

DO YOU REALLY WANT TO BE A LEADER?

*If your actions inspire others to dream more, to learn more, to do more,
and to become more, you are a leader.*
—JOHN QUINCY ADAMS

We challenge you to ask yourself, "Do I want to be a leader?" If your answer is yes, ask yourself a second question: "Am I willing to continually evolve who I am and what I do in order to lead others to achieve great things?"

We have often heard executives say that their jobs would be easy if they did not have to deal with people. You may have had one of those executives as a boss, in which case you know how uncomfortable it feels to work for them. We understand that building relationships and developing others are rarely easy. Yet successful managers and leaders see these roles as a vital and rewarding part of the job—not as a nuisance.

After each promotion, your job will be more complex, the scrutiny more severe, the consequences of failure greater, and the need to align and inspire people more intense. Furthermore, your success increasingly depends less on what you do and more on your vision of the future and how effectively you motivate others to achieve it. For those considering the journey from individual contributor into management, ask yourself the following questions before making a decision:

- Will I prefer management tasks to acting in the role of expert?
- Can I transition from receiving kudos to giving them?
- Will I enjoy the administrative tasks that managers must do?

- Am I willing to have my success depend on how well others perform?
- How effective will I be in working with a rainbow of personality styles?

For those currently in management who are considering the leap into leadership, remember that being an effective manager does not guarantee success as a leader. Leaders operate in an arena that has few boundaries. Many managers struggle when they move into a position where their options and responsibilities become virtually limitless. As a high potential, you will be well served to learn the essential skills at each level prior to jumping to the next, because learning skills and using them at the same time can be risky. To be a great leader, ask yourself:

- What are my motivations for being a leader?
- Will I receive satisfaction from developing the capabilities of my people?
- Can I provide vision and strategic direction to the organization?
- Is it important to me that my customers and suppliers succeed?
- Am I willing to consider new factors like social responsibility and globalization?

For some, leading in an increasingly complex world is second nature; for others, it is an overwhelming challenge. How will you hold up knowing that the professional survival of hundreds or potentially thousands of people depends on your vision, your strategies, and the relationships you build?

HOW GREAT LEADERS TREAT OTHERS

Simply put, leaders connect with people. The breadth and depth of those connections determine a leader's ability to influence; and the greater the influence, the greater the alignment and results. Great leaders

- Have a style and a voice that fit their organization and enable them to form bonds with their followers and ignite their passion.

- Beget great followers. Leaders learn their people's objectives and guide them toward achieving their full potential.
- Address small conflicts to avoid larger ones later. They know intuitively when things do not seem right, and promptly hold the conversations required to fix them.
- Know that creativity cannot be forced. They enable creativity in the natural flow of business by providing the time, the space, and the conditions for people to be creative—then they cultivate the fledgling sprouts of innovation.
- Celebrate their people. They are liberal with praise and realize that their personal success is rooted in their people's successes.

GREAT LEADERS COMMUNICATE EFFECTIVELY

In a world where time is precious, many executives have become tactical in their conversations instead of strategic, and problem focused rather than opportunity driven. They sometimes use technology to bypass the potential messiness of face-to-face communication and truncate conversations as soon as possible. Yet your job is to lead people and maximize an organization's success. The fact is, the more time you spend in up-front conversations, the less time you are likely to spend clarifying objectives and solving problems. Great leaders

- Cultivate a culture of possibilities and opportunities.
- Are open to what other people say. They are willing to change their minds and, by doing so, enable others to change and grow.
- Know that asking questions is an effective technique. Whereas managers usually answer questions, great leaders routinely ask them. They coach rather than command their people toward creativity and innovation.
- Build a culture of feedback that aligns people behind shared objectives and actions that proceed directly toward the desired result.
- Focus on what is right (rather than who is right) to defuse tension, reduce resistance, and produce better decisions.

GREAT LEADERS GROW THEIR PEOPLE

The business world does not reward high potentials for what they know; the rewards are based on the results they produce by motivating others. Great leaders are catalysts for getting things done—through others. They grow their people's skills, understand the objectives, and have a willingness to cooperate with each other. Great leaders

- Are learners. They acknowledge that they know only a portion of what needs to be known and consciously seek to learn from others before making a decision and galvanizing action.
- Foster learning in others. They gently push people out of their comfort zones, encourage them to acquire new skills, get them to connect and align with each other, and accept well-intentioned mistakes as learning opportunities.
- Look for the root causes (not symptoms) of a problem in order to take more effective actions and avoid unintended consequences.
- Embrace change. They know that world-class performance requires cutting-edge solutions. They tell others how a change might impact them, and maintain alignment by obtaining feedback early in the change cycle.
- Institutionalize learning in the culture. Great leaders know that by teaching others, they learn as well. They make learning an essential component of every conversation.

WHAT GREAT LEADERS BELIEVE

Like everyone else, executives make decisions based on their own beliefs. Although treating beliefs like facts can obstruct a conversation—especially when people are reluctant to allow their beliefs to be challenged—some beliefs support effective leadership. Great leaders believe that

- Good enough is not good enough. They know that if they accept mediocrity, they will seldom achieve more. Great leaders leverage the strengths of high potentials to push the organization to achieve excellence.

- Any problem can be reframed as an opportunity. Leaders who seek to solve problems tend to see everything as a problem. Great leaders look for opportunities and often find them in situations that others see as problems.
- They are personally responsible for every outcome. They take responsibility for a negative outcome rather than allocating blame. When a mistake is made, they discuss it, minimize the impacts, learn from it, and move on.
- Their actions speak louder than their words. Great leaders willingly live their values—they do not opportunistically modify or excuse themselves from them.
- Diversity and inclusion are essential to success. Great leaders do not hire diverse people and listen to their ideas just because it is politically correct. They do so to obtain different points of view that improve results.

The leadership traits listed in the previous four sections are based on simple concepts—but they are not always easy to follow. Once you have a clear philosophy and apply it consistently, it will become the core of who you are as a leader.

SAME PLAYING FIELD BUT A WHOLE NEW GAME—TWICE

When you move from individual contributor to manager, even in the same organization, everything changes. All the technical skills you learned and everything you have done to be successful up to this point in your career become less important. You actually could limit your success if you hold on to them too tightly. Your new management position includes such tasks as

- Parceling work, assigning it to others, and motivating them to complete it
- Setting goals and establishing schedules for others
- Accurately measuring the performance of others (as well as yourself)

- Resolving conflicts with and among others
- Giving feedback to others—even if it might be perceived as negative

Notice that the word "others" appears in all five tasks. Building relationships and developing others become more important than technical knowledge and skills. Your performance will be measured not by the quality and quantity of work you do but by the actions your team takes and the results they produce. Even if you are a world-leading expert in the area you manage, you must adapt your mindset and use a different set of skills to manage others and lead them to develop their technical expertise.

The shocker for many managers is that moving from management into leadership is a second transformational change. The things you will be expected to accomplish as a leader that are generally beyond what you did as a manager include

- Providing vision, direction, and inspiration to others
- Developing the management skills and emotional intelligence of others
- Reaching out to external stakeholders
- Assessing and responding to an ever-changing world

Conversations become more complex in leadership positions because they extend out to executives in your organization and other key stakeholders. Your focus will be on vision and strategy instead of tactics and schedules.

Success is far from automatic after a promotion because executives must employ a different mindset and use a blend of old and new skills. Surprisingly, most organizations offer support only after a new manager or leader delivers mediocre results or struggles to build the relationships essential for success— an unpleasant situation for everyone. Effective leadership conversations will help you avoid being the recipient or the deliverer of the difficult feedback that surrounds such career derailments.

When asked initially about his goals, Phil, an experienced project manager, said, "Ultimately, I want to own my own company because I like the freedom and perks that business owners enjoy. But I despise the conversations required to resolve conflict, build relationships, and negotiate with clients."

As an individual contributor, Phil received kudos from everyone and five-figure bonuses from the boss for resolving complex software issues in elegant ways. He often got product out the door ahead of schedule with little help. He was given the project management position when, after working around the clock to finish a large system for a major client, he insisted that the boss promote him.

Floundering and miserable from the start, Phil was two months behind and well over budget partway through an eighteen-month project. His staff's morale was low, and two of his people had quit. He claimed that the project was failing because his staff was incapable of following instructions. Frustrated, Phil finally realized, "It's not them—it's me who is getting in our way. My optimal position is not to lead or manage others. I was attracted by the prestige and financial benefits of a leadership position, but now I realize that my real satisfaction lies in the accolades of being the technical guru." Phil went back to serving the company well in that capacity.

For some of you high potentials, the best use of your abilities may be in a capacity other than leading people. For example, if your passion lies in being a technical expert, many organizations offer a career track for subject-matter experts that would tap into and develop your technical skills. Or you may decide that you want to be a leader, but not *the* leader. Others of you will settle for nothing less than the equivalent of CEO. The bottom line is that you have options and must make a choice.

Whether you choose to be a leader or not, determine the role you want before applying compensation and perks as a litmus test. Doing what you love is preferable to working unhappily just for more money. You will feel rewarded every day if you follow your passion. Instead of coming in the form of annual bonuses, your rewards may be simply doing what you love.

IT'S NEVER TOO LATE

It is your choice to be a great leader, a great manager, or a great individual contributor—and you could even change your decision today. Consider which of the following statements is most true of your long-term professional goals:

- Without doubt, my goal is to get promotion after promotion until I become the top leader. I am willing to do whatever it takes to reach that goal.
- I am content with my current position. I want to learn more about what is needed to be successful here, and then I may stretch for a promotion.
- I enjoy working in my current position, and, despite the perks and higher pay that would accompany a promotion, my choice is to continue in this position.

In making your choice, be honest about who you are; what skills and relationships you have; and your willingness to continually improve your management and leadership skills, increase the scope of your responsibilities, and work with a broad range of people and organizations. Throughout this book, we provide concepts, techniques, and case studies that will expand your leadership and management mindsets and challenge you to realize your full potential—at whatever level you choose.

CHAPTER 2

WHAT BLEND OF MANAGEMENT AND LEADERSHIP MINDSETS IS BEST?

Management is efficiency in climbing the ladder of success. Leadership determines
whether the ladder is leaning against the right wall.
—STEPHEN COVEY

L eadership and management mindsets are two sides of the same organizational coin. When you are operating in the management mindset, your
conversations focus on quantitative goals, deadlines, and measureable results.
Within the leadership mindset, the conversations focus on the future and how
people will grow. Combining both mindsets in appropriate ways and at appropriate times will produce top-notch results in your organization.

Figure 2.1 contrasts activities typical of executives operating in a management mindset with those typical of a leadership mindset. Most executives
regularly toggle between the two mindsets during a business day to produce
the results expected of their position. As you climb to positions of higher
responsibility, you will find yourself spending an increasingly higher percentage of your time operating in the leadership mindset, yet some activities in the
management mindset will still be necessary to achieve your objectives. This
chapter will guide you to consciously make the shift more easily and to hold
conversations that blend the two mindsets in a mix appropriate to your position and the situation at hand.

All of the management and leadership activities listed in Figure 2.1 are
essential for success, yet their focus is different. The management mindset
focuses on getting things done through others, whereas the leadership mindset considers future possibilities for the organization and its stakeholders

Management Mindset		Leadership Mindset
Tightly Knit Team	M..............................L	Large Stakeholder Group
Transactional Relationships	M..............................L	Trusted Relationships
Leveraging Resources	M..............................L	Leveraging People
Investing in Technology	M..............................L	Investing in Developing People
Objectives and Tactics	M..............................L	Global Vision and Strategy
Problem Oriented	M..............................L	Opportunity Driven
Clearly Defined Boundaries	M..............................L	Unlimited Possibilities
Executing the Agreed-on Plan	M..............................L	Introducing New Actions
Using Resources Efficiently	M..............................L	Creating Additional Resources
Making the Numbers	M..............................L	Focusing on the People

FIGURE 2.1. Management and Leadership Mindsets.
Where on each management-leadership continuum do you currently focus? Where should you be focusing?

and how to build the organization to achieve them. Your leadership mindset defines the objectives; your management mindset ensures that those objectives are met.

We have left the era when management and leadership were separate and unequal positions, when managers could operate in silos and concentrate only on tasks within their responsibility, leaving leaders to ponder the future and look horizontally across the organization. As a high-potential executive in today's world, you must instead consciously know when and how to shift from one mindset to the other to produce results that satisfy the responsibilities of your hierarchical position.

You need to make this shift whether you are in a business, government agency, nonprofit, educational institution, or the military. Only the specific weighting of each mindset varies depending on the type of organization, its mission, and its values. Regardless of your position, you are not either a leader or a manager—you are both a leader *and* a manager. You, and everyone around you, must blend the two mindsets appropriately in order to create a high-achieving organization and find the optimum balance between meeting current targets and pursuing future opportunities. The unique blend of the two mindsets that is suitable for your position will strongly influence the conversations you have with your people.

CONVERSATIONS MAKE THE DIFFERENCE

Executives use conversations to engage, connect, align, direct, and motivate people—but their results vary widely. For example, consider the conversations, strategies, rallying cries, and results of two well-known leaders who gave voice to inspiring visions: John F. Kennedy, president of the United States from 1960 to 1963, and Dr. Andrew von Eschenbach, director of the National Cancer Institute (NCI) within the National Institutes of Health (NIH) from 2001 to 2006.

After extensive conversations with cabinet members and technical experts, Kennedy felt confident in challenging Congress and the American people: "I believe this nation should commit itself to achieving the goal, before this decade is out, of landing a man on the moon and returning him safely to the earth. No single project in these times will be more impressive to mankind; and none will be so difficult or expensive to accomplish."

In the months prior to this call to action, Kennedy held conversations with his top advisers and the brightest scientists in the country, who cautioned him that the United States lacked the fuels, the materials, the engineering skills, and the budget for such a gargantuan project. His answer was, "Now we have a list of things to do. Let's get started! I'll get the money." In giving this famous speech, Kennedy met his commitment to obtain funding for the man-on-the-moon project and ignited the imagination of both young and old about future possibilities.

He also appointed Wernher von Braun, who designed German rockets during World War II, to organize what became the National Aeronautics and Space Administration (NASA). The organization was deluged with applicants for virtually every position; its pivotal interview question was, "Do you believe we can land a man on the moon and return him safely in this decade?" Any applicant who hesitated in answering yes was dismissed. The conversations focused on how—not if—the goal would be achieved. Based on the clear vision broadcast by Kennedy, the interviews were an effective early use of the management mindset. The NASA team became opportunity driven rather than problem focused.

Dr. von Eschenbach approached his grand vision differently. He had a distinguished career in oncology as president of the American Cancer Society, prior to being appointed in 2001 as NIH-NCI's director. In 2003, in the "Annual Report to the Nation on the Status of Cancer, 1975–2000," coauthored by the NCI and the Centers for Disease Control and Prevention, von Eschenbach surprised most NIH-NCI scientists by challenging them to erase the suffering and death caused by cancer—and to do so by the year 2015. He said, "One of every two men and one of every three women during their lifetime will hear the words: 'You have cancer.' One American every minute is dying from this disease. It is an old and enormous problem. But I want to talk less about the old problem and more about fresh thinking."

His vision was vigorously supported by Congress and the American Association for Cancer Research. At the time, NIH-NCI was a thirty-year-old organization with a proud history of success. After receiving the challenge, NCI physicians and scientists, in private conversations among themselves, focused almost exclusively on the difficulty of achieving the goal and on their concern about the false hope it might engender in the public. They wondered why such a proclamation was needed and were alarmed that it might divert resources from ongoing programs. They felt neither a connection with von Eschenbach nor an alignment with his vision.

EFFECTIVE CONVERSATIONS CREATE ALIGNMENT

Both leaders promoted a clear vision of the future and set arguably clear long-term goals. Let us consider from several leadership and management perspectives the events that followed and the results that were achieved.

First, the goal Kennedy set, though difficult and challenging, had well-defined success criteria that stimulated creativity and passion. The ensuing conversations focused on building a team to achieve the goal based on the clear vision of landing a man on the moon and returning him safely to earth. Further, once that goal was achieved, the technologies and strategies could be applied to exciting future projects. In contrast, the goal von Eschenbach set was open to interpretation. Did he mean no one would ever die of cancer? Did he include all types of cancer? Should people focus their research on cure or prevention? Therefore, conversations among NCI oncologists and scientists questioned whether the goal was achievable, as there were so many strains of cancer, and were concerned that an approach that worked for one cancer might not work with others.

A second pivotal difference was in how the leaders built relationships. Kennedy had the stronger power base on which to build relationships, yet von Eschenbach arguably had a more noble cause. Kennedy's conversations stimulated focus and enthusiasm in his followers, and he cemented their commitment by delivering on his promise to get money from Congress for NASA. In contrast, von Eschenbach's conversations were ineffective in dealing with his followers' doubts and dissention. He left uncomfortable questions unanswered—even basic strategic questions—which caused experienced researchers to fear failure rather than to focus on success.

A third difference had to do with the early decisions made on each project. For example, Kennedy appointed von Braun to lead the mission because of his proven rocketry expertise; von Eschenbach made no analogous appointment. The criteria von Braun used to select NASA employees produced a staff that saw challenge as an exciting adventure rather than as a mountain to climb. Conversely, von Eschenbach did not provide a strategy that was in synch with NCI's culture and ongoing projects and that would mobilize its extensive expertise and resources toward achieving the new goal.

In the end, of course, the actions these leaders initiated produced very different results. NASA landed men on the moon and returned them safely in 1969, six years after Kennedy's death in 1963; cancer remains a major health threat to this day. Kennedy blended the leadership and management mindsets effectively to produce an extraordinary result, whereas von Eschenbach and his key people operated primarily in a management mindset. He focused on the goal rather than on motivating people to achieve it. Von Eschenbach's results are typical of well-meaning high-potential executives who are not effective at blending conversations in the management and leadership mindsets to achieve the desired results.

YOUR GENERATION INFLUENCES YOUR MINDSET

One challenge facing most organizations in the United States and many abroad is generational mindset biases. The top executives we speak with—most of them from the baby-boom generation—often complain about the work ethics of Generations X, Y, and Z. They are concerned about the inability of older executives to work effectively with high-potential younger employees. (As an indicator of which generational group you are in, ask yourself whether you take a new electronic product out of the box and start using it, or whether you read the instruction manual first. Older generations expect the instructions to be extensive and clear; younger generations feel that if a product needs directions, then it is not well designed.)

The top executives ask the same question of both groups: "What are you thinking—why can't you connect and align with each other?" Baby boomers describe the younger generations as spending too much time socializing and being creative (the leadership mindset) and not being willing to work hard to get today's job done (the management mindset). One baby boomer executive bemoaned, "How can they expect to get ahead without paying their dues and learning the fine points of their jobs? They won't be ready for a promotion until they work the way we always have. They just don't understand how the system works." For example, in some high-powered accounting, engineering, and law firms, the younger generations are reluctant to work long hours the way the older executives did to get ahead, and that endangers the business model of using high billing hours from junior associates to support the salaries of seasoned partners.

At the same time, younger workers complain about their bosses' unwavering focus on getting the job done, about how long it takes to move up the leadership ladder, and about their lack of participation in strategic conversations and decisions. They say heatedly, "At companies like Facebook and Google, my contemporaries are included in strategic conversations, and promotions happen faster than here. I shouldn't have to wait three years to get promoted just because that's how long it took my boss and his boss. The world moves faster today—my organization is lagging."

The two generational groups rarely have productive conversations with each other because they are approaching the discussions from conflicting mindsets. As a high-potential executive, you must bridge these points of view—get each group to look at the issue from the other's mindset as well as from its own. Previous generations faced this problem too, but it is more intense today because communications across global markets are significantly faster and easier for everyone.

HARNESSING GENERATIONAL MINDSET DIFFERENCES

Unlike baby boomers, today's high potentials grew up in a connected world saturated with information. Arguably, the younger generations spend more time making connections than completing work. Because the focus on people comes more naturally to them, they tend to be more comfortable operating in the leadership mindset than in a get-it-done management mindset. Conversely, baby boomer executives often have a laserlike focus on producing results and making the numbers. Of course, both mindsets are essential for success, so each group must leave room for the other to express itself. The most ineffective thing either group can do is to demotivate the other by ignoring or minimizing its leadership or management tendencies.

Marcelo, who became a division president in a public company after thirty-plus years with the firm, told us about his experience: "During a meeting, one of my young high potentials—who had been invited to observe the discussion—blurted out an idea during especially tense negotiations with a strategic supplier. At first I was angry because his participation was unexpected and, frankly, unwanted. I felt like firing him. Yet the supplier loved the idea, and it broke the logjam. Later, I realized that his idea was both creative and apropos. It enabled us to complete the negotiations and nail down a win-win long-term contract. I promoted him instead."

The world Marcelo had grown up in was quite different—concealing information was a way to demonstrate power. Beginning as an apprentice, he copied the methods senior workers used to get ahead, and managed just as his bosses had managed. Creativity was somebody else's job—someone high up in the company hierarchy. Even though that approach had produced success for Marcelo, the meeting with the strategic supplier changed his thinking: "Now, before every critical meeting with stakeholders, I hold a brainstorming conversation with key executives and high potentials from several areas of the organization. I challenge everyone to leverage one another's experience and knowledge to come up with the next great idea. This bridges generational gaps and breaks down silos."

Another complaint we occasionally hear about the younger generations has to do with their strong sense of entitlement. They grew up in a system that awarded trophies for playing a sport rather than for winning a championship. They earned a degree, so the world now owes them a living. This issue, though common, seems to play out more at the individual level than as a true generational trait.

For example, Joyce is an executive who has two adult sons, each of whom is on a different end of the entitlement spectrum. She told us about them: "My husband and I were downsizing, so we asked our sons to take away as much of their childhood things as they could from our old house. One took only two trophies; they were from tournaments where his team was the league champion and he made significant contributions to their victories. He threw away scores of awards that he called 'showing-up trophies.' Our other son insisted on keeping every award he had ever received and asked us to continue storing them for him."

She considers those behaviors when she hires new employees and has conversations with her high potentials. Like Joyce, you must be aware of your generational bias toward either the management or leadership mindset, and harness that bias in your hiring and promotion decisions and in your leadership conversations.

CHAPTER 3

HAVE YOU HAD LEADERSHIP CONVERSATIONS TODAY?

The single biggest problem in communication is the illusion that it has taken place.
—GEORGE BERNARD SHAW

You speak with bosses, peers, direct reports, and other stakeholders nearly every business day, but are they effective conversations that blend the leadership and management mindsets appropriately? Conversations in the leadership mindset build respect and trust, encourage bidirectional feedback, create learning experiences, and elicit the best from everyone, including you. Those in the management mindset involve processing information, evaluating alternatives, completing tasks, and meeting deadlines. Together, the conversations create alignment, inspire innovation, mobilize change, and produce superior short- and long-term results.

A VIRTUOUS CYCLE OF LEADERSHIP CONVERSATIONS

There are four types of leadership conversations:

- **Building relationships** that enhance decision making and coordinate action
- **Developing others** in a manner that achieves and perpetuates success
- **Making decisions** that are understood, supported, and executable
- **Taking action** to produce the desired results in a timely manner

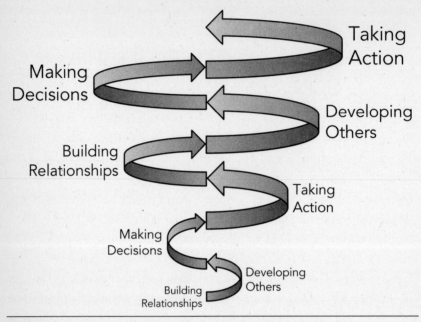

FIGURE 3.1. Leadership Conversations Create a Virtuous Cycle.
Effective leadership conversations produce an upward spiral in performance.

Figure 3.1 shows that each leadership conversation increases the power of the next in a virtuous cycle. Building relationships and developing others produce better decisions and more effective actions. Successful actions in turn strengthen relationships, and the cycle continues, building an increasingly stronger enterprise. Taken together, the four types of conversations are a foundation for leading and managing through complexity and change. An executive who lacks proficiency in or ignores any of the four is likely to experience inferior results.

Leadership Conversations to Build Relationships

Leaders build relationships that attract, motivate, and inspire followers. How well do you know the desires and abilities of each of your people? How closely do those desires and abilities align with your organization's goals? How regularly do you provide useful feedback? Would any of your people leave if they received an enticing job offer? People, and your relationships with them, count. If that understanding is not in your DNA, reconsider your desire to become a leader.

For example, Martin received survey feedback that was much lower than before—his people were in revolt. As second in command of a large office in a services firm, he had advanced rapidly and was heir apparent to the senior partner, who planned to retire soon. Martin wanted that job, but the new feedback jeopardized his chances. Considering that Martin had built productive relationships in the past, it was not clear why he was experiencing this problem, so his boss provided an external coach. Early in the first session, the coach asked Martin, "What is your job?" He responded by itemizing the professional services that his staff provided to clients.

The coach continued to prod: "What else?" Martin detailed additional issues his staff resolved and the regulatory filings they prepared. The coach listened silently until Martin blurted out, "Do you mean mentoring and training those ungrateful kids who leave after we teach them everything? If I have to continue doing that, I may shoot myself!" The coach looked on as Martin whispered, "Did I just say what I think I said?" Yes, he had. He was operating in a management mindset entirely focused on project results rather than on building relationships with his people. That mindset did not align with his position, let alone with the promotion he wanted. Martin understood: he could change his attitude and rebuild relationships with his people, or give in to his resentment and potentially lose his job. After bringing significantly more of the leadership mindset into conversations, Martin and several of his people continued to rise as high potentials.

Effective relationship-building conversations are essential to enable you and your people to connect and align to produce superior results. Part 2 of this book provides tools and techniques for building relationships by learning the new rules, knowing your strengths and shadows, fostering a relationship culture, and embracing differences.

Leadership Conversations to Develop Others

Once you choose to be a leader, you inherit the responsibility to develop your people—to have conversations that encourage them to stretch and that address new possibilities. If you focus only on today's management tasks and this year's goals, you limit your success as a leader and possibly jeopardize the future of the organization. Furthermore, the lack of developmental conversations and stretch assignments could drive away your high potentials, leaving you with those who only do exactly what you tell them. Your job as a leader is to provide the environment and the resources for your people to meet their career goals and increase the organization's capability. After all, is that not what you also expect from your boss?

If you think you control your organization, you need only consider earthquakes and tsunamis that disrupt commerce, volcanic eruptions that interrupt travel plans, and renegade employees who take irrational actions for you to see how important developing others is to your success. When you develop people, you must anticipate both the unexpected and the more predictable industry-wide and company-specific upheavals. When you hold open conversations about progress, opportunities, and problems, your people will learn and grow rapidly—and so will you.

Developing others cultivates people who are more capable of assisting you in building productive relationships, making better decisions, and taking effective actions. Part 3 provides techniques and tools to meet the challenge of developing other high potentials, filling the succession pipeline, providing actionable feedback, and celebrating success, all of which enable you and your organization to win the battle for talent.

Leadership Conversations to Make Decisions

What would your organization's future look like if you made decisions by throwing darts at a dartboard or reading a deck of tarot cards? What would your results be if you did not research critical issues or ignored key facts? What roadblocks would you encounter if you failed to consider relationships and personalities in your decisions? How effective can your decisions be if they are made without engaging the knowledge and experience of the high potentials in your organization? Decisions are the knives that whittle a universe of possibilities into future potential.

The IT division of a company that delivers its product electronically held a strategic workshop. It was late January, and they had not set goals for the year; their decision-making process was broken. The group split into teams to explore ways to get back on track. When Helmut, the division head, received their feedback, he paled. He thought that everyone agreed with his approach to upgrade the architecture, but instead found that the team had stopped talking to him. They detached from his decisions—and from him. To make matters worse, his decisions had become increasingly flawed because they were based on incomplete data, due to the lack of useful feedback during decision-making conversations.

The architecture redesign project was in danger of failing, and everyone's job was at stake. The next day, Helmut offered to resign. But the other division heads told him that he was still the best person to lead the effort and that they were willing to give him another chance. Without the blunt feedback, the technology upgrade could have failed, resulting in mass firings. Instead, Helmut reengaged with his team to review earlier decisions, listened attentively to their feedback and suggestions, and modified the direction of the redesign project. With the feedback and decision-making processes back on track, they transitioned successfully to the new architecture on schedule later in the year.

You employ the management mindset to make decisions based on numbers and facts, whereas you use the leadership mindset to consider the people who will participate in making and executing the decision. When you blend these mindsets properly, you can make decisions with confidence that the people will perform and the numbers will work. Part 4 looks at how to develop the judgment gene, become curious, ask great questions, and find the third alternative—the one that exceeds everyone's expectations.

Leadership Conversations to Take Action

In today's always-connected, instant-information digital world, you rarely need more data—you need more effective action. A never-ending search for more information is often a sign of being stuck in the management mindset. Do not wait for the perfect time to start—respond now to the changes you sense around you. Take one small action and follow it with another in order to avoid analysis-paralysis. Do not let an opportunity evaporate while you search for the perfect solution—because it usually does not exist. What appears to be an ideal approach today might be less than ideal if you wait too long to implement it.

Some of our case studies do not have a happy ending; this is one. High-potential executives from four government agencies held a planning workshop to determine how they could work together more effectively. They moved decisively through the process of defining performance gaps and identifying areas to improve. They selected nine new initiatives and prioritized them based on cost, risk, and return on investment. But when it came to allocating staff and funding, the process came to a screeching halt. The agencies did not have sufficient resources available to begin even the highest-priority initiative.

The facilitator asked the executives, "What will you stop doing in order to begin the new initiatives?" They could not agree on ways to free up resources, so they compromised by adding the initiatives to the following year's budget request. Predictably, Congress not only did not approve the budget increase but actually cut funding from the previous year's level. The nine innovative and strategically relevant initiatives were never implemented.

Ending or curtailing old actions is as important as starting new ones, yet it is often more difficult. When you are considering a new start, quantify the time, the people, and the other resources that will be required. Do the same for activities you plan to stop. Because it is unlikely that you will have more time or resources in the future, the amount you save from activities you stop must at least equal what you need for the new starts.

By using conversations that align and motivate people, effective leaders tear down barriers that interfere with putting decisions into action. Planning conversations set expectations; feedback conversations compare in-process results to the plan in order to fine-tune the next actions. Part 5 provides tools and techniques that produce organizational and personal success through strategic planning, managing change, inspiring people, and learning from successes as well as failures.

THREE PERSPECTIVES IN LEADERSHIP CONVERSATIONS

Figure 3.2 shows that conversations can be conducted from three perspectives. The most effective leadership conversations touch all three in a way that fosters innovation and breeds trust and respect:

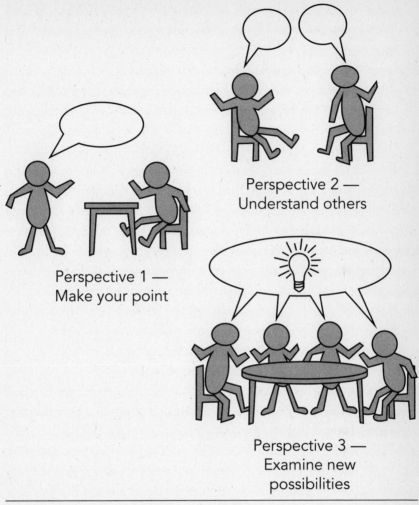

FIGURE 3.2. Three Conversation Perspectives.
The most productive leadership conversations employ all three perspectives.

Perspective 1: idea exchange. Each person conveys his ideas to the others. The criteria for success in idea exchanges are that each person states his position and intentions clearly and presents new ideas and pertinent facts for others to consider.

Perspective 2: understanding what others say. Each person seeks to understand the points that others are making, as well as the context and emotions behind their words. Operating in this perspective, people ask probing questions of each other. When done well, everyone feels heard and understood.

Perspective 3: exploring possibilities. Participants explore the what-else or what-is-missing aspects of the topic by looking at a bigger picture. Conversations held in this perspective frequently combine ideas from several individuals in bold, innovative, and strategically valuable ways.

Few people routinely engage all three perspectives in their conversations; the ability to employ all three is a mark of a great leader. The order in which the three perspectives are addressed varies. For example, a visioning conversation held in the leadership mindset might begin in the third perspective, move to the second to explore ideas, and conclude with the leader communicating decisions in the first perspective. Conversations held in the management mindset often remain in the first and second perspectives. They focus on what each person must do to get the job done because boundaries on the possibilities are already established and are not open to debate.

Which perspective is the most important? It depends on your objective. If you must quickly win a point in the management mindset, focus on the first perspective (yours) by conducting a monologue that convinces others— commonly called a "pep talk." Curious people naturally focus on the second perspective because they want to learn as much possible. But beware: these same people are sometimes reluctant to voice their own views. Visionary leaders who consistently extend boundaries often have conversations in the third perspective and instinctively tap into the experience and knowledge of their people by using the second perspective. In general, the most stimulating conversations occur in the third perspective. Learning happens in all three.

BLENDING TWO MINDSETS, FOUR TYPES OF CONVERSATION, AND THREE PERSPECTIVES

At any given moment, a leadership conversation may involve one of twenty-four distinct yet equally useful combinations of the two mindsets, four conversation types, and three perspectives. Consciously choose the mindset, type, and perspective appropriate for the situation, and shift to another combination to propel the conversation in the direction it needs to go. Conversely, recognize when one of your people shifts the conversation to another combination; that shift reveals the individual's thinking about the matter at hand and is valuable information to a leader.

Executives who primarily operate in the management mindset (getting things done) reduce potential conversations with their people (and the possible results) by up to 50 percent. Similarly, executives with a command-and-control style frequently ignore the third perspective (additional possibilities), thus narrowing their potential conversations by one-third. Furthermore, those who do not consciously develop their people reduce the content of their conversations by one-fourth. If an executive did all three of these, she would engage in only six of the possible twenty-four conversations required to be a great leader.

STANDARDS FOR LEADERSHIP CONVERSATIONS

Effective leadership conversations (1) ensure that everyone shares the same information and understanding of the goals, (2) mitigate cultural and other differences that block innovation, and (3) produce agreement to work in unison toward the agreed-on result. Effective conversations are dialogues—not monologues—and end with a conclusion that satisfies individual and organizational needs. The organization wins in effective conversations, and every participant shares in the success. Conduct conversations that are direct, open, honest, and caring:

- **Direct.** You discuss alternatives with people who hold views different from yours and avoid sidebars with those who are sympathetic to your position.
- **Open.** You are willing to change your mind, but are not required to do so. Most executives are adept at convincing others. But to promote

innovation and create unity, you must also give others the opportunity to influence you.

- **Honest.** You are transparent about your objectives and do not have a hidden agenda. You do not pull rank, leave out key details, or exaggerate.
- **Caring.** The conversation yields results that meet your needs and the needs of others. Use an optimistic and empathetic voice and avoid body language and tones that feel like an attack or denigrate the ideas of others.

Whenever possible, prepare for your leadership conversations in advance. Clarify in your mind the context of the conversation, your goals for its outcome, and the learning objectives. Map out the conversation in terms of the twenty-four combinations of mindset, perspective, and type—where do you intend to start and finish? You may want to obtain inputs from those who cannot be present during the conversation. Be sensitive to what others want from the conversation too—their desired outcomes may be different from what you assume them to be.

To avoid speaking at each other rather than with each other, ensure that you are in the proper frame of mind for the conversation and ascertain that others are as well. If the conversation gets heated, you may want to suggest a cooling-off period. If it gets emotional, ask the group what is needed to defuse the emotion. At the end of each conversation, validate a common understanding of the conclusions and schedule follow-on conversations if necessary. Consider your conversation successful if, after you and the other participants process the outcomes, everyone has made her points clearly, had her questions answered, and is in alignment regarding the course of action to be taken and her role in that approach. Apply these criteria to your next leadership conversation.

CHAPTER 4

WHERE DO YOU STAND ON THE LEADERSHIP LADDER?

*As you become more clear about who you really are, you'll be better
able to decide what is best for you—the first time around.*
—OPRAH WINFREY

The definition of "high potential" varies from organization to organization, yet high potentials are universally expected to outperform others at the same level. Thus, as a high potential, you probably have been given challenging and important assignments. In that high-risk, high-reward environment, it is crucial to have conversations to learn what is expected of you and to be sure that the high potentials who work for you know what you expect of them.

We once toured a castle in France built in the Dark Ages when lawlessness was rampant. No castle lord could trust the others, yet no one lord could repel an invasion on his own—a life-or-death issue. The most striking feature about the castle was its seven distinct areas inside the outer wall, each separated from the others by a drawbridge. When there was no risk of attack, the lords lifted the drawbridges and lived independently. When danger, such as a Viking invasion, was imminent, they lowered the bridges and fought together. There is a parallel between the lords of the Dark Ages and executives in many of today's organizations: they work together in crisis but operate in silos when pursuing day-to-day objectives.

Even in the twenty-first century, differences remain between the roles of managers and leaders and how their success is measured. As you reflect on your conversations, think about whether you possess the skills required for your current position and whether you are encouraging your people to develop the skills they need for their positions; if not, change your conversations. Plan how you will prepare yourself and your people for the next promotion. To facilitate discussions in this book, we have divided managers and leaders into four categories according to their skills and maturity level:

1. **First-line managers** supervise others to provide essential services or to direct team projects. They accept responsibility to accomplish more than they can do alone and to work closely with and guide others. The key lesson that a first-line manager must learn is that his role in each of the four conversations is truly different than it was when he was an individual contributor.

2. **Managers of managers** are often considered the go-to people for getting things done. Their jobs are no longer technical. Rather, they are a nearly equal blend of management and leadership. They must build their people skills in order to select and grow first-line managers. Their challenge is building relationships with peers, and they must be proficient in all four leadership conversations.

3. **Executive leaders** have operational and organizational responsibilities that require them to balance their individual goals with organizational objectives. They convert the organization's vision into an executable strategy, which requires a unique blend of management and leadership skills. Executive leaders become students of best practices, build strategic partnerships and external relationships, are innovative in planning the future, and coach their high potentials effectively.

4. **CXO leaders** know the value of relationships in making decisions and taking action. They create a compelling vision for the organization and engage internal and external resources to bring the vision to life. A CXO must focus on developing others—especially if she covets the CEO position—because her team's collective success will define her success and her reputation.

Figure 4.1 summarizes the maturity levels through which high potentials evolve as they grow from first-line manager to CXO leader. Look at the

	First-Line Manager	Manager of Managers	Executive Leader	CXO Leader
Building Relationships	Learns the value of relationships and how to use them	Learns to manage across as well as up and down	Includes other industry leaders in network	Engages broad network of strategic partners
Developing Others	Develops the technical skills of his or her people	Learns to coach first-line managers and direct reports	Coaches and mentors others as an essential task	Builds culture to develop people at all levels
Making Decisions	Considers resources to be a constraint	Engages team in decisions and in securing resources	Uses best practices and is open to mentoring	Makes decisions based on the vision and the strategic plan
Taking Action	Directs people to complete specific tasks	Coordinates across teams to achieve larger goals	Converts vision into strategy	Empowers the enterprise to succeed

FIGURE 4.1. Maturity Levels for Managers and Leaders.

Consider the maturity expected at your level and the next higher level during each leadership conversation.

attributes in the Building Relationships row and circle the one that best describes you today. Do the same for the Developing Others, Making Decisions, and Taking Action rows. Do not be surprised if you put yourself in a column different from your position. If you are like most people, your leadership skills will vary, so it is important for you to identify your unique strengths and potential blind spots.

Next, ask others at work to evaluate your performance in each of the four conversation types and compare their feedback to your self-evaluation. Any row where their response differs from yours represents fertile material for a conversation that will align your collective viewpoints and possibly give you a few things to change in order to realize your full potential.

In today's fluid workforce, some managers and leaders have come full circle and returned late in their careers to individual contributor status as board members, consultants, and professional coaches. From experience, they know that the answers to leadership questions are not static and must be reexamined each time an executive is promoted, when organizations increase in size by 50 percent or more, when a game-changing technology emerges, and when market demands shift. The need for effective conversations is never ending because answers that worked last year may not work today. These grey-bearded individual contributors have been learners for decades. They have absorbed leadership lessons from successes as well as mistakes and have become experts in blending the management and leadership mindsets to suit evolving situations and higher positions.

TEN WAYS TO PRACTICE GREAT LEADERSHIP IN EFFECTIVE CONVERSATIONS

1. **Know your people.** What are the professional goals and personal priorities of your high potentials? If you do not know them, what does that tell you? Leaders connect and align with people; the greater the alignment, the better the results.
2. **Invest in people.** Leaders invest in growing their people's skills, aligning their goals, and encouraging them to cooperate. The more time you invest in up-front conversations, the less time you are likely to spend later to resolve problems.
3. **Balance your conversations.** Are you spending sufficient time in conversations with your high potentials—balancing the need to explore alternatives, develop a plan, take action, assess results, and provide feedback?
4. **Use both mindsets.** Regardless of your position, you must both lead and manage in order to create a high-achieving organization. What blend of the two mindsets is appropriate for your current position and current challenges?
5. **Hold all four conversations.** During the past week, did conversations with your people build relationships, develop others, make decisions, and take action? Which, if any, of the four was missing? Consider emphasizing that type in the coming week.
6. **Use all three conversational perspectives.** Recall a meeting that addressed a strategic topic. Did each participant have an opportunity to express her views, ask questions about others' views, and explore additional possibilities? If not, which perspective dominated, and which was absent? How did that limit the outcome?

7. **Set priorities.** Are priorities for your organization clear and concise? Could your team accomplish more if it had fewer priorities? Have you held a conversation with each of your people to discuss what constitutes "doing a good job"?

8. **Avoid unnecessary conflict.** Depersonalize your next difficult conversation by focusing on *what is right* rather than *who is right*.

9. **Mentor and coach.** High-performing organizations provide mentoring, coaching, and training for new managers and leaders because they know how difficult the transition can be. Did you receive such assistance following your last promotion? What assistance have you been providing to the high potentials on your team?

10. **Set expectations.** Ask your boss what traits are most important for high potentials who want to advance in your organization. Be sure that your high potentials also know what is expected of them.

PART 2

CONVERSATIONS TO BUILD RELATIONSHIPS

Relationships enable leaders to develop others, make great decisions, and take powerful actions. They are an essential ingredient in effective leadership conversations and the catalyst for achieving orders of magnitude more than you could alone. The ability to continually strengthen existing relationships, build new ones, and blend relationships into strong teams is fundamental to success.

Building relationships is not a task on a to-do list that you attend to from time to time. Rather it is something you need to do well—consciously and unconsciously—every minute of every day. Conversations with your bosses, peers, direct reports, and other stakeholders are the lifeblood of your business relationships.

Part 2 opens by describing the new rules for leadership success (Chapter 5) and explaining how your relationships define you (Chapter 6). Then it points out that your strengths can at times have a shadow side that inhibits the clarity of your thinking and the durability of your relationships (Chapter 7). Next it encourages you to focus on people as individuals (Chapter 8) and extols listening, transparency, and authenticity as attributes of effective leaders (Chapter 9). Part 2 closes by focusing on a leadership skill that is especially vital in a global economy: embracing differences (Chapter 10). Taken together, these chapters will assist you in building relationships more consistently and at higher levels.

CHAPTER 5

LEARN THE NEW RULES

I suppose leadership at one time meant muscles.
But today it means getting along with people.
—MAHATMA GANDHI

How well do you understand the rules of today's global economy? Here are a few probing questions to ask yourself:

- Would my boss hire me today if I interviewed for my job?
- Does my team consistently produce extraordinary results?
- Have I demonstrated the ability to lead others to success?

If you hesitated in answering yes to any of these, you may be spending too much time doing your job and not enough time building relationships and expanding your knowledge to prepare for future positions. Today, relationships and adaptability are valued more highly than seniority, experience, and advanced degrees. For some, that is great news. For others, it is an unwelcome introduction to the new rules.

A seasoned executive with twenty years of experience lamented to us that he had lost his job and could not find a new one despite multiple interviews. He had consistently achieved his key goals, and his academic credentials were impeccable. He assumed that his resume would give him the inside track to a senior position. What he missed was that credentials are now the price of entry; they are no longer a guarantee of success. He was interviewing because his prior company had been acquired by a larger firm. He found himself competing for his old position against well-qualified candidates who could do his job at a lower salary. He had not invested in building external relationships and acquiring the cutting-edge knowledge required to justify his high salary. The rules had changed, but he had not.

KNOWING THE LEADERSHIP RULES

In the Industrial Age, intelligence, education, and determination were enough to succeed. But today's global economy follows new rules. You are more likely to be valued and rewarded for who you know and the results you get others to produce than for any technical skill you may possess. If you are not expanding and blending your leadership and management mindsets continuously, you risk waking up one day to find that what you are doing is no longer needed, your function is being offshored to India or China, or your team is being replaced by a new technology or streamlined process.

In contrast, proactive executives recognize the opportunities presented by evolving markets, new technologies, and changing demographics. In such a fast-paced environment, knowing the rules is more essential than ever before, for several reasons:

- Leaders in many organizations direct diverse global operations and have trusted relationships with a broad range of peers across their industry.
- The type of relationships leaders must build has changed. They form connections to motivate people rather than demand results through a command-and-control style.
- Leaders stimulate creativity and growth by asking great questions, listening to the answers, and asking more questions. It is not their knowledge that counts; what matters is how fast everyone learns and how effectively the learning is shared and applied.
- Today's leaders must be concerned about much more than producing top-line and bottom-line results. They are expected to be conscious of the social impacts of their operations and to develop people for future positions.

If you do not learn the rules or do not follow them, there will be professional and human consequences to pay regardless of whether the rules are anchored in society or unique to your organization or industry. You must adapt.

Rule: People Skills Trump Technical Skills

As a leader, you can get by with superior people skills and mediocre technical skills, but the reverse is high risk. Actions that produced success just a few short years ago are inadequate in today's business world. It is your responsibility to incorporate the new rules into your leadership persona and to teach them to those you lead.

For example, a retired three-star admiral tells the story of an executive officer (his second in command) whom he evaluated to be superior in technical skills yet lacking in people skills. He mentored the officer on the technical side, but overlooked the people-skills issue because that would have entailed an awkward conversation. When the admiral's rotation came up, he transferred to another billet and lost contact with the officer. One day, the officer called in a panic. He had been relieved of command for what he called "a petty people issue," and he asked the admiral to intercede. The admiral denied the request. Years later, he was in a seminar when he overheard the commander who relieved the officer and the officer's replacement discussing how hard that incident had been on everyone. As he listened, the admiral felt remorse because he had ignored his executive officer's lack of emotional intelligence and thereby doomed him to failure despite his superb technical skills. The admiral had ignored one of the new rules: people skills are more essential to success than technical expertise.

Rule: Be Clear About Your Values

Few people have precisely the same values. That is why you must communicate yours if you want them to be understood. One manager, Mike, clashed with the women who worked for him. Senior leaders feared that he might be hostile to women because he was not sharing information with them. When confronted with this assumption, Mike laughed and countered, "That's ridiculous—I have two daughters who are striving to succeed in business. Every fiber in me wants women to succeed in business."

So what was the real issue? In an attempt to build trust, Mike had confided changes he wanted to make to coworkers who happened to be women, and they had shared the ideas with others. In his mind, they had violated his trust, so he stopped sharing information with them. During coaching, Mike came to see that people have different values and that he could not expect everyone to share his values—or even know what they are—unless he discussed them. Issue resolved. He told his staff, "Trust is my top priority." They agreed to respect that value, and open conversations resumed.

If values (think computer hardware—hardwired) are the basis by which you lead, then beliefs (think software—reprogrammable) are what drive your decisions and actions. Beliefs fall into two groups: enabling ("I am" or "I can") and limiting ("I am not" or "I cannot"). In Mike's case, he shifted from a limiting belief, "I am not willing to discuss ideas with people who don't share my values," to an enabling one: "I can work with people with different values as long as we understand and respect each other's values." Understanding and respecting the values of others—and clearly sharing yours—are critical for sustained success in a diverse business world.

Rule: Pay It Forward

It is essential to build new relationships proactively, because when you really need a relationship, it is too late to develop it. Chen, a communications industry entrepreneur, volunteered to serve on the board of directors of a nonprofit organization. During his tenure, the nonprofit went through a crisis related to the alleged misappropriation of funds by its executives. Even though his schedule was jammed with work for his own fledgling company, Chen paid it forward by working long hours to resolve the matter. Other directors instead resigned because they were reluctant to spend the time or to be associated with the scandal. Chen and Rachel, another board member, worked closely during the crisis, including making nightly calls to discuss each day's events.

When the crisis abated and his term ended, Chen left the board. Years later, he ran into Rachel while making a sales call at the firm for which she was a senior executive. She told him that she had been impressed by his integrity and willingness to work tirelessly to resolve the nonprofit's issue. He won the contract, and Rachel's company became his largest client.

Chen's reward for his pay-it-forward investment did not come when or how he expected. It rarely does. When you help a relationship partner, you make a deposit in the relationship bank. When you require a favor or do something foolish, you make a withdrawal. Effective leaders have large balances in their relationship banks because they have paid it forward for years. As a leader, you owe it to your followers to demonstrate pay-it-forward behaviors and teach them how to pay it forward too.

Rule: Compete Vigorously—but with a Long-Term View

Many executives see business as competition among organizations and individuals. They encourage their people to "conquer" customers and "attack" competitors. Today's leaders, in contrast, understand that business is a complex ecosystem in which organizations thrive by building relationships that adapt to change. If you win today's transaction but damage an important relationship in the process, you may actually have been the big loser, because bitter relationships are rarely forgotten. As a leader, you may compete at the transaction level, but in the long term, you must form strategic partnerships to grow your industry and serve all your stakeholders.

The competitive spirit is useful in both the management and leadership mindsets. In the leadership sphere, it stimulates innovation and creates value for stakeholders. In the management sphere, it spurs a team to operate at high levels in order to outperform competitors. However, competition can be destructive when it is directed inside an organization or toward the wrong objectives.

For example, two sales managers in a large pharmaceutical company were licking their wounds after losing a promotion to a third colleague whom they had not seen as a serious contender:

"Frankly, Jack, I thought you were my only competition for the promotion, so I watched your numbers as closely as my own. Now I see that Sue was developing her people, implementing new sales strategies, and building trusted relationships in addition to meeting her numbers."

"Yes, Bill, we both missed out. I thought all that counted was the numbers—that's how I got to be a sales manager. But the reality is, all three of us exceeded our goals by roughly the same amount. Yet Sue also set the stage for an uptick in sales over the next several quarters, which made her a clear choice for the position. What I'd like to know is how she did those things while still meeting her numbers. Maybe she would mentor us so we can do the same."

"Let's visit Sue to congratulate her, offer our support, and ask her to share her secrets. After all, she is our new boss."

Clearly, Sue was seeing the big picture and blending the management and leadership mindsets as she won sales, exceeded goals, and mentored her people. Yet there was more to her conversations: she valued excellence more highly than beating competitors. Excellence enables you and your team to win over and over again. When relationships are strong, you can meet any challenge and solve any problem. But if your relationships are broken, that alone can impede your success.

Rule: Think "Yes-And," Not "Either-Or"

Either-or means that one party is right and the other is wrong, which can lead to toxic power struggles. The either-or mindset is incredibly limiting. You are not either a manager *or* a leader, you are both. Yes-and means you are combining the best of your ideas with the best ideas of others in a way that works for everyone. The accepting nature of a yes-and attitude strengthens relationships and expands an organization's capacity. "Yes, Jackie, that is a great idea, and what if we also . . . ?"

Your purpose as a leader is to motivate people to achieve holistic objectives. Think in terms of your team reaching its goals *and* other teams and the organization as a whole achieving its goals. Imagine the positive effects such an organization-wide point of view would produce. When each part of the organization takes responsibility for its success *and* the success of the other parts, people look across boundaries to identify priorities, give and request assistance, and cooperate to achieve shared goals. Whereas this urgent need to work together is obvious in the midst of a crisis, the sense that cooperation is vital often gets lost in routine, everyday business transactions.

As you move up the leadership ladder, will your existing mindset allow you to compete with the market instead of your peers? Look beyond your silo. You are not responsible solely for finance, sales, engineering, or whichever piece of the organization you personally oversee. Avoid competing for resources to build your area at the expense of other parts of the organization that may need the resources more urgently. Reaching your goals is important, but success ultimately will be measured by how well everyone aligns to achieve the organization's mission. If one fails, all will struggle. Playing on the leadership team requires you to collaborate with people who are different from you. Yet mutual trust and respect enable you to work together to produce results that competitors with a self-centered point of view may think is impossible.

Rule: No More Command and Control

You have no doubt seen people who bullied their way to the top using command-and-control tactics. What you probably have not seen is how often we are called in to coach executives to use a more motivating style. Those executives are under crushing pressure from their bosses to change, and they speak candidly about their predicament:

"I was blindsided by the expectations when I moved into a corner office. I kept pushing people around the way I always had and got hammered by the CEO for not being a team player. I never saw it coming."

"It took me a long time to realize that beating my peers was not a viable advancement strategy at the top. We all wanted that next promotion, but demonstrating teamwork and motivating others to do the impossible was the way to get it, not superior individual results."

"I see now that I got this job in ways I am not proud of. I wanted the promotion so badly that I was blind to how I manipulated people to get it. I keep getting called on the carpet by the CEO—most recently in his staff meeting this morning—for not working with my people to create leadership depth and bench strength."

"I lost my job and was sent to a nonleadership position because someone told my boss how poor my relationships were with peers and direct reports. I only focused on managing up. The CEO said she was surprised at how little respect and trust others had for me. Connecting with people had never been a priority for me."

One common fallacy about being in a leadership position is thinking that everyone will adapt to you and trust you merely because of your title. "Now that I'm the boss, here is how we will do things." We often see this belief play out in mergers when employees of the acquired company are expected to adopt the practices and culture of the acquirer. "Welcome aboard. Listen carefully to your new goals and how we will measure your performance." Mergers have a higher probability of success when the cultures are blended and conversations are held to align everyone behind a shared vision. "Welcome aboard. Let's start this meeting by seeing how we are alike or different in core business processes. Let's get off to a great start by identifying several that we can all rally behind." A shared vision strengthens relationships and avoids a power struggle to determine who will be the top dog.

Rule: Match Culture with Objectives and People with Culture

Because culture determines what an organization can achieve, it follows that the culture must align with the organization's key objectives. You should choose (or develop) a culture that fits your leadership style, and hire and train people who will thrive in that culture. In small organizations, culture serves as a conscious filter that naturally leads to the hiring of like-minded people. IT companies like AOL, Google, and Microsoft are famous for their distinctive start-up cultures. We all have seen brilliant programmers who produce top-notch products single-handedly. If independence is a cultural value, these programmers are good hires. However, if teamwork is a prized value, they will be a disruptive influence no matter how brilliant and competent they are.

For many positions, attitudes and behaviors are more important to hiring and promotion than are experience and skills. For example, are you hiring and training people who build relationships quickly and easily? Are they willing participants in open and honest conversations? Are they comfortable accepting and giving feedback? Having the necessary skills and experience should be the go–no-go criterion for even scheduling an interview—as it will probably be when you interview for your next promotion. Ensure that the people you hire and promote will either thrive in your current culture or function as catalysts to change the culture if that is appropriate.

THE COMMON THREAD

If all the new rules were rolled into one, that rule would be "Leadership is about connecting and aligning with others." High-potential executives ask questions and listen to their people and their peers. They understand and follow the leadership rules and adapt quickly to evolving priorities.

At each higher level, culminating with becoming the CEO, you will have more independence, less supervision, and greater responsibility than in any previous position. Furthermore, those above you, especially the CEO or a board of directors, will have less time available to develop your skills—often assuming that you already have them. That is why onboarding programs and other forms of postpromotion assistance are increasingly popular and why more leaders are using executive coaches today.

Your success as a leader derives from what you accomplish with and through others. Develop relationships before you need them. The most effective relationship builders begin their conversations by asking, "Tell me about yourself. What are your talents? What are your goals? How can we best work together to achieve them? How can I help you?"

CHAPTER 6

YOUR RELATIONSHIPS DEFINE YOU

Some of the biggest challenges in relationships come from the fact that most people enter a relationship in order to get something. In reality, the only way a relationship will last is if you see it as a place you go to give, and not a place you go to take.
—ANTHONY ROBBINS

How do you view the people you lead? How do you form relationships? What unique contributions do you make to relationships? Your responses to questions like these are the basis of the relationships you have today and those you will build in the future. They reveal what you stand for and define the reputation—your leadership brand—that you bring into every conversation. To the extent that your reputation is authentic and you are faithful to it, you create connection and alignment with those around you. Your brand is the platform on which you build relationships with others.

Sam, the CEO of a training company, spent several hours a week reaching out to others in five- to ten-minute phone conversations that were as varied as the people he called. He asked great questions and ended each call with an agreement to speak again during the next few months. Sam rarely asked the person for anything during the calls, yet took careful notes about what he learned. At the time, the other executives in the firm wondered why he spent so much time making such calls when there were so many challenges to be dealt with.

Yet precisely because of these calls, whenever the company faced a major issue or opportunity, Sam was able to reach into his contacts list and find the name of a person who would help. Whenever the company needed to hire a key employee or contact a potential new customer, supplier, or investor, his call was taken by the person who could fill the need. Sam's brand was that he could always secure resources for the people in his organization and would also help people in other organizations obtain what they needed. They were eager to take his calls and looked forward to having conversations with him. When making these calls, he operated in a leadership mindset.

ESSENTIAL RELATIONSHIP-BUILDING SKILLS

As you move into positions with increasing responsibility, you will need more and deeper relationships. In addition to internal relationships, you must develop an ever-widening circle of relationships with customers, suppliers, competitors, industry leaders, financiers, and professional advisers. Collectively, these people are called stakeholders—they affect your success and are affected by your performance.

Figure 6.1 summarizes the relationship-building skills required at each rung on the leadership ladder, along with the perception of relationships typical at that level. As you move into the upper leadership levels, your technical skills—what you know—become less important. What counts is whom you know and, perhaps more important, who knows and trusts you. Top leaders usually have the broadest and deepest relationships and, ideally, will teach you how to form and strengthen yours.

	First-Line Manager	Manager of Managers	Executive Leader	CXO Leader
Essential Relationship-Building Skill	Learn basics of relationships: what they are and how to use them	Deepen use of relationships to achieve goals and help peers achieve goals	Form teams that integrate cross-division and external partners	Build external network with long-term strategic view of the industry
Perception of Relationships	Considers relationships as lying inside the organization	Displays pay-it-forward and win-win thinking	Sees how the organization fits into the industry	Grows network to suit a changing world

FIGURE 6.1. Relationship-Building Skills.
As you climb the leadership ladder, your relationship skills deepen and your perception of relationships broadens.

Stakeholders are essential to achieving your goals. Your job is to identify and build relationships with them. Find personal ways to connect and create alignment. One CEO of a Fortune 500 company was known for writing notes—over twenty thousand in one year—to virtually every fellow traveler, employee, customer, and supplier he met while visiting his company's facilities. Each note acknowledged what he had learned, expressed appreciation, or asked for more information. He wrote them in the car on the way to and from the airport and while waiting for flights. His assistant took the letters and mailed them the next day for maximum impact. The longer he continued this practice, the more that people reached out to him during his travels and the more strategic information he was given—just by connecting in this personal way. His brand was one of listening and responding, of caring and connecting with others.

MULTIMEDIA RELATIONSHIPS

Communication has always been a keystone skill in relationships, but now we are all having conversations with more people, more often, through more media than ever before. In this digital age, conversations are multimedia interactions that include emails, blogs, instant messaging, texts, tweets, video-conferencing, Facebook, LinkedIn, and Google+, among many others, in addition to face-to-face meetings and old-fashioned phone calls.

Electronic conversations efficiently deliver facts and figures, yet they convey little, if any, emotion. They are easily misunderstood and can become grenades that explode in the receiver's inbox rather than tools that strengthen relationships. Unfortunately, when some people receive a grenade email, their first instinct is to lob one back. "I can't believe he said that and copied our boss. I'll set the record straight so he won't mess with me again." This response initiates an email battle when the goal should be to build relationships. Emails can erect walls when you should be building bridges.

Another unfortunate trend we see today is for people to email or IM a coworker rather than walk down the hall to have a conversation. Even worse, they copy others on the email, many of whom feel compelled to respond. Consciously or unconsciously, these individuals avoid the personal interactions that make conversations work. Then they are surprised when a message is misinterpreted or people are not aligned behind a key strategy. The real problem is that they have not held conversations that build relationships. Without question, we support using multimedia communications to open doors, schedule appointments, and reach out to those you cannot meet face-to-face. But they are not a panacea for resolving issues, nor do they replace the synchronous conversations that solve real problems and create real opportunities.

Ineffective communications create narrow relationships, which produce ill-advised decisions and uncoordinated actions that yield poor results. Conversely, great conversations follow the same path but in a virtuous cycle, one that substantially increases the potential for extraordinary results. Many executives work in a virtual environment today and have limited opportunities for face-to-face conversations. If you are one of them, the phone or Skype provides additional richness in the conversations (if you pay attention to inflections, tonality, pauses, and the pace of the conversation in addition to the words) and enable you to receive the unspoken as well as the spoken messages.

THE INCREASING IMPORTANCE OF RELATIONSHIPS

The way you relate to others evolves as you grow from individual contributor to manager, and again from manager to leader. Often the promotion to first-line manager is given as a reward for superior technical skills or the willingness to work long hours. Relationship-building skills may be secondary. If you think back on your promotion from individual contributor to first-line manager, you may recall being tempted to use the same skills that made you successful in the past. But in the new position, you realized that your performance was measured not by your actions but by your team's results. As a neophyte manager, you learned to build and strengthen relationships with your direct reports to complete assigned work. You only succeeded when your team succeeded. In some cases, your direct reports may have been your peers prior to the promotion. So you were challenged not just to build but to change the nature of these relationships. Similarly, if you are a manager of managers, your performance is defined by how well your managers perform and the collective results they produce.

Leadership positions require deeper relationships and broader conversations than management positions. Furthermore, being a good manager far from guarantees that you have the skill to succeed as a leader. Upon taking a leadership position, your scope expands; your decisions are of greater consequence; and their implementation depends as much on evoking trust, respect, and passion as on your people's skills. You must deal with a wider circle of stakeholders and surround yourself with thought leaders, because tomorrow's opportunities will grow from today's conversations.

Figure 6.2 illustrates the progression from targeted to trusted relationships in your life as an executive. The process begins by identifying people who could contribute to your current and future success—targeted relationships. After finding opportunities to meet them, you develop and nurture a tentative

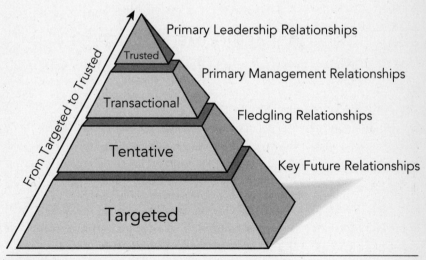

FIGURE 6.2. The Progression of Relationships.
Relationships enable you to benefit from high-level opportunities—but they take time and focus to develop.

relationship. When you get to know and trust each other, the relationship becomes an asset for both of you—a transactional relationship. The process culminates when you hold intimate conversations about issues and opportunities without a personal agenda. Such trusted relationships are critical to success at the highest levels.

Trusted Relationships

Trusted relationships are the most personal, valuable, and usually longest lasting. They are a safe haven that welcomes conversations on virtually any subject—each other's objectives and challenges being the primary focus. The conversations usually involve big-picture topics and mentoring. The first person you call when you uncover a critical issue or want to blue-sky an idea is someone with whom you have a trusted relationship. "Peter, I don't have a clue why my team and my company are stuck. Can we meet later today and mull this over?" Conversely, when this person calls you, you will drop what you are doing to accept his call. He helps you recognize underlying problems and uncover hidden solutions because he knows your goals and understands your strengths and weaknesses—and you do the same for him. Each party knows that the other will not abuse the relationship for a one-sided gain. This does not mean that a trusted relationship partner will not ask you for an order or that you cannot ask him for one. Rather, you can trust that the order he suggests will meet your needs and be on fair terms—and he expects the same from you.

Trusted relationships often exist between senior executives in different organizations and can lead to an extraordinary solution to a critical problem. For example, a major hospitality chain switched from one soft-drink brand to another virtually overnight. The change seemed abrupt to outsiders, but a trusted relationship existed between the two companies' top executives. The hospitality company was in danger of not making payroll—and its executive was willing to share that sensitive information with his trusted relationship partner in the search for a solution. The soft-drink executive offered that his firm would cover the other company's payroll if the hospitality chain would adopt his brand as the exclusive soft drink at all of its properties. It was a major win for both companies. Business deals crafted through trusted relationships frequently create huge opportunities and have enormous long-term impacts on their organizations.

Transactional Relationships

Transactional relationships are less personal and are used in the management mindset to accomplish specific business objectives. They are defined by what each party can do for the other to reach near-term objectives, seldom extending into career or personal areas. Ongoing relationships with customers, peers, and suppliers often lie in this category. The following conversation between a buyer in a midsize electronics company and a key supplier is typical of a transactional relationship:

"John, we just received a provisional order for five thousand [units of our core product], but the customer needs delivery in ten days. I know it's asking a lot since our contract gives you a lead time of twelve days, but if you could deliver the [key parts] in a week, I can meet their deadline. It would impress the customer, help me make my quota for the quarter, and mean a lot to my company."

"Harry, I'll get back to you in thirty minutes, but I think we can adjust our production schedule and work some overtime to get the [key parts] to you in a week. We anticipated this kind of situation when we set up our sole-sourcing agreement, and I won't let you down. We may have to add a 5 percent overtime charge. Can you cover that?"

"Absolutely, John. That would be a win-win for me, you, and the customer."

Transactional relationship partners trust and respect each other because they frequently work together and consistently treat each other fairly. These relationships develop with go-to people whom you can count on to get the job done. Likewise, they trust that you will meet your end of the bargain. You may have this type of relationship with someone in accounting who responds quickly to your requests for financial data, a customer who depends on you in tight situations, or a helpful waiter who shows you and your guests to your favorite table with a panoramic view. The conversation is less strategic than in a trusted relationship, yet the results are vital to your success—and the other person's too.

Tentative Relationships

Tentative relationships are "prerelationships"—you must learn more about each other before relying on the relationship for a make-or-break transaction. If you received a phone message or email and set it aside with an intention to respond later today or tomorrow, you have a tentative relationship. Neither of you knows the other well enough to make your conversations an instant top priority. You may have spoken briefly at a conference or heard the person's name from a transactional partner, or she may be calling because of your reputation in the industry. You may invite her to lunch or ask her to join you in whatever common interest you share. If you are fortunate, those interests will push a tentative relationship into the transactional category. It usually takes several minor transactions before you trust each other enough to work together regularly.

Target Relationships

To achieve your goals, there are people with whom you should have a relationship but do not—those are target relationships. You do not know them, but you do know that you will benefit from what they offer and that they will benefit from knowing you. How can you identify and reach out to these individuals? We suggest that you construct a target relationship pipeline by writing their names down and contacting at least one of them every week. Be creative and aggressive in adding names to the list. That list is your path to future transactional and trusted relationships. Establishing contact with the target relationships within your organization is relatively easy, and you can build external relationships by attending networking events and joining your industry's association. In addition, use social media like LinkedIn and Facebook to contact target relationship partners, but consider the appropriateness of business versus personal media and the context in which you use them.

NOT HAVING A RELATIONSHIP CAN BE COSTLY

No matter how many relationships you have, you always need more. Furthermore, as we noted earlier, when a relationship is needed but does not exist, it is usually too late to form it. One CEO described the relationships he wished he had built. As a senior executive in a Fortune 100 firm, he was regularly invited to join the company's lobbyists on Capitol Hill to meet the congressional committee members who set policies in his industry. He declined the invitations, saying that he had more important work to do.

Instead, he focused on building relationships with the financial institutions, large customers, industry peers, and key employees who were critical to his current success. He consistently produced impressive growth through these relationships. He told us, "When I visited our facilities, I would see individuals working at their stations and have lunch with them. I would get to know them on a personal level, share information to build trust, and let them know I cared. It wasn't a trick—the trick was that I really cared, and they felt it and responded."

However, declining those congressional visits was something he regretted a few years later as the CEO of a government services firm. While he focused internally, a crisis exploded when a government agency tried to debar his company from working with federal agencies, based on untrue allegations. The CEO, angered and alarmed, called his congressmen and asked for help. The requests fell on sympathetic but deaf ears because he had not previously developed relationships with them. After lengthy negotiations, the CEO agreed to leave his position as part of the settlement with the government to reinstate the company. This CEO hit a speed bump in his career, not because he did not value and build relationships, but because this talented relationship builder did not reach wide enough. He had built relationships for expected events, but not for the unexpected. Fortunately for this executive, within a year, he became CEO of another company primarily through the industry relationships he had built.

CHAPTER 7

KNOW YOUR STRENGTHS AND
THEIR SHADOWS

We talk about quality in products and services. What about quality in our
relationships, quality in our communications, and quality in our
promises to each other?

—MAX DE PREE

A 2011 study looked at whether extroverts or introverts were more effective as leaders.[1] To align our definitions: extroverts gain energy by sharing ideas in a group and lose energy working alone. Conversely, introverts value the opportunity to evaluate a situation and consider alternatives thoroughly; they lose energy when participating in meetings where rapid-fire choices must be made. The study found that leaders of both types were equally effective—as long as they surrounded themselves with people of the opposite style. The least effective leaders were found to be those who surrounded themselves with people like themselves. As a high potential, be aware of your strengths and your people's strengths. Understand that each of your strengths has a shadow side, and consciously construct a team that has complementary strengths.

For example, the new, strongly extroverted group vice president of a large firm called a two-day off-site with his mostly introverted executive team. The group spent the first day imagining possibilities and considering new ideas; the facilitator purposefully kept the discussions broad. After dinner, the group president pulled him aside and said, "The meeting isn't going well—we haven't made any decisions yet. This off-site must produce clear goals." The facilitator responded, "Trust the process. You'll see decisions tomorrow." The group president reluctantly gave him until noon the next day for key decisions to be made.

That evening, the IT executives held impromptu conversations to exchange views on the concepts that had been presented during the day. They pondered the alternatives and discussed them again at breakfast the next morning. When they reconvened, the discussions were lively and focused. Decision after decision was made with near-unanimous agreement. The group president was amazed. He always considered his ability to make rapid decisions to be a strength, but he learned a valuable lesson that day about giving people—especially introverts—time to consider alternatives. When he acknowledged this "aha" moment to the executives at the end of the off-site, their relationship was off to a great start, and everyone was aligned behind the group's clear goals.

EACH STRENGTH HAS A COMPANION SHADOW

Few things reveal leadership strengths and shadows more vividly than high-pressure situations—an impending deadline, extra scrutiny from the boss, a conflict among top executives, a high-stakes decision. During the stress of these situations, consider that

- Any strength taken to excess can become a shadow that derails the relationships required to achieve success.
- Embracing and integrating the strengths of each person will maximize the team's power and minimize its collective shadows.
- Over time, you will develop new strengths and workarounds for your shadows.

Knowing and acknowledging your leadership strengths and their companion shadows establishes a robust foundation for relationships. For example, one top CIO in the U.S. government describes his leadership strengths and shadows to his people as follows:

- **My Style:** I'm blunt and transparent. I like debates and direct feedback. I ask a lot of questions—don't take them personally. I delegate and I encourage calculated risk-taking. I like structured processes and procedures. I insist on a family-friendly team—your family comes first.
- **What I Expect from You:** Fierce loyalty. Represent the organization well at all times. Do a quality job on time. Don't give up. Be creative—a person

who says it can't be done is often interrupting a person who is doing it. Mistakes are okay as long as they are made with the best intentions and we learn from them. Be accountable. Follow official policies. Focus on the customer. Be nice.

- **Joint Responsibility:** Communicate well and often. Teamwork means we watch each other's backs. If you need help, ask for it. We will succeed if we work as a team, or fail working as individuals. Always close the loop.
- **When to Contact Me:** With ideas, recommendations, feedback, or complaints. When things are going very well and not so well. Don't let me get blindsided. If you need help, I'm accessible 24/7.
- **My Vision:** Success is when: (1) every employee is excited about what he does; (2) every government employee wants to work for us; and (3) every federal agency wants to use us as their trusted IT partner.

He has this conversation with each new hire to define their relationship, communicate expectations, and establish how best to interact. This welcome-aboard message begins the leadership conversations in his organization.

GETTING STARTED ON THE RIGHT FOOT

The early conversations between executives and their direct reports establish the blend of management and leadership mindsets that persists throughout the relationship. For example, consider the following conversation between an executive leader and high-potential manager who has just been hired into the organization:

"I look forward to us getting to know each other, and see you as a valuable addition to the team. We have a lot to accomplish and can only meet our stretch goals by working closely together. For the moment, let's not talk about the goals. Instead, let me tell you a bit about our culture and about what makes me tick as the boss, and ask you to share the same about yourself. To start, tell me, why did you choose to join our team?"

This conversation—and therefore, the relationship—opened in a leadership mindset, while the management-mindset conversation about goals, roles, and resources was put on hold temporarily. Beginning the conversation by connecting with one another increases the likelihood that a relationship will be created that can endure future challenges. A typical response by the new manager might sound something like this:

"Thanks for asking. I sensed this was a great place to work—that people matter here. In my last position, everyone had a different idea about how the job should be done, and competition was intense. The boss blamed us when things didn't go well and took credit when they did. We rarely knew what he was thinking, and his conversations with us were merely appeals for us to work harder and do more. I came here because this organization uses a more people-oriented approach."

By creating a safe place for the new manager to reveal what was important to him, the boss gained critical insights on how to motivate him. The conversation also validated the boss's policy to focus on relationships and attitudes in his hiring decisions. The boss continued the conversation:

"I've arranged for you to meet key members of the team over the next few days. Get to know them as trusted and respected colleagues as you dive into the new position. Then we'll have the conversation about goals and mutual expectations. Our team enjoys work, and we build relationships to ensure that everyone succeeds. That's why our customers love us, and that's how we out-perform our competitors and the other divisions."

The messages exchanged during this conversation clearly establish that the boss, the new manager, and others—the people, not just the results they produce—are critical to the team's performance. The new manager both relaxed and became more excited, and the boss felt good about the hiring decision. As a high potential, you probably have already participated on both sides of similar conversations. Conversations to build relationships are largely about making conscious connections that lead to alignment in decisions and actions.

DEVELOPING UNCONSCIOUS COMPETENCE IN RELATIONSHIPS

The conscious competency model illustrated in Figure 7.1 describes the process for developing a new strength.[2] To understand the model, begin with (A)

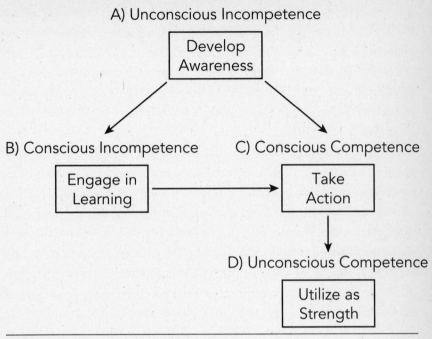

FIGURE 7.1. Conscious Competency Model.
Building strengths is a process that starts with awareness, may entail learning, and is developed by taking action.

unconscious incompetence, which is the state of not knowing that you need to know something. A skill that is not a current strength but that you recognize as important and that you acknowledge as necessary to learn is called a (B) conscious incompetency. When you become aware of the new skill and work to become proficient, you have a (C) conscious competency. When the skill becomes second nature—a (D) unconscious competency—it is a strength that you rely on naturally.

As a practical example of the model, consider breathing: for most of us, this is a fully developed unconscious competency. Yet the ability to consciously control breathing is advantageous in stressful situations. For example, scuba divers are acutely aware of how their breathing varies when they are calm, exerting effort, or in panic mode, because that skill can save their lives. They are unconsciously competent in breathing under all, not just normal, circumstances. New divers must learn to control their breathing under all circumstances because breathing underwater is different than doing so on land. It takes practice to breathe smoothly and manage an air supply. Novice divers gulp a tank of air in fifteen minutes, whereas the same tank may last an experienced diver an hour. The conscious competency model is relevant to leadership because building relationships is as essential to leaders as breathing properly is to scuba divers.

Observe what others do who are proficient relationship builders. Become aware of what you do not know and learn what you need to know. For instance, you may have noticed that some successful leaders are outgoing and some are curious. Now isolate the traits of being outgoing and curious—become conscious of their importance. The next step is to determine if you are competent in these two traits. If not, identify what keeps you from being outgoing or curious (or both) so that you can learn what you need in order to become competent at them. Becoming consciously competent, you will meet people and use curiosity as a basis for building interesting relationships. As you develop these traits, you will find yourself being outgoing and curious in your relationships without consciously trying. Then you have achieved an unconscious competency that you will use naturally and continually.

RECOGNIZING THE SHADOWS

The process of becoming unconsciously competent in a new skill is as important as the competency itself. Most of us have worked with someone whose strength was an ability to quickly assess a situation, decide what to do, and direct others to take action. Look at that style in terms of the conscious competency model. For those executives, springing into action is an unconscious skill they habitually employ when facing tight deadlines or perceived threats. In routine situations, that approach can be a shadow in terms of inhibiting their teams' professional growth and long-term performance.

A team's performance generally can be enhanced by identifying the strengths required to perform a task (becoming aware), considering whether you possess them (a conscious competency) or need them from someone else (a conscious incompetency). When you blend the strengths of each team member to complete the task, the team usually will be more creative, find a more effective strategy, and align better for execution. Just as important, the team feels vested in the strategy and forms more productive relationships—the shadows have been erased by the collective strengths of the team.

Furthermore, think about the mindset of an executive who immediately springs into action. He is relying solely on his skills to devise the strategy, set the schedule, and push people into action. Thinking much like an independent contributor, he feels confident in setting the agenda by himself and using people like marionettes. That executive is unconsciously incompetent (a shadow area) relative to

- Developing others by allowing them to set the agenda
- Freeing himself to work on more complex parts of the task
- Recognizing that teamwork is essential for superior long-term results

Engaging the strengths of others—particularly in your shadow areas—will instill the team with confidence in your leadership skills and your ability to build relationships.

There is another lesson in observing executives who spring into action—they must learn to engage in leadership conversations. These executives tap their personal strengths but ignore the strengths of others. What might happen instead if they posed leadership questions to the group, such as "Take a few minutes to identify your strengths relative to this task and describe them to us" or "What obstacles do you think we'll encounter, and how should we conquer them?" Questions like these take less time than you might think, and save time during subsequent steps because they engage all of the group's strengths and build relationships that are useful today and strong in the future. In the long run, conversations that connect and align make a larger contribution to a group's performance than any "perfect" plan a leader might dictate all by himself.

As a leader, use both mindsets to define success criteria and determine which (and whose) strengths to call on. Determine what the team has the ability to do before deciding what it will do: "What skills or competencies is the team missing?" Independent contributors usually define their own success criteria—after all, they are experts in a narrow range of tasks. Managers focus on completing the task as quickly as possible in order to move to the next one. Leaders concentrate on delivering value to stakeholders and building relationships in the process, even though that approach may initially take more time. In addition, bring all three conversational perspectives to the meeting-room table: hear everyone's ideas, understand what they are saying, and explore new possibilities as appropriate to the task at hand.

FOCUS ON STRENGTHS

Some executives attempt to convert weaknesses into strengths rather than leveraging existing strengths. The feedback they provide and formal performance reviews they hold often examine weaknesses in excruciating detail. There are few surprises because the reviewer and recipient both recognize them. The review process often ends with a plan that attempts to transform weaknesses into strengths, the underlying assumption being that everyone should be capable in every area. That is an unrealistic expectation that devalues unique skills. There are some things that a person may never be good at doing. A more effective approach in today's collaborative, crowdsourced world is to match people in teams that collectively have all of the strengths needed to produce an extraordinary result.

Building on your strengths is a natural and essential part of climbing the leadership ladder. Get feedback, be coached and mentored, and obtain training in areas that are vital for your success. Observe your boss's strengths and shadows—which could you use now, and which might you use when her job becomes yours? Successful leaders expand their effectiveness by leveraging strengths and working around weaknesses. There may come a time when your strengths are insufficient for your position. If you develop new strengths and relationships, you can thrive. If you do not, your status as a high potential will be at risk.

CHAPTER 8

PEOPLE AREN'T MACHINES

People will forget what you said. People will forget what you did.
But people will never forget how you made them feel.
—MAYA ANGELOU

Some executives devalue their people by treating them like machines. Those executives implement processes and procedures to maintain control, and are disappointed when their people respond by waiting to be told what to do. By contrast, effective leaders sense that their organization is a collage of individual aspirations and expectations connected by a higher purpose and shared successes. Those leaders reach out to each person in their domain to build relationships that are collaborative and creative. They have conversations that motivate and inspire, as well as ones that provide clear direction.

With tunnel-vision intensity, command-and-control executives tell their people what to do, how to do it, and when it must be done while discounting or ignoring their people's ideas. Tyrone, a sales manager under pressure to increase sales in a difficult economy, is one example:

Tyrone: Be in this office at 8 am for the next four Monday mornings to make telemarketing calls to potential clients in your territory. No excuses, just be here. I also want to accompany you on at least four sales calls each week, even if it means canceling other plans you've made.

Susan (top sales rep):   In twenty years as one of the company's top ten sales reps, I've had more success making face-to-face calls on referrals than telemarketing. I can connect far better with prospects in person than over the phone.

Tyrone: If I make an exception for you, everyone will want exceptions, and they don't have the experience or selling skills that you do.

Susan: The goal is to increase sales, right? Trust the salespeople to increase sales in ways that work best for them, and tailor your support for each person. The new sales reps will probably benefit from telemarketing experience.

Tyrone: We want everyone to use the same selling techniques, so set a good example by doing it our way.

Susan: As an alternative, I'd be willing to teach face-to-face skills to the others by having them ride with me. I also could assist you in working with each person to help him or her find the most effective selling method. There is a better way than chaining everyone to a phone.

Tyrone: Sorry, no exceptions. We'll do this my way.

The result of treating Susan and other sales reps like gears in a sales machine? Sales plummeted, and Susan and two others left the company. Soon thereafter, Tyrone lost his position and returned to being a salesperson. One common reason coaches are brought into organizations is to address the inability of an executive to treat coworkers, customers, and other stakeholders with respect—to value who they are as well as what they can contribute.

By blending the management and leadership mindsets, you will find that differences between you and your people lead to conversations that identify effective approaches and develop a deep appreciation for each other. When executives ignore their people's ideas, the issue can be a lack of emotional intelligence. In an effort to prove they are right, these executives focus on things they want done instead of how their people can best accomplish them. Unfortunately, they often are not conscious of how their actions are seen by others, which leaves them unable to build the relationships required for success.

PEOPLE HAVE FEELINGS

Feelings count. You may have coached sports teams, managed projects, supervised functional groups, or led organizations. Every time you were called to lead, people expected you to be an expert—even if you were not. They also expected you to get to know them, tap into their highest potential, and mold them into a winning team. Those relationships had a common characteristic: everyone contributed because the group's objective was bigger than any one person could accomplish alone. The challenge was to get each person to align with the others and perform together at an optimal level. That challenge required you to build a relationship with each of them, to talk to them using all three conversational perspectives, and to inspire them to do their best.

At the start of each new leadership assignment, the objective may have been outside your people's comfort zone, and their enthusiasm may have been diluted by fears, doubts, or concerns. Those feelings are a natural part of anything new. Yet stepping through them is what separates winners from losers.

Build relationships by empathizing with your people as they experience feelings that may be similar to those you felt when you were in their shoes—and ones you may feel again after your next promotion. Encourage them to embrace their feelings and conquer them as a team. One source of competitive advantage in today's global economy is the ability to sense and respond to market changes faster than competitors. If your relationship with each person includes being in touch with his or her feelings, you have a huge advantage in reacting to change.

THE LEGENDS IN YOUR ORGANIZATION

Recall your first day in your organization. What legends did your new colleagues relate to you? Who were the heroes, and what were their stories? What values did they embrace? What behaviors were acceptable and unacceptable? What importance was attached to building relationships? Those legends, heroes, stories, values, and behaviors define the culture of your organization and the relationships that bond people together. Were you expected to focus on internal conversations, external collaboration, or both? To what extent did your organization share information with outsiders to form strategic partnerships? The culture of an organization may not be obvious at first, yet it becomes apparent when you listen to the stories people tell. They give you a peek into what traits are admired and considered as important for success.

A company set a goal to earn recognition for its government clients for the results its clients achieved. One team pursued that goal vigorously. They identified awards available to government employees and linked the project's results to the award criteria. Within three years, the government's project manager was selected as a Top 100 IT executive. Members of the project team were given a bonus because their client won the award, and they attended the award ceremony to celebrate the client's success. A few months later, the team won a multiyear contract renewal and received another bonus. The client succeeded, the project team earned two bonuses, and the company secured a multiyear contract—everyone was a winner. This approach to building relationships became a legend in the company—a legend that brought the company's values to life.

You cannot determine an organization's culture by evaluating its balance sheet, seeing its offices, or reviewing its organization chart. These kinds of information may provide clues, but only conversations with its people will reveal the culture behind the public façade. The culture began with the founders' vision, values, and beliefs, and evolved over time. Some organizational cultures never seem to change, others change gradually, and still others morph virtually overnight. A healthy culture is an environment where people can succeed individually and collectively through teamwork.

THE ELEMENTS OF CULTURE

Relationships are the cornerstone of culture, and high-performing organizations reshape their culture as their strategy and objectives evolve. Reshaping the culture is a key part of a leader's job. The following four elements of culture guide relationships and set the expectations and acceptable behaviors for an organization:

- **Mission:** the big picture of what the organization wants to accomplish
- **Vision:** where the organization is going—what the future holds for everyone

- **Goals:** measures of success, usually quantitative
- **Values:** how people treat others and expect to be treated

In aligned cultures, these elements guide people toward high levels of success. They establish the purpose for building relationships, developing others, making decisions, and taking actions. Your organization's culture influences the relationships that are formed and the conversations that are held—or not held.

Mission

A mission statement is a broad definition of what the organization seeks to accomplish—it is the backbone of culture. It should be part of conversations both inside the organization and with external stakeholders. A mission statement describes the organization's relationships, markets, customers, and product or service offerings rather than the organization itself. It often can be a succinct statement with social significance. For example, the mission of one company was to "Help Government Change." That may sound altruistic, but it was an effective business strategy because change in government is a growth market. When the company's customers achieved their change goals, they awarded new contracts to the company to assist with additional changes. That mission statement identified potential customers clearly: federal agencies that want to change. So agency leaders who were change champions were the customers with whom this company built relationships.

Vision

The organization's vision is a picture of the future that touches hearts, stirs emotions, and links people together—it is the soul of culture. The vision is the reason why people work hard even when it is difficult to do so. Conversations that address vision can be highly effective. However, any inconsistencies between the way people experience the organization and the vision its leaders espouse will erode the culture and adversely affect performance. Ask your people to describe your organization's vision. Invite them to tell stories that show how the organization is working to turn its vision into reality. If they cannot answer quickly and clearly, it is time for a leadership conversation . . . or perhaps a new vision.

Goals

Goals define the future of an organization because they determine relationships that must be formed and actions that must be taken. Setting quantitative goals is a prerequisite to developing an effective strategy and an executable plan. Where do new goals come from? Usually they emerge from the conversations leaders hold with their people when they sense change in their environment. Compelling goals are often set without concern for how they will be achieved or the resources that may be required—those are details to be ironed out during planning. Goals are not feel-good objectives that you and other executives develop at an off-site workshop. Rather, they are accomplishments that need to be discussed thoroughly, measured objectively, and rewarded generously. Your organization's overall results will be directly proportional to the effectiveness of the conversations you have while setting goals.

Values

Values that everyone embraces are the conscience of an organization. Most people are reluctant to abandon their personal values when they go to work—they want relationships at work with people who hold similar values. So during interviews, they look for organizations where their values align with those of the organization and its leaders. For example, one company had four values that were embedded so deeply that people treated them like rules:

- **Integrity.** I do what I say I will do—every time. (This value encouraged people to say no when they had doubts, which also meant that a yes was a commitment that everyone could count on.)
- **Win-win relationships.** I will help all stakeholders, customers, and partners and each of us accomplish their objectives in every transaction.
- **Personal responsibility.** When a problem arises, instead of casting blame, I will ask, "How can I help fix this problem, and what must I do better next time?"

- **Open and honest conversations.** I will constructively discuss what I believe with people who are directly affected by my beliefs.

Values define the relationship among employees, customers, and stakeholders and define how each person expects to be treated. Every organization has underlying values even if they are not written. Identify and discuss your organization's values with job candidates to improve your opportunity to make great hires who fit the culture.

CHANGING RELATIONSHIPS CHANGES THE CULTURE

Aligning people behind a new culture requires time and consistent action because cultural changes affect relationships and alter people's interactions. Possibly the most important relationship-building conversations you will have will involve recognizing success beyond obvious rewards like bonuses, salary bumps, and promotions. Ask, "What will it take to get you truly excited about working here?"

Nonfinancial recognition is more powerful in building relationships and motivating cultural change than financial rewards. If an employee is motivated only by financial rewards—rather than by culture and purpose—she will leave your organization if she is offered a more lucrative compensation package.

A second culture-changing conversation has to do with how ideas are recognized—especially those that seem off the wall at first. The contribution of an idea should be acknowledged even if that idea is not implemented. "Howard, that's a great idea. Let's hold off on implementing it until we measure how the current initiative is working. Thanks for presenting it." That response will be better received than "Not now, Howard. That's not what we're going to do."

To build strong relationships, increase the frequency of your conversations and focus their content. Even embrace people who resist change, and determine what is behind their resistance. If you can resolve a resistor's concerns and gain her support, she will become a positive force to influence others to adapt as well. "Cathy, I really want to work closely with you, and I respect your ideas. What change in our plan would turn you into a proponent of this idea?" Remember, it is not the organization that changes; it is people who change. And it is the job of every leader to motivate positive change. Once everyone is aligned with a change, it is your job to consistently steer the organization toward the new mission, vision, goals, and values.

Pamela was an engineer who had worked diligently for fifteen years in the male-dominated culture of a federal agency. Although she had equal opportunity, she felt like an outsider simply because she was the only woman in the department. Headquarters selected her for an award based on her technical achievements and consistent performance. As a surprise, Pam's manager scheduled a meeting to present the award. When he called her up to receive the award, instead of coming to the podium, Pam left the room, cleared her desk, and went to HR to resign. Her manager was stunned that anyone would act like that after being chosen for a prestigious honor. He assumed that she would react as he would have. Months later, he learned why she left. Pam told him, "I worked fifteen years to gain respect for my technical skills because I was seen as a woman doing a man's job. It's only been in the last two years that relationships here have changed and they finally accept me as a full member of the team. The public award ruined it all."

So why did Pam leave? When the award was announced, she saw in the faces of her colleagues that she was no longer one of them. She was afraid they would once again set her apart because she had an award that none of them had; she did not have the heart to rebuild her relationships. Despite supervising Pamela for years, her manager was unaware of her concern about being treated differently when he decided to give her the award publically. Because the manager had not cultivated a close relationship, he was unaware of the potential issue; he treated her as he would want to be treated instead of asking her what she wanted.

In your role as a manager, your relationships largely will be transactional, focused on completing tasks efficiently according to established processes and standards. However, this does not mean that your people are gears in a machine. Use the leadership mindset to discover, understand, and address their feelings, needs, and goals in your conversations. In your role as a leader, your responsibilities become larger, more complex, and more critical to the organization's success. Therefore, you must build relationships whose bonds are deeper and in which respect crosses ethnic, gender, cultural, generational, and distance boundaries. Do not assume that you know your people's needs, desires, or aspirations—learn what they are thinking and feeling by reaching out to them. Listen carefully to their spoken and unspoken responses.

CHAPTER 9

DON'T LET THEM ASSUME THEY KNOW WHAT YOU'RE THINKING

Assumptions are the termites of relationships.
—HENRY WINKLER

People who work for leaders and managers who are open in their conversations about objectives, priorities, concerns, criteria, and time constraints are more likely to operate in alignment with each other. The absence of clarity about those factors leaves people guessing—and running an organization on guesswork is risky. Furthermore, leaders and managers are human, and they have good days and bad days. But their attitudes and moods—good or bad—are a tsunami that engulfs their domain. A buoyant, optimistic mood tends to improve performance; a surly, pessimistic outlook often has the opposite effect.

For example, one CEO was known for exceptionally broad mood swings. Three executives took turns calling him as he drove to work each morning and asked random questions. What they were really doing was ascertaining his mood. When news of a good mood spread, people would line up outside his door to discuss issues and make requests. When they learned about a bad mood, they would literally hide. With coaching, the CEO learned to leave his moods at home. This bolstered his relationships at work and led to more consistent performance throughout the organization.

YOU ARE ALWAYS UNDER A MICROSCOPE

As a successful executive, you know how to prepare for and perform at high-visibility events like presentations and when chairing meetings. You are primed at special events to make a good impression. But do you realize that you are always under a microscope? Do you understand the broad impact you have on your people's effectiveness and satisfaction even in moments when you are not conscious of your actions? Do you know that your people analyze every word you say and everything you do in order to learn how to succeed? Executives often underestimate how closely they are watched. As important as it is to orchestrate big events, it is the little moments—an acknowledging glance, a small compliment, or a few words of encouraging feedback—that determine how your people feel about you, their jobs, and their ability to succeed.

Among the most crucial conversations you will encounter are impromptu incidents that are uncomfortable. You will not know they are coming and usually cannot prepare for them in advance. Those are moments when you must address someone who failed to finish a task on time, missed an important detail, or treated someone else inappropriately. Handling those moments in a way that builds trust and respect—yet sets and enforces standards—will go a long way toward building effective relationships.

"JR, the conversation you had this morning with Jose accusing him of lack of effort didn't go well. Let's meet later today to see what we can do to get things back on track." Recognize that no matter how you handle these situations, the individual is likely to become emotional. Listen for that in his response.

"Boss, I'm sick about the way it turned out, and I'm afraid Jose is really mad. But I couldn't just let the matter go by without doing something. I'm not sure there is anything we can do to fix the situation."

React positively to his statement and the emotions behind it. Do not ignore the problem—rather, turn it into a learning experience. Make it clear that the incident does not irreparably damage your relationship or his chance for future success.

"Yes, he might be mad, but the purpose of our meeting will be to come up with a solution that mends the fences. Once you process what happened, we'll have a conversation to figure out steps to take to resolve the issue."

Remember: everyone is watching what you do—or do not do—in the uncomfortable moments that set the boundaries of acceptable behavior. Your people will only wade into uncomfortable situations and fix them if you model constructive behaviors in such situations.

It takes years to build a reputation and a relationship, but one thoughtless moment can undo everything. Making a bad decision, rebuking a high potential with an offhand remark, or losing your temper will damage relationships. Yet most of the time, your people will not confront you about such behaviors. Do not assume that your actions will be forgotten or forgiven—they will not. Be aware of what you do, acknowledge when you make a mistake, and make a sincere effort to fix it. Handle every faux pas with the individual in mind. Most relationships can be restored with a sincere apology promptly delivered.

Some people are comfortable when you take a humorous approach to acknowledging and apologizing for an error. Others may be affronted by humor because they feel that it belittles them or the issue. Be conscious of how your people react to what you say. Ask for feedback. Some people want to know the corrective actions you will take; others will be satisfied with an apology. Know and study your people just as they know and study you.

LISTENING

When we became coaches, we thought we were intuitive and perceptive. We were trained to understand and accept the answers that clients gave. Yet in those early days, we now see, we tried to guess what our clients would say rather than listening to them. Our guesses were wrong most of the time—we understood that we sometimes missed what they were really saying. Those difficult sessions showed us the key to effective conversations: listen to what people say (and do not say), reflect on the information they provide, ask questions, and only then prepare a response.

The internal conversations people have often obstruct their ability to listen. They may mull over an issue for hours or days—in the car, the shower, or other places where they have a moment to think. They solve the problem in their minds without knowing the perspectives of others. But an effective conversation requires at least two people, and they both must offer their ideas and share their feelings. Use the salient parts of your internal reflections to plan a synchronous conversation with others that improves relationships and results. Having real conversations will prevent you from assuming that you know what people are thinking and what they will say. Be transparent and look for connection and alignment.

TRANSPARENCY

Transparency enables people to feel trusted and connected in an organization. It also allows leaders to be open and honest about their objectives, motives, and capabilities. Being transparent by acknowledging weaknesses will engender trust as long as people do not perceive the weaknesses as a barrier to success. Examples of being transparent about one's weaknesses include statements such as these:

"I have difficulty remembering names. Please introduce me to our clients when we circulate during the event."
"I am creative, but sometimes I don't get the numbers exactly right. Please double-check them and don't hesitate to tell me when I'm off the mark."
"We're entering uncharted waters relative to customers for the new product line, so our sales forecast isn't as solid as we'd like. Please provide customer feedback as soon as you can."

Few organizations are fully transparent—some information is embargoed. You face two challenges in transparency: (1) the need to pass on vital information in a timely manner and (2) the need to be forthright that some information must be held closely. The critical areas where transparency is essential are

- Organizational objectives and concerns
- Changes in strategy and priorities
- The criteria and timetable for advancement
- Processes and techniques that enable people to perform better

Clearly, information related to confidential personal matters, legal issues covered by nondisclosure agreements, and merger-and-acquisition transactions cannot be shared openly. Keep in mind that the higher you rise in an organization, the more that people will look to you as the source of information and the more constraints you will have on what information you can and cannot share.

AUTHENTICITY

From the moment you were born, you began developing emotional intelligence by smiling, crying, and making cute gestures. At first your actions were automatic, but soon you noticed that people reacted to the things you did. You started engaging those reactions purposefully to satisfy your need for food, comfort, and attention. Your need to express desires and emotions to others did not decrease as you grew older. Rather, your actions became more complex as your desires grew and your emotions became more intense. Sociologists say that up to 85 percent of the messages we send to others are nonverbal. As a leader, realize that you are continuously conveying information to your people whether you intend to or not—even when you say nothing, you still are sending messages.

On the positive side, you can connect and align with others through dynamic nonverbal interactions—if they match your words. Trust evaporates and problems emerge if there is a gap between what people hear you say and what they see you do. Authentic conversations close the gap by allowing full disclosure and setting clear expectations. When you hold effective conversations, your people will not need to speculate among themselves, make assumptions, or analyze the possibilities on their own.

You could go to extraordinary lengths to present a brand that defines who you are and what you stand for, and broadcast that brand on social media sites. But if the brand substitutes for effective one-on-one conversations, it will not carry you across the finish line. Humans thrive in relationships. They want face-to-face interactions during which they look in your eyes to assess your trustworthiness. People are hardwired to act that way, and they will subconsciously see microexpressions that you are not even aware of.

Therefore, it is essential to design the message they are receiving to ensure that it matches your intentions. When you are authentic, you influence others easily because your words and actions present a unified picture of who you are. Being authentic means that what you think, what you say, and what you do are in alignment. Being who you are means being authentic without hiding anything. Tell your story: how you came to be the way you are and what you may want to change about yourself to become more effective as a leader. When you are authentic, you encourage others to be authentic too— and authentic conversations build authentic relationships.

HAVING THE RIGHT CONVERSATIONS

Leaders hold the right conversations with the right people at the right time to build relationships that create alignment and connection. Conversations conducted in the first perspective tell people what you want them to know and are used by virtually all executives. However, in the extreme, that practice hamstrings an otherwise effective organization. Conversations in perspectives two and three can bring people together—lack of such conversations can drive them away.

For example, Raul, a senior executive in a county government, was proud of his open-door policy. But when we asked how many people had actually walked through his door last week to have a conversation, he hesitated and said, "Last week ... no one. I wonder why?" Interviews with his key people revealed the reason. They all managed multiple projects. When they came to his office seeking advice on a project, he always provided insightful sugges-tions. But when they tried to leave, he would ask probing questions about their other projects, which they were not prepared to discuss. So no matter how useful his insights were, the risk of being caught without up-to-the-minute status on every project outweighed the value of receiving assistance on the priority project. Armed with this insight, Raul promised his project managers that he would stop asking about other projects when they came to him for assistance. With clear boundaries set, the free flow of information resumed.

CHAPTER 10

EMBRACE DIFFERENCES

*The biggest mistake is believing there is one right way to listen, to talk,
and to have a conversation—or a relationship.*
—DEBORAH TANNEN

Kate, a competitive rower in the United Kingdom, was much shorter than the other seven women in her boat, yet she was equally passionate about rowing. To gain her seat, she trained harder, longer, and more intensely than the others, who had an easier time because of their height. Everyone showed up differently prior to a race. Kate was focused and quiet, some chatted and giggled, others wandered off alone, and one energetically tried to rouse team spirit. Those differences stopped them from rowing as a team. The seven felt pressured by Kate; she felt they were blasé. After losing a race for the first time in more than a year, everyone was upset.

The coach encouraged them to examine their personalities and realize that they each offered something special. Kate could assist others in getting "into the zone" before a race, and the others could assist her technically and emotionally by helping her relax and enjoy the race. All it took was an understanding and patient conversation. They went on to have a blistering win-loss record that season, and the relationships remain strong to this day. Kate learned three lifelong lessons:

- There are several different ways to achieve the same goal.
- A team must work together even if the members work differently.
- Patience and learning produce mutual success and, just as important, fun.

How you react when you encounter people with different points of view defines you as a leader. Leaders who recognize the significance of today's multicultural workplace embrace diversity as a strategic necessity. They understand that an organization that welcomes and respects people regardless of race, religion, gender, sexual orientation, age, or other characteristics has a strategic advantage because it will attract top talent globally. They have seen how organizations that tap into diverse perspectives routinely produce better products, grow faster, and deliver superior customer service. In contrast, some executives see diversity as an altruistic concept that rewards people based on factors other than results. Most executives are somewhere in the middle. They acknowledge the human benefits of diversity, but do not know how to use it to drive superior results and separate their organizations from competitors. This chapter offers pointers to assist you in embracing diversity and inclusion.

OPEN YOUR MIND

Leah, a high-potential executive responsible for enterprise growth in an accounting firm, described her reaction to meeting new people:

"I look for people to teach me new ways to reach our goals. I get especially excited when I'm with people from different backgrounds who have a new perspective about delivering services and building the firm. In fact, my job is to stimulate innovation by coaxing new ideas out of them. If I'm not meeting new people every day, I'm not doing my job properly."

Leah's open mind helps her arouse creativity in others and recognize the value they contribute. Her attitude shows new people that she values her time with them. To be open, you do not have to change your mind, but you must be willing to do so. Closed-minded executives often listen with negative body language that looks like a neon sign on their forehead flashing no. Their people feel devalued and eventually stop providing ideas. Open-minded executives lean into a conversation (sometimes physically) to learn more. They ask insightful questions and build relationships by respecting the ideas of others.

Being open is especially challenging for those who operate in a purely management mindset and focus on deadlines. Leadership flexibility is required to suspend judgment and consider a new idea at the eleventh hour. When an idea at first does not appear to make sense but is passionately presented by one of your people, take time to understand her thinking as well as how the idea fits the big picture. Look for the link that could produce a major breakthrough. Ask why instead of telling her why not.

For example, a new product manager was assigned to women's brands in a large consumer products company. By the end of his first day, he was somewhere between nonplussed and angry, as he knew little about the women's brands but felt very knowledgeable about brand-name products for men. Afraid that his marketing career might end before it started, he found the courage to ask his boss how the company could make such a mistake. He participated in his first leadership conversation that day when his boss said, "It's not what you know that counts. It's hearing what each consumer wants that successfully positions a product. How easily could you keep an open mind were you to manage products that you use every day?"

Although the new product manager never found a reason to use the products himself, he spent days watching women use them and asking what they preferred and disliked. Thanks to the effort of the entire marketing team, his product went from number three to number one in its category. Had he followed his initial instincts and insisted that he be assigned to men's brands, he would have missed the building blocks of building relationships: be curious about differences, ask questions, and listen carefully.

ENCOURAGE DIVERSITY AND INCLUSION

Understanding the principles of diversity and inclusion and being able to build relationships and connect with people who are different from you are critical to success. Historically, executives have not been adept at inclusion, so it is not easy to find great mentors in this area. At the same time, the emphasis on diversity and inclusion is intensifying because populations are becoming more diverse, international affiliations are expanding for many organizations, and government mandates require organizations to accommodate ever-broadening types of diversity.

There are so many types of diversity that it is easy to unknowingly or unconsciously offend others or trample on their beliefs. Some areas of diversity, such as age, gender, language, race, and disability, are easy to identify because we see or hear them. Other areas—nationality, sexual orientation, level of education, political leaning, religion, and spiritual beliefs—are subtle and usually become apparent only during personal conversations. Still other types of diversity, such as learning style, military service, and genetics, may require in-depth conversations to discover.

Leadership practices and attitudes vary widely from group to group, so seek to understand how and why those practices and attitudes developed the way they did. For example, insightful conversations about diversity and inclusion are common in Europe because of the number of different cultures, languages, and religions that coexist in a small geographical area.

For example, at the end of one leadership presentation in Germany, the audience was quiet. Being from the United States, the speaker was puzzled and asked, "What was it about tonight's presentation that dampened the conversation?" One listener hesitantly volunteered that "it's complicated to aspire to leadership in Europe because of how diverse the region's leaders have been just in my lifetime." That comment led to an enlightening discussion of how to put leadership principles into practice across borders. By accepting that members of the audience had different but equally valid thoughts on the topic of leadership, the speaker and audience gained several new insights:

- New relationships thrive when you reach out to people with trust and respect, hear what they say, and react appropriately—especially when they have different cultural or religious beliefs or different personality styles.
- Most people accept that differences of opinion exist and that their opinions may not prevail—but they expect to be heard. Attempting to avoid conflict by ignoring dissenting opinions tends to deepen the conflict.
- When people disagree with you or do things you do not want them to do, it is not insubordination—it is an opportunity to learn and strengthen the relationship.

In coaching, we often hear impassioned pleas ending with "I just don't understand why they won't do it my way." We respond to that frustration with a simple question: "Why do you expect them to be like you?" When this does not make the point, we ask a follow-up question: "Will you agree to do it their way instead of expecting them to do it yours? The logic is the same." At that point, people usually see that anyone can be intractable in her way of doing things. Consider differences to be a productive topic for a leadership conversation—not an excuse to argue.

MAKE DIVERSITY WORK

Gretchen grew up in Denmark, went to college in England, and got her first job in Germany. After positions in Berlin, Paris, and Madrid, she transferred to New York. The cultural collision started the first Friday evening when she declined an invitation from her colleagues for hot dogs, beer, and a baseball game at Yankee Stadium. Gretchen's curt response and apparent lack of interest caused them to label her as standoffish and arrogant. Soon, revenue in her department flatlined as her people gave only lip service to her decisions. Eventually, she was replaced and transferred to France. Gretchen's style, effective in Europe, did not mesh well with a more informal business style in the United States. If effective conversations had occurred between Gretchen and her boss and between Gretchen and her people, she may not have been derailed. High potential for leadership across international boundaries was squandered.

Making diversity work is so crucial to success in today's globally connected world that some organizations have appointed a chief diversity officer to cultivate diversity and inclusion. It is not diversity itself that matters. Rather it is how effectively you lead a diverse workforce to achieve the organization's goals. There is no cookie-cutter definition of diversity—few practices work equally well in the United States, Europe, China, and, say, Brazil. Yet diversity must be accommodated in business strategies because diversity in the customer base is increasing as rapidly as it is in the workforce.

When you look around the table during your next meeting, you are likely to see customers and stakeholders of various races, religions, physical abilities, sexual orientations, and generations. You and your team must address that diversity in order to develop and deliver products and services that meet customers' needs. Further, as workforce diversity increases, the ability to build relationships with diverse people is necessary to give everyone a path to reach his full potential. Empathize with and include those who are different from you rather than dismissing them or isolating yourself from them.

TEN WAYS TO PRACTICE GREAT LEADERSHIP IN BUILDING RELATIONSHIPS

1. **Use electronic media carefully.** Next time you want to send a negative email, do three things first: (1) save a draft with no addressees (in case you hit Send by mistake); (2) consider what your family would say if it appeared on Facebook; and (3) use it to plan a conversation. Then delete it and speak with that person.

2. **Network.** Start a list of target relationships by identifying ten new people who could help you professionally over the next five years. Also identify what you can do to help them. For each person, identify scenarios where you could meet him or her.

3. **Stay in touch.** Who are your key stakeholders? What techniques do you use to stay in touch with them on a regular basis?

4. **Know your strengths and shadows.** What are your greatest strengths as a leader? How does overusing those strengths sometimes have negative effects?

5. **Follow the rules.** To what extent do you and other leaders in your organization follow the rules established for your people? To what extent do all of you hold each other accountable to those rules?

6. **Set big goals.** Use leadership conversations to set goals with your people. Ensure that the goals are set high enough to achieve everything you, your people, and your organization are capable of achieving.

7. **Be authentic.** Identify an area where you have not been completely open about yourself. Have a conversation with your people that reveals your humanity in that area.

8. **Find out what others are thinking.** When your boss, a peer, or a direct report stakes out a position or offers an idea that does not make sense to you, ask questions to find out what she is seeing that you are missing, or vice versa.

9. **Think *yes-and*.** Are you weighing two alternatives or considering the ideas of two people? Instead of using either-or thinking, ask yourself how you could embrace both of them.

10. **Use conflict constructively.** During your next meeting, purposefully use constructive conflict to explore controversial ideas and bring out new points of view. Ask (a) "Why can't we do both?" (b) "Is that the best we can do?" or (c) "What else could we do?"

PART 3

CONVERSATIONS TO DEVELOP OTHERS

The demand for proven leaders exceeds the supply—so much so that head-hunters prosper even in soft economies as organizations offer enormous compensation packages to attract superstars. The problem is that everyone pursues the same proven leaders. Organizations that consciously grow their future leaders instead of bidding for outside talent are far more likely to consistently produce better results.

Most executives spend considerable time minimizing risks in their strategic decisions, but skip such thinking in personnel decisions. Developing high potentials reduces the risks inherent in leadership-level hiring decisions. To win the battle for talent, your organization must ensure that an effective leadership development and retention program is a core element of its long-term strategy.

Part 3 presents a bottom-to-top succession strategy that will help your organization win the battle for talent (Chapter 11), and addresses the special challenge of leading other high-potentials (Chapter 12). It provides tips for holding baseline and feedback conversations (Chapter 13) that form the foundation for success, and shows how integrate training, mentoring, and coaching into your daily routine to eliminate obstacles that block progress—yours and your people's (Chapter 14). We close by focusing on effective ways to recognize your people's accomplishments and celebrate their successes (Chapter 15).

CHAPTER 11

THE BATTLE FOR TALENT

The only thing worse than training employees and losing them is
not training them and keeping them.
—ZIG ZIGLAR

Do conversations similar to this occur in your organization?

Janet: "We work in a fast-paced environment, with so many new people that it's nearly impossible to know who is right for a new project. We consistently hire outside managers when we need them, and that approach is creating chaos. Each of them was hired for a specific project, and they struggle because they don't know how we do business. Frankly, I think we aren't using the talents of the people we already have, and we're missing some key leadership skills."

Steve: "We don't have time to think about ways to develop our people. We work with top-notch recruiters who have always delivered the right person at the right time. Why should we change how we operate?"

Janet: "With all due respect to you as CEO, the wheels are coming off. Clients are complaining because we cobble together teams that may or may not work well together. Turnover is twice the industry average because our people don't feel connected to their work, to us, or to the company's culture. Besides, recruiting fees are so high that we've had to cut back on training to stay within the budget."

During this conversation, Janet shifted from a management to a leadership mindset to envision the workforce of the future. Steve is operating staunchly in a management mindset that focuses on meeting near-term deadlines. Neither of them knows his or her people well enough to accurately measure the risk of reassigning or promoting them, or which skills and additional people they need to sustain the company's growth. Furthermore, they lack a reliable process for developing the relationships, skills, and mindsets that their people will need to succeed in future positions. The conversation continued:

Janet: Bottom line, Steve, we're spending too much time onboarding people and investing too little to develop the potential of those we already have. To sustain our growth, we need a strategy—especially for the high potentials who are the company's future leaders—to develop our people and align them with our culture, growth strategy, and business processes.

Steve: Okay, Janet, come up with a plan to systematically develop our people and build the skills and attitudes we need. I'll review it with you and present it to the executive team at the strategic planning off-site next month.

The management mindset, of course, is essential to getting things done. Steve and Janet initially treated people like commodities to be allocated to the most urgent project; and when necessary, they just went out and bought more. In the short term, that approach worked, but performance eventually deteriorated because the people were not increasing their capabilities—they were just getting the job done. Acknowledging their problems, Steve and Janet's conversation switched to a leadership mindset when they committed to develop their people to support the growth strategy.

Blending the management and leadership mindsets is also critical in making technology investments. Operating in a management mindset, many executives use technology as a tool to improve efficiency and reduce errors— they want to get more done with fewer people. When executives use a leadership mindset, technology is seen as a way to leverage people's skills and develop their capabilities more rapidly. That approach consistently produces superior results because high potentials become vested in the company's strategy and consider themselves to be key players in its growth. They willingly adopt new technologies instead of fearing them.

BUILD VERSUS BUY

Unfortunately, a common approach for handling high potentials is to promote them into key positions with the expectation that they already know what they need to know to succeed. Too often they receive minimal assistance to understand, let alone conquer, challenges of the new position. In short, conversations do not take place to develop a plan, set expectations, define metrics, and mentor the high potentials. If you do not invest in developing your high potentials, one of three things is likely to happen:

- They will succeed on their own (which may be how you did it).
- When results fall short, you will step in to fix the problem.
- Eventually the high potentials will leave, be demoted, or be fired.

It is more effective and easier on everybody to eliminate the fix-it-later process by having developmental conversations early and often with your high potentials.

Organizations that lack an effective leadership development program are forced to buy talent in the open market—a time-consuming, expensive, and risky approach. The issue is not merely that organizations do not grow the leadership, management, and technical skills of their people. The real problem is even more troubling: an organization underperforms when it does not develop its people. Yet few organizations view coaching, training, and developmental assignments for high potentials to be a vital part of their growth strategy. The problem starts at the top when CEOs neither mentor their CXOs nor insist that the CXOs mentor their direct reports.

Executives who consider a job to be a set of tasks miss the importance of developing people. Each leadership level involves new priorities, more complex skills, and a different blend of leadership and management mindsets than the previous one. The conversion of success at one level to success at higher levels requires you to mentor people rather than just assume that they will be able to do the new job. The need to mentor is even more urgent when you fill a leadership position with outside talent. Those who are also moving up a leadership level when they join your organization are particularly at risk. In addition to tackling new responsibilities, these executives must build new relationships, learn new processes and tools, adapt to a new culture, and deal with resentment from insiders who may have wanted the position. They will require more mentoring than an executive who is promoted from within.

Hiring exceptional employees makes sense, of course, when new viewpoints or new skills are needed, but it is not sustainable as the primary way to find leaders. Hiring leaders costs too much and is more prone to mistakes than promoting an employee who has institutional knowledge and established relationships. Furthermore, many high-priced business stars change organizations so frequently that they fail to master the skills required at one leadership level before moving up to the next. You might just be hiring someone else's problem.

START WITH THE RIGHT PEOPLE

Building a staff stocked with high potentials starts with candidate interviews at every level, especially individual contributors.

"Paul, in evaluating you for your first job out of college, we want to understand your interest in and passion for future management and leadership positions as well as your fit with our culture and your ability to perform in this position."

"I'm glad to hear that, because I see myself as a good fit for your company and that you are striving to do special things here. I want to work in an organization that has advancement potential and will develop my skills."

"That's great, Paul; let's start by having you tell me a bit about yourself and what you want to accomplish over your career."

Using resumes, references on the Internet, and social media as a base, interviews should confirm the candidate's achievements, validate his or her skills against the position's requirements, and—most important—ensure that the candidate fits your culture.

Great organizations have a culture that accelerates growth in people who embrace its values and that rejects those who do not. When we are asked, "How do I hire people who fit our culture?" we answer quickly: "Look for people who are attracted by your mission, goals, and values—and be sure that you retain those people."

When evaluating candidates for promotion, avoid the trap of assuming that the best salesperson, engineer, or other individual contributor will be the best manager. Instead, promote the candidate who demonstrates the potential to manage and lead. "Jackson, you didn't earn this promotion because you are one of the top salesmen. Your sales record is extraordinary, but you were promoted because you exhibit the mindset and behaviors that we believe will make you a great manager."

High potentials are defined as much by how they think as by the skills they have. Specifically, they

- **Have a passion for the work they do.** They pursue the organization's goals with diligence and intensity.
- **Collaborate with others.** They share information, are open and honest, and volunteer to help others. When things go right, they share credit; when things go wrong, they do not blame someone or something else.
- **Are curious learners.** They are willing to take calculated risks, learn from the results, and adapt to a fast-changing environment.
- **Do what they say they will do.** Because they consider their word to be their bond, they are careful about what they promise and rarely overcommit.

These criteria are uncomfortable for executives who are accustomed to making hiring and promotion decisions based on the best technical skills or as a reward for past performance. It is more effective to evaluate individual contributors in terms of their aptitude to become a first-line manager; evaluate first-line managers in terms of their executive potential; and so forth. When you understand that you are not just filling an open position but are building the organization's leadership inventory, the hiring and promotion process takes on greater importance.

YOUR RESPONSIBILITY TO DEVELOP OTHERS

Next to making strategic decisions, a leader's most important responsibility is to develop her people. Why? Mistakes in hiring and promoting have near-term negative effects on results. Most promotion mistakes happen because the leadership bench strength is shallow and leadership conversations are either trivial or nonexistent. The most effective leadership development programs are constructed to produce a stream of great candidates that flows steadily from the bottom to the top of the organization.

Most executives acknowledge their responsibility to develop people. Yet few know how to do so—and even fewer make it a priority in their daily agenda. Today's business imperatives tend to trump tomorrow's strategic priorities. Yet with a bit of planning, you can meet short-term objectives and grow your people concurrently. Start by asking why some of your best strategies produced mediocre results, why crucial deadlines were missed, and comparing your turnover to industry standards. Because these are all people issues, assume that you will need to mentor your people to resolve them. As a high-potential executive, you have felt the pressure of preparing plans, working with limited resources, meeting tight deadlines, and achieving stretch goals. Share your stories with your people in everyday conversations to explain how you conquered those challenges. Encourage them to have the same conversations with their people.

We asked a friend who was appointed to a CXO position in a public company, "How did you get where you are?" He replied, "I'm here today because I always did what I love. But just as important, I'm here today because people along the way recognized my potential, mentored me, pushed me to grow, and insisted that I develop my people."

This CXO learned that developing others unlocks one's own potential. High potentials by definition have most of what is required to succeed—your job is to help them develop the rest. That entails guiding first-line managers from an individual contributor mindset to a management mindset, and managers of managers toward the leadership mindset, as shown in Figure 11.1. Model and teach leadership behaviors so that your direct reports will recognize the value in teaching their people. That approach deepens leadership bench strength and provides a stream of succession candidates.

	Management Mindset	Leadership Mindset
Building Relationships	Build transactional relationships to get the job done	Build trusted relationships to envision and achieve goals
Developing Others	Teach people what they need to know for their jobs	Build an organization that will prosper long after you have left
Making Decisions	Make decisions based on the best technical approach	Choose courses of action that stimulate long-term growth
Taking Action	Provide resources and push people to get the job done	Balance the importance of long-term and short-term results

FIGURE 11.1. Cultivating a New Mindset.

Help first-line managers develop their management mindset and managers of managers develop their leadership mindset.

HOW DEEP SHOULD SUCCESSION PLANNING GO?

Organizations of all sizes stumble when an executive leaves and a replacement is not ready to step up. Especially at the CEO level, the new executive is frequently an outsider, because no internal candidate has been developed who meets leadership standards set by the board. Typically, the outsider does not have relationships with members of the company's management team, who are instinctively nervous about the new CEO's agenda. Or the board may select the insider with the best CXO performance record, even though he may lack the vision needed to lead the company as CEO. Organizations that have trouble filling CEO vacancies usually have equal difficulty in filling lower-level positions. They urgently need a bottom-to-top leadership development strategy that supports continuity of operations.

Succession planning is often equated with replacement planning, particularly in large organizations. Key executives officially designate multiple candidates as their potential replacements, and those candidates are put through rigorous training and evaluations. However, those programs are flawed if they are based on the premise that tomorrow's leadership requirements will be the same as yesterday's. Leaders must adapt to changing technologies, markets, alliances, and demographics. In addition, globalization, mobile communications, outsourcing, and mergers have eliminated positions while also creating positions with new leadership challenges. Replacement planning is inadequate in this scenario. Instead, positions should be defined flexibly in terms of the evolving needs of the organization and its stakeholders. That approach develops loyalty and builds a pool of leaders who can direct new strategic initiatives or replace departing leaders.

Too much emphasis is placed on succession planning for CEO and CXO positions and not enough on other leadership positions. Evaluate your organization's leadership development program in terms of the steady flow of talent it does (or does not) produce for open leadership positions. Effective programs start by hiring individual contributors who have the desire and aptitude to become managers. Each successive leadership level is built primarily by promoting high potentials from lower levels. Predictable changes occur in each promotion from individual contributor through corner-office positions.

From Individual Contributor to First-Line Manager

You probably spent your early employment years as an individual contributor in sales, marketing, engineering, production, accounting, or another specialty. You contributed by completing tasks according to a schedule and standards set by your first-line manager. When you sharpened your skills and earned a reputation for quality and reliability, you were given more complex tasks. As a high potential, you learned to plan work so that it would get done on time, and you embraced the organization's values. When your skills and productivity were among the best and you collaborated effectively with others, you were promoted to first-line manager. You were (we hope) among the lucky few who received coaching and mentoring in the role and mindset of first-line manager so that you could understand and master your new challenges.

As a first-line manager, you applied multiple management skills, including dividing objectives into tasks, assigning tasks, setting schedules and standards, measuring performance, providing feedback, motivating others, interviewing new employees, and training people to fill your job. Some of these skills may have been new to you. However, you were able to perform them well once you realized that your performance was measured by the quantity and quality of results that your people produced. Your performance did not depend on how much you did yourself. If you managed poorly, you spent a lot of time putting out fires. If you managed well, you had time available to invest in innovative ideas and new opportunities.

From First-Line Manager to Manager of Managers

The biggest change in moving from first-line manager to a manager who manages other managers is that your new job is no longer technical. As a first-line manager, you would still make occasional technical contributions and judgments. That will seldom work as a manager of managers. The additional skills required to be successful involve selecting the right people as first-line managers, assessing their capabilities, and coaching them to become effective managers rather than doers. Generally, for the first time, you also will be required to look beyond your function and contribute to strategic planning for your organization.

It is hard to be an effective manager of managers if you insist on making technical contributions. If you did not master the leadership skills of a first-line manager, you are at risk of failing at this level. Two early symptoms of problems are that you

- Chose first-line managers based on technical rather than management skills
- Hold first-line managers accountable exclusively for technical results, rather than primarily management results

If you are doing either of these, you are limiting your success, limiting your people's growth, and disrupting the upward flow of high potentials. Instead, mentor and coach your direct reports to be effective managers, and be patient as you repeatedly lead them through the feedback cycle. One of the most difficult conversations you will face as a manager of managers will be the one in which you return a technically competent first-line manager to individual contributor status because of his or her inability (or unwillingness) to develop a management mindset.

From Manager of Managers to Executive Leader

You may think that being an executive who leads a multifaceted operation would be similar to managing other managers. But it is much more than that:

- When you exchange interesting ideas with technically savvy individual contributors, you are bypassing two management levels; so you must develop communication channels that keep everyone in the loop.
- Some of your direct reports may manage functions that are foreign to your experience; so be prepared to learn a new vocabulary, deal with new concepts, and address unfamiliar challenges.
- You will be leading a diverse team of managers who have varying and often conflicting needs, so emphasize the importance of teamwork.
- You will be allocating valuable resources to competing functions and projects, often without being sure which will produce the best rate of return; so formalize the decision-making process that is used within your domain.
- You will be the primary strategist for your business segment. Your people will offer ideas, but they will look to you to combine them into a cohesive plan.
- You will be a key player in developing the enterprise strategy, a task that will require a large chunk of your time and force you to delegate more than you did in previous positions.

Furthermore, your successes and failures will now be visible to the CEO and other top executives. In order for you to produce a sustainable strategic advantage, your focus must shift from "How do we do this best?" (management mindset) to "Is this the best thing to do?" (leadership mindset). Reblending the two mindsets is the top challenge that executives face at this level. They sometimes put too much focus on short-term results or attempt an elegant long-term strategy that produces weak short-term results. Your job is to be better than your competitors by being innovative in delivering products and services, building lasting customer relationships, and improving efficiency.

You will enjoy significant autonomy and see direct links between your actions and your results. In addition to integrating multiple functions, you will also find yourself working with a variety of people and facing multifaceted cultural issues. You frequently will be pushed to make trade-offs among production, revenue, profit, people, and innovation goals, and, at the same time, to implement strategies that will produce superior results years into the future.

Entering the C-Suite

You have worked your entire career to create this opportunity. You delivered top-notch results and learned valuable leadership skills as you mastered previous roles. Because you have managed a major business area successfully, managing across a portfolio of business areas should not be a problem—yet there are a few new wrinkles. As an executive leader, you focused on the success of your business unit, but as a CXO you also must value—and contribute to—the success of your peers. This may be awkward for those who enjoy receiving personal accolades for spectacular results. A CXO who does not value the success of executive leaders and other CXOs usually will fail to support them adequately and thus fail to meet the CEO's expectations.

Leading across a portfolio of business units is very different than directing a single unit. You must become proficient at asking the right questions and analyzing the right information in order to select the best strategy. You must continue to motivate the high potentials who work for you—the best of whom lust after your job—even as you prepare them to step into it. Other vexing strategic questions you will face include, "Are our business units synergistic?" "Which units should we shrink, expand, or change to improve our market position?"

Leadership is holistic at the CXO level. CXOs must be shrewd in assessing the organization's core capabilities and resources—especially its people. The laser focus that helped you succeed earlier in your career could become a liability if it interferes with your ability to understand the big picture. And these are only the internal portions of your new responsibilities.

As CXO, you must be a visionary thinker who grasps the importance of global trends while, at the same time, ensuring that mechanisms are in place to deliver quarterly results. The trade-offs can confound the best leaders. The organization's long-term success hinges on a few pivotal decisions each year. The challenge is in knowing which of your thousand decisions are in that category. Similarly, your organization's growth will be accelerated or retarded by your effectiveness in building strategic partnerships in your industry and sister industries. Possibly the most exciting aspect of being a CXO is the opportunity you have to inspire employees to achieve greatness. Leadership conversation skills will be among your most prized and powerful tools in winning the battle for talent.

CHAPTER 12

THE CHALLENGE OF LEADING OTHER HIGH POTENTIALS

Before you become a leader, success is about growing yourself.
When you become a leader, success is all about growing others.
—JACK WELCH

Sylvia personified high potential. After being valedictorian at an elite all-women college, she earned an Ivy League MBA and was recruited by a prestigious consulting firm. Her track record on strategic planning engagements with large companies was nearly flawless. Clients were amazed by her insights and work ethic. Soon she was managing major clients, often exceeding their expectations, and growing revenue. Even though she received top performance ratings and big salary bumps, her senior partner said it would be a few years before she would be considered for partner.

Frustrated, she resigned and quickly found a position as section head in corporate development with a Fortune 500 company. From the start, she received accolades because her group consistently produced insightful analyses. After a year, she was promoted to manage a department with a dozen first-line managers, one hundred professionals, and a support staff. To shorten a long and painful story, the department's performance deteriorated because of her lack of leadership, and two years later she was fired.

Sylvia was a brilliant individual contributor who did not learn first-line management skills before being promoted into a manager-of-managers position. Her high potential was wasted because neither the senior partner at her first consulting firm nor either of her bosses at the Fortune 500 company mentored her to develop her management and leadership mindsets.

By definition, you and the high potentials who work for you have the ability to be great future leaders. Conversely, you also have the potential for catastrophic failure if you rise too fast without grasping the leadership differences between successive positions. By holding leadership conversations that help high potentials achieve the appropriate blend of leadership and management mindsets, you can make the difference between their success and failure—and yours too.

ASSESSING POTENTIAL

High potentials often can be identified by their rapid rise through the ranks, as illustrated on their resumes. What resumes don't show is that many superstars have yet to learn the leadership skills required for the next level. High potentials often get the benefit of doubt in personnel decisions because of their extraordinary past performance. As a result, they can zoom up the leadership ladder so quickly that they don't have opportunities to learn vital lessons. Unfortunately, if you do not know the skills required at each level and how to develop those that may be missing, the first indication of a problem may be a shocking career derailment like Sylvia's.

High potentials usually have the following characteristics:

- They demonstrate the intelligence, ability, judgment, and emotional intelligence commonly found in top leaders.
- They have a genuine passion for business and sometimes come across as ambitious and aggressive—they want it all and they want it now.
- Many have advanced rapidly without managing through the full cycle of (1) analyzing a problem, (2) developing a solution, (3) gaining buy-in, (4) implementing a plan, (5) evaluating in-process results, and (6) making adjustments to improve the outcome.
- They tend to be process oriented. They understand work flows, problem solving, and how to put together a team to get the job done.

A person can only be labeled as a high potential if she is expected to excel in the future on the basis of her ability to build relationships, apply accumulated technical and professional skills, learn and adapt to change, and tackle complex tasks. A person's potential can and often does change over the course of a career because of acquired skills, the changing nature of jobs, emerging technologies, and new relationships. Because people sometimes reinvent themselves, keep an open mind about who in your organization is a high potential.

High potentials should be evaluated in terms of three categories:

- **Expert potential:** ability to do more complex tasks in the same field (example: a manager who has the technical skill to lead a team in developing a cutting-edge technology)
- **Growth potential:** ability to lead bigger projects at the same level (example: a manager who is happy in his or her specialty who could lead that function for a larger team)
- **Promotion potential:** ability to deliver results at the next higher level (example: a proficient first-line manager who may have potential to become a manager of managers)

For the purposes of both succession planning and candidate selection, these categories offer a common language for decision-makers in discussing high potential. Likewise, the three categories are useful in performance reviews, career counseling, and interviews. Do the high potentials who work for you have the potential to be high-level experts, to do bigger jobs, or to be promoted? Making this distinction will enable you to coach them more effectively about future opportunities and to recommend appropriate training.

DEVELOPING LEADERSHIP SKILLS IN HIGH POTENTIALS

Each promotion requires a high potential to learn new ways of leading and to leave some old ways behind—even though the old ways produced success in the past. The five attributes that change significantly after each promotion are

- **Skill requirements:** the capabilities required to achieve objectives
- **Priorities:** the things that are most important to do first
- **Measures of success:** the criteria for "doing a good job"
- **Time frames:** the time horizons that govern the work
- **Relationships:** internal and external people who are vital to success

Some high potentials persist in using the attributes of their old positions; or, even worse, they may not have learned the key attributes of that position. Similarly, if you did not learn how to perform at a previous level, you will have a hard time mentoring your direct reports in how to perform at their level. As a result, you could be less effective as a leader in your new level, and the development of your people may be adversely affected.

Although high potentials may excel in such management areas as risk taking, finance, and planning, they may be weak in leadership areas, such as people selection, performance assessments, and coaching—if they continue thinking like individual contributors. In coaching engagements, for example, we frequently hear direct reports complain that their bosses treat them like robots and expect them to do exactly what they are told. Coaching your high potentials on how to value and develop people is a high-priority conversation.

Well-defined leadership requirements for each position are essential in providing targeted assistance to high potentials. One-size-fits-all training generally is only marginally effective. Evaluate a person's readiness to move to the next level by considering his ability to fulfill the needs of the new position rather than by looking solely at the results he produced in the current one. As we discussed in Chapter 11, one real benefit of developing high potentials is that you will win the battle for talent by growing your own stars instead of being compelled to offer astronomical compensation packages to hire them.

Developing leadership skills in high potentials is not an HR function. Rather, it is a strategic imperative that should be championed by leaders at all levels and in all departments, including HR. Make it part of the culture and demonstrate its importance by modeling it yourself. Expect performance gaps initially whenever one of your high potentials is promoted into a new position. No matter how skilled or successful she was previously, every time a person moves up a level, she enters a new world that has new lessons to learn. Hold conversations to identify and close such gaps in yourself and in the high potentials who report to you.

DEMAND MORE FROM YOUR HIGH POTENTIALS

One of your goals as a leader is to coach high potentials to achieve excellence. Start by ensuring that they have the knowledge, tools, and attitude necessary for their positions. Hold a conversation to explain the strategy and to specify what you expect from them. For example, consider Matt, a high potential who was just promoted to first-line manager reporting to you. You know Matt's superb record as an individual contributor and are thrilled to have him on your team. Yet you also know that the move to first-line manager is especially difficult. A good way to begin Matt's tenure would be to engage in a conversation about your expectations and his challenges as a first-line manager. Those include the skills of

- Communicating expectations and objectives to his people
- Defining and assigning tasks to be done, and establishing schedules
- Delegating work to his people instead of doing it himself
- Providing resources, measuring performance, and giving helpful feedback
- Building effective relationships with you, his peers, and his people

Guide Matt to plan his first tasks carefully. Conversations take time, but if he is a typical new first-line manager, Matt will want to charge ahead to do things rather than plan what must be done. Caution him instead to prepare before acting. Mentor him in filling the vacancy that his promotion created, and ensure that he considers how well the candidate fits the culture. As an experienced leader and coach, you can assist Matt in using a mindset appropriate for these and other tasks. Do not wait for him to struggle.

One thing that retards the growth of high potentials is not asking enough of them—especially those who have been recently promoted to first-line manager or manager of managers. Instead of treating them like overgrown individual contributors, ask more of them. Encourage them to participate in budget development and strategic planning. Have them give a presentation on a vital topic at your next meeting. Challenge them to do considerable research and stretch their boundaries. Perhaps ask them to prepare and justify the budget for their operation; ensuring that work is done at the right cost is an increasingly important skill these days. One significant benefit of asking more from high potentials is that it softens any unrealistic expectations they may have about how fast they should advance to the next position. It helps them realize how much they still must learn.

DON'T MISS THE SIGNS OF TROUBLE

If you do not ask the right questions and then hold the necessary conversations, poor performance may be just around the corner. If people tell you what you want to hear, are reluctant to put an issue on the table, withhold negative information, or think they can fix problems alone, trouble is coming—or has already arrived. When the meaningful part of a conversation takes place in the hallway after a meeting without including you as the leader, problems can go unresolved, and opportunities may be missed. In our experience, the signs of trouble are more noticeable at lower levels in the organization. This means that you and other leaders need to walk the halls and visit remote offices to see firsthand how your people are doing. Observe the conversations and interactions that take place between your direct reports and their people.

As you visit with your people and engage in casual conversations, use this list of ten warning signs that your people may be focusing too much on management and not enough on leadership:

1. Technical people have management titles but no one to supervise.
2. Executives work in their offices all day with the doors closed.

3. Executives have a line of people outside their doors waiting to ask questions.

4. Executives treat questions from their people as if they were interruptions.

5. Executives spend most of their time resolving technical or quality issues.

6. Executives fix mistakes rather than teach people to do the work properly.

7. Executives do the work themselves because they can do it faster and better.

8. Executives distance themselves from their people's problems and failures.

9. Executives do not require their direct reports to develop their people.

10. Executives spend all of their time on today's issues and little on tomorrow's possibilities.

Also look for favorable developments during your tours and conversations. It is not enough just to take notes. Transform your findings into recognition for people who are doing well and into feedback, coaching, or process changes when they are not.

DELIVERING FEEDBACK

The objective of feedback is to assist another person in reaching agreed-on goals. A few minutes of well-delivered and well-received feedback can produce behavioral changes that drive more effective actions. Yet if someone stood in front of you right now and said, "I want to give you feedback," how would you respond? Common reactions include "Oh no, how can I avoid this conversation?" "What did I do wrong?" or "Is it time for another review?" Such reactions are signs of a negative feedback culture. In contrast, reactions like "Great, your office or mine?" or "I'll clear my schedule and see you in ten minutes" indicate a culture where feedback is both expected and appreciated. Ideally, feedback should be permission based, which is yet another reason to cultivate strong relationships with your people. If you actively work to develop others and are seen as a leader who makes cooperative decisions, your people will relish feedback from you and apply it to improve their actions and results.

For example, let us assume that there is a woman in your group, Lois, to whom you want to provide feedback. You observed Lois interrupting your boss several times in today's staff meeting despite your having given her feedback in the past about not interrupting others. After the meeting, your boss pulled you aside and suggested that you no longer bring her to the meetings. You are concerned that her inability to participate in the meetings could interfere with your grooming her to take your position and, in turn, even endanger your potential promotion. At the same time, one idea she suggested during the meeting was brilliant, and you want to acknowledge that contribution. To give feedback to Lois, ask her whether she is willing to hear it and where she would like to have the conversation. Within reason, grant her request, but be clear that you are not asking whether the feedback conversation will happen, just when and where it will occur.

When you provide feedback to Lois, you are not telling her who she is. Rather you are describing how you and others experience her. Keep judgments out of feedback. Lois is not good or bad, right or wrong. You are not trying to change her as a person; you are just asking her to modify some behaviors to enable her to reach her goals. This key distinction depersonalizes feedback, usually calms emotional situations, and reduces the need for Lois to defend herself. Feedback is vital to success because it provides clear direction instead of allowing people to make assumptions about their progress.

THREE-PHASE PROCESS FOR GIVING EFFECTIVE FEEDBACK

There are three phases in the feedback process: preparation, delivery, and follow-up. Be sure you systematically engage all three and remain focused on why you are providing feedback.

Phase 1—Preparation

For example, before speaking with Lois, be clear about the goals that you will be assisting her in reaching. Are they her goals, the group's goals, your goals, or some combination of all three? Think through the impact, context, observations, and next-step aspects of the feedback you will deliver. Prepare emotionally to have a difficult conversation—should it turn into one—by focusing on what is right, rather than on who is right. Consider holding the conversation in her office or a vacant conference room in case she needs time to think alone after hearing your feedback. Giving Lois the choice of time and place establishes that she is a full partner in the conversation.

Phase 2—Delivering the Feedback

As we noted in Chapter 3, great conversations are direct, open, honest, and caring. This applies doubly to feedback conversations. You may collect information from others in order to provide clear feedback to Lois, but do not discuss the feedback with them—only gather facts. As you talk, be open to her responses. Do not exaggerate or conveniently forget to mention relevant facts. Openness and honesty may seem challenging, but they leave no room for doubt, confusion, or misunderstanding. Your feedback to Lois is about how you perceive her performance. Could there be a more important time to be caring? The following elements are essential in effective feedback conversations; they can be addressed in any sequence:

- **Impact.** Tell Lois that your boss suggested that she no longer attend his meetings, and express your concerns about grooming her for a promotion if she is excluded. Also tell her that the perceptiveness of some of her contributions during the meeting validates your confidence in her ability to think strategically and eventually be promoted.
- **Context.** Remind Lois of the earlier conversations you have had with her about interrupting others, especially your boss. Discuss how important her attending these meetings is to her getting your job when you are promoted, and that you consider her to be a prime candidate for that promotion (if this is true).
- **Observations.** Describe the interruptions, repeating to the best of your ability the actual words Lois and others used during the meeting. Also restate the idea she offered that you found to be strategically useful. If you stick to observations, this will be an easy part of the feedback. However, things will get dicey if you mix judgments with observations.

- **Next steps.** First, ask her to continue her great strategic thinking. With respect to interruptions, you might ask Lois to say nothing at the next meeting unless she is asked a direct question. Ask her how she could avoid interrupting your boss and offer to assist in that behavioral change. Be prepared that this might be a difficult conversation if the interruptions are symptomatic of a larger issue she has with your boss, her current position, her career path, or even you.

Give Lois the opportunity to reflect on what you have said, respond to your questions, and ask her own questions. Listen to her concerns and address any issues she may have. If you would like to know more about her new strategic idea, this would be a good time to inquire further. Ask what she heard and what new actions she intends to take based on the feedback.

Phase 3—Follow-up

Feedback conversations are rarely completed in one session because assisting people to change a behavior or take different actions is a process, not an event. In this case, you hope that the feedback after the next several meetings will be to tell Lois that she is doing a good job listening and not interrupting, and that she continues to contribute great ideas. Be conscious of how she receives your feedback. As in any conversation, it is not what you say that counts; it is what Lois hears. Be mindful of her expressions, the questions she asks, and how she participates. Monitor her emotional state and be willing to take a break for a few minutes if need be. Sometimes people need a break during a feedback conversation because of the amount of information involved, the broad implications of the requested behavioral change, and their emotional state.

BUILDING A FEEDBACK CULTURE

Do not reserve feedback for a formal performance review. In fact, no specific incident should be cited in a review that has not been discussed previously. The effectiveness of feedback is highest when it is delivered close to the event and the person has a chance to correct the behavior before a formal review. If casual feedback conversations succeed in fixing the concerns, avoid bringing them up in any formal review unless it is to tell the high potential how well he is working at reaching his goals.

The purpose of a formal performance review is to evaluate results against last year's objectives and to agree on objectives for the coming year. It is also an opportunity to discuss the progress that has been made (or not made) as a result of informal feedback conversations during the year, and to have the high potential recommit to making and sustaining behavioral changes.

You may be concerned that you do not have time to provide feedback to your people. But when giving and receiving feedback become second nature and embedded in the culture as a competency, an average feedback session takes from fifteen seconds to a few minutes. People crave feedback. In the average workplace, people receive five negative messages for each positive one. As you invest fifteen to thirty minutes per day in one-on-one feedback conversations throughout your team, reverse that ratio to motivate them. When they make a habit of observing their behavior and its effect on others, the feedback conversations will get shorter, and they will perform better because the feedback both motivates them and keeps them on track. Remember, a leader's job is to grow people and assist them in taking powerful actions. Feedback conversations are central to both of these. Building a feedback culture has other benefits too. Actions become more efficient and conflicts decrease, both of which save time. People perform better in the presence of feedback that is clear, concise, and caring.

The three-phase approach described earlier also is useful in requesting feedback and provides an opportunity for you to model effective ways of receiving feedback. Go to someone who regularly observes you at work and ask her for feedback on aspects of your performance and behavior. If she does not know how to provide feedback, ask questions that lead her through the "impact, context, observations, and next-steps" phase. No matter what you hear, thank her. At the end of the feedback session, restate what you heard and summarize the actions you will take as a result of her feedback. Follow up later with her and ask how you are doing. Asking for feedback in this manner shows how important feedback is to you and helps embed it in your organization's culture.

CHAPTER 13

CONVERSATIONS YOU MUST HAVE

A competent leader can get efficient service from poor troops, while on the contrary an incapable leader can demoralize the best of troops.
—GENERAL JOHN J. PERSHING

In developing others, you must engage in two kinds of critical conversations to create alignment and eliminate assumptions—both yours and theirs:

- **Baseline conversations** set mutual expectations; define ground rules; provide metrics to evaluate performance; clarify boundaries; and establish alignment around strategies, objectives, and tactics.
- **Feedback conversations** maintain alignment, address changes and unexpected developments, and resolve issues in order to follow an effective path toward the agreed-on objectives.

You might currently avoid these conversations because they can be difficult, time-consuming, and uncomfortable—especially if not handled properly. Or you might use the excuse of having to finish a high-priority task to evade or truncate the conversations. Hold these conversations—nothing is more urgent. If you do not hold them, the actions you and your people take will be based on differing assumptions and will deliver less than optimum results. Even worse, sidestepping baseline and feedback conversations can undermine relationships and limit your ability to develop others. An additional irony is that dealing with the chaos of misalignment usually takes more time than proactively engaging in up-front conversations to avoid it.

Olivia was promoted to vice president, overseeing 120 people in a financial services company. After two months in the new job, she asked her boss for an outside coach to assist in the transition. The boss agreed to a three-month, thirty-hour coaching program. During the first session, Olivia mentioned that two men who reported to her had previously been her peers. The coach asked, "What baseline conversations did you have with them when you took the new position?" She looked puzzled for a moment and acknowledged that she had not held baseline conversations with them or any other member of her team.

Olivia had simply assumed that they would treat her differently now that she was the boss, but had not discussed her expectations with them or asked them what role they wanted her to play in their development. The coach role-played with her to prepare for her first real leadership conversation. The coaching engagement ended after only three hours when Olivia realized that holding baseline conversations, rather than making assumptions, was a better way to build effective working relationships.

Get to know your people before crunch time so that you will be prepared to guide them when challenges emerge. Make it a point to speak with them regularly, even when there are no pressing business topics. Ask about their goals and discuss what they might do to achieve them. Provide feedback and offer to mentor them. We sometimes are asked how often baseline and feedback conversations should be held. There is no pat answer, but frequent conversations are essential for building relationships and maintaining high performance levels. You probably will not be able to address all four types of conversation unless you meet with each of your people at least monthly, and possibly weekly for high potentials. Routine feedback should occur on a daily basis as situations present themselves.

Several events should automatically trigger a baseline conversation: a merger or reorganization, a shift in strategy or priorities, a new customer or strategic partner, a new person joining the team, or a key person leaving. Public and private feedback conversations are appropriate when someone performs especially well, a major goal is achieved, or a breakthrough occurs. Likewise, it is vital to have feedback conversations—even if they are uncomfortable—when attitudes are poor, relationships are strained, a project is botched, or a customer is lost.

Baseline and feedback conversations should be dialogues. Avoid jumping to conclusions or forcing an answer. Look for a new view that might not have occurred to either of you before. Although the list of topics that could precipitate a baseline or feedback conversation is long, the following sections cover a few events and situations that are likely to trigger conversations with high potentials and other direct reports, either individually or as a group.

BASELINE CONVERSATIONS TO SET EXPECTATIONS

One of the early conversations when someone joins your team should be to set mutual expectations about character and courage, align belief systems, and lay the foundation for trust and respect. For instance, you might describe character as a moral compass, but note that character without courage is impotent. Similarly, courage without character is risky. Character is more than just knowing right from wrong—it is doing the right thing every time. Or you may talk about trusted relationships and provide your views on earning respect, accepting responsibility for results, doing the best job possible, and putting team success ahead of personal success. Ask him if it is possible to lead without trust or to gain trust without integrity, good character, and genuinely caring about others. The key is that the new person fully participates in the conversation.

You also might set expectations about balancing the competing demands of financial success, growth, and social responsibility. Tell your people what you expect from them relative to environmentally sustainable business practices, collaborating with others, and accepting the sometimes higher cost of those two approaches. Encourage high potentials to be creative in transforming those practices into a strategic advantage.

For example, a business owner promoted a high potential to manage sales for a new type of customer service agreement. Three months later, he complained that "she's not doing a good job." When we asked him what the guidelines were for doing a good job, he stammered and said, "I'm not sure. I just expected more sales than I'm getting." The baseline conversation that followed set month-by-month sales goals, developed innovative promotional strategies, and allocated advertising and other resources in a way that both the new sales manager and the business owner accepted—and those goals were achieved. Months later he told us, "She's the best promotion I ever made—especially now that I'm a better leader."

BASELINE CONVERSATIONS ABOUT PERFORMANCE STANDARDS

If you were to ask five top leaders from five organizations what they considered the definition of doing a good job, each would offer a compelling and unique answer. Your definition may well be the sixth. Likewise, each of your high potentials has his or her definition. Therefore, a baseline conversation about goals and performance metrics is essential to align your high potential's definition with yours. The product of the conversation should be a clearly written statement on goals and metrics that covers the following results as appropriate to the position:

- **Financial results:** revenue, budget, costs, profits, and growth rate
- **Customer results:** branding, satisfaction, retention, and acquisition
- **Production results:** quality, deadlines, and development of new products
- **Relationship results:** new and stronger internal and external relationships
- **Social results:** community involvement, charities, and environmental protection
- **Leadership results:** developing people, building culture, and communications
- **Personal growth:** training, academic degrees, and professional certifications

In creating this agreement, ask your high potential what she expects to achieve in each area. You often will be surprised and delighted by her response. The agreement might specify quarterly, annual, and multiyear objectives. Of course, the agreement is bidirectional. What will you and your organization do to help the high potential fulfill the agreed-to objectives and realize her full potential?

BASELINE CONVERSATIONS ABOUT RELATIONSHIPS

In our experience, baseline and feedback conversations about relationships are the ones that executives sidestep most frequently. For example, Brady had worked for the company since earning his MBA and, after eighteen years, was one of five executives on the strategic leadership team. He managed nearly half the revenue and directed several strategic initiatives, including acquisition of a firm that now reported to him. Abruptly, the CEO called Brady into his office and said that the former CEO of the acquired company had complained about Brady's harshness and unrealistic goals, so oversight of the acquired company was being transferred to another executive.

Brady was furious. Not only was he not consulted about the reasons for the transfer, but he did not get a chance to address differences with the former CEO or present his view of the "harshness and unrealistic goals." Obviously, the CEO had not held effective baseline or feedback conversations. He had failed to address the former CEO's complaints earlier with Brady, undercut Brady with a preemptive decision, and failed to fully evaluate the situation before taking action. But the CEO's primary failure really occurred months earlier when he did not hold a three-way baseline conversation with Brady and the former CEO relative to goals for the acquired company and the expected relationship between Brady and the former CEO. Your direct reports must know your expectations not only in regard to performance but also in regard to the roles they will play and their working relationships.

BASELINE CONVERSATIONS ABOUT PRIORITIES

This can be hard to hear, but you may be causing your people to work on the wrong priorities. If this is the case, it is likely that you are not working on your top priorities either. Unless you are an individual contributor, you should be leading and managing, not doing production work. Getting your people what they need to be successful is your top priority. One way to determine whether you are working on the right things is to ask your high potentials if they are receiving the direction, support, resources, and coaching they need to get the job done. You may not like their answers, but now you will have a prioritized to-do list.

Your calendar is another indicator of whether you and your high potentials are working on the right priorities. The items on your schedule are what you consider to be top priorities. The higher your position, the longer the time horizon should be for the items on your calendar. A short time horizon, say a few weeks, might be appropriate for a first-line manager; a horizon of years would be typical for a CXO. If a CXO's calendar is filled with meetings about near-term topics, her short-term goals may be met, but long-term results may be in jeopardy because the future is not receiving the planning attention it needs. Similarly, an executive leader whose calendar is crammed with production review meetings rather than strategic planning is also not adequately addressing the future.

Another indicator of whether your high potentials are working on the right priorities is the plans they submit for your review. The sections that receive the most space, the most thought, and the most research reveal their priorities (and to some extent, their strengths). If the plan is unclear or based on questionable assumptions, the high potential may not value or be good at planning (a vital skill at any level), and it would be an appropriate time for a feedback conversation to get him back on track.

FEEDBACK CONVERSATIONS ABOUT ACHIEVING GOALS

Once performance goals are established, periodic conversations are necessary to compare results to the goals and adjust strategies when necessary. Consider Marilyn, for example, an attorney who seemed destined to be a star. She had great client skills and was brilliant at settling complex issues. Revenue from her clients grew steadily, and after two years she was put in charge of a group of clients who generated over $5 million in annual revenue. She was on the fast track. During her annual review at the start of each year, she was given aggressive targets for revenue and new clients, but fell short of those goals three years in a row.

We spoke with Marilyn shortly after she received a termination notice, and asked, "What happened? You looked like a sure bet to make partner." She answered sadly, "I thought things were going well. Each year my bonus was larger. My revenue grew steadily even though it was short of the targets. I thought that's all they were—just targets. I met with the partner monthly, but our conversations were usually about tactics relative to individual clients."

After a painful pause, she added, "There were no consequences for missing targets—until now. I wasn't coached or mentored, and suddenly my job and potential partnership are gone."

We see this cycle repeatedly: promote or hire a hero, admire his initial performance, let him do things on his own, give him big goals, and then part ways after a few years because he fell short of expectations. The problem usually can be traced back to lack of clear initial goals or lack of frank, regular, and useful feedback conversations to guide the high potential toward achieving those goals.

FEEDBACK CONVERSATIONS WHEN ROLES GET TURNED UPSIDE DOWN

When roles and relationships get turned upside down, as often happens in crisis situations, straighten them out. Consider Ava, a registered engineer, who was promoted from lead engineer to project manager in a nationwide engineering services company. As project manager, she directed seven people on one big project and three smaller ones. After two weeks in the new position, Ava told her boss, Justin, that the big project was behind schedule. Justin, concerned that the client would be upset if the deadline were missed, told Ava, "Do what it takes to meet the schedule. I'll handle your other projects." After a month of extensive overtime, the big project finished on time, and the client was delighted. Ava and Justin got bonuses from the boss for their heroic efforts and long overtime. Justin also told his boss, "Ava has high potential—she'll be my replacement when I'm promoted."

You may be thinking, "What's wrong? They got the job done." That would be your management mindset speaking. By management standards, Ava and Justin did a super job; but, unfortunately, they turned leadership roles upside down to do it. Justin set a precedent by assuming control in a crisis and turning project managers into highly paid individual contributors. As a result, project managers did not learn to allocate resources in a crisis—a key lesson for first-line managers. And Justin, as a manager of managers, failed to implement a process to share resources in crisis situations. He reacted like a project manager and abandoned his leadership responsibilities. Several feedback conversations should have taken place in this situation:

- Ava should have asked Justin for assistance in managing multiple projects while respectfully declining to revert back to her old job.
- Justin should have used feedback conversations with first-line managers to identify problem projects early and work as a team to finish them on time.
- Justin's boss should have provided feedback to mentor him in how to develop the skills of a first-line manager.

It is hard to tell when people are working at the wrong level because the management focus is on getting things done—the long-term leadership costs of not developing people are ignored. In this case, everyone felt good about Ava and Justin's accomplishment; they were unaware that they had laid the foundation for future project and leadership issues.

FEEDBACK CONVERSATIONS ABOUT UNDERPERFORMANCE

One of the most uncomfortable yet essential feedback conversations you will face is counseling a high potential whose underperformance is adversely affecting the morale and performance of the entire team. The underperformer may be misusing resources, focusing on the wrong priorities, operating at the wrong level, or causing personnel conflicts. This person must be mentored, coached, moved to a lower level, or asked to leave.

Short tenures are a sign of the times, but they also can be an indicator of weak leadership. So, before taking rash action, determine why performance has dropped. Provide a factual performance assessment and discuss what is happening. People with outstanding past performance records may struggle with the responsibilities of a new position or a difficult situation for several reasons:

- They do not have the qualifications or personality you expected.
- The mindset that made them successful in the past has now become a liability.
- They fail to develop relationships with their boss, peers, or direct reports.
- They are unable to deal with the broader requirements of the new situation.
- A personal issue is interfering with their performance.

Of course, it is also possible that organizational factors such as inadequate resources or fuzzy job responsibilities are affecting performance. If so, take it upon yourself to fix those conditions. It is essential to conclude the feedback conversation with an action plan that (1) defines what each of you will do to ensure that performance improves, (2) specifies the metrics that define improvement, and (3) establishes progress milestones. In addition, discuss potential consequences should performance not improve. Consider the situation to be an opportunity to employ your mentoring and coaching skills.

FEEDBACK CONVERSATIONS ABOUT TIMELINESS

Your timeliness (or lack thereof) as a leader sets an example for your people. Maybe that is why completing work on schedule and showing up on time are common issues that few executives are willing to address. To accelerate the growth of high potentials, coach them regarding their choices, actions, reactions, and priorities—and insist that they be on time. For example, in terms of skills, Larry was a high potential. But he was consistently late to meetings and behind on projects. He worked long hours to achieve miraculous recoveries, but his tardiness disrupted the office routine and annoyed clients. The office joke was that Larry was born late and had never caught up. He had a microwave mentality: a self-limiting mindset that led him to do everything as fast as possible and always at the last second.

Rather than arriving at a meeting a few minutes early fully prepared, people like Larry think, "If I arrive early, I'll waste time waiting. Besides, I can finish one more task before I go." When he was lucky, Larry was not the last person to arrive; but when he was, he often disrupted meetings. If you tolerate a Larry on your team, you are lowering standards and sabotaging your team's efficiency. Lead by example: start and end meetings on time. Hold baseline and feedback conversations with each Larry on your staff to set timeliness standards and show him the adverse impacts of his behavior.

FEEDBACK CONVERSATIONS WITH YOUR BOSS

Are you courageous enough to have a feedback conversation with your boss when he or she is disrupting work, acting like a jerk, or being abusive or unethical? One CEO was lucky enough to have a high potential tell him, "John, you may be the best project manager in the entire company, but your job is CEO. Do your job and let us do ours. We are fully capable of getting everything done without your micromanagement." John was working at the wrong level. As his company grew, he moved quickly from a first-line manager to a CEO whose role was to forge strategic alliances in the industry. Like everyone else, bosses struggle with blind spots and lightning-fast changes. In some cases, they were promoted because of their past performance rather than their leadership skills. This is just one of a thousand topics that could necessitate a feedback conversation with your boss.

Be empathetic in feedback conversations with your boss because one day you may find yourself on the receiving side of a similar conversation with your high potentials. Initiate the conversation by explaining what you are seeing and how you believe the organization can be more successful. Ensure that the conversation engages all three perspectives: what each of you is seeing, understanding each other, and exploring new possibilities. Feedback conversations with your boss are also different from conversations with direct reports because you are likely to be assigned most of the action items at the end. Keep in mind that the purpose of any feedback conversation is to assist people in reaching agreed-on goals—not to cast blame. In our experience, upward feedback is as necessary and common in high-performing organizations as are downward and peer-based feedback conversations.

WHEN ROUTINE CONVERSATIONS DO NOT WORK

What do you do when baseline and feedback conversations do not work? When routine conversations fail to produce the results you seek, use one or more of these approaches:

Examine your relationship. Ensure that your relationship is deep enough for the person to accept coaching and mentoring from you. If it is not, hold a relationship-building conversation to establish mutual trust and respect. Approach the conversation with the mindset that you share an issue—not that the other person is the problem. Frame the conversation jointly as an opportunity to improve performance, and identify the benefits that each of you will realize by working together more effectively.

Are external factors affecting performance? If a personal issue outside of work is compromising performance, do not attempt to empathize by saying you know how the other person feels. Even if you have experienced a similar problem, you cannot really know how he feels. Instead ask, "I can't imagine how you feel; would you tell me?" If he says no, respond with, "I am here when you're ready. Can we talk again tomorrow?" If he continues the silence, it may be wise to engage HR in the situation.

Discuss the person's goals. Assuming the relationship is on solid ground, have a deeper developing-others conversation. Learn what matters most to this person. Discuss her career goals and demonstrate that you are committed to assisting her reach the ones that you both agree are realistic. Then link the difficult issue at hand to reaching her goals.

Are they seeing a new you? As a high potential, you are continually learning new skills and exhibiting behaviors that enable you to perform at higher levels. Yet unless you share that learning with your people, it can take a long time before they see, understand, and accept that you are acting differently and that they can respond to you differently. To work powerfully with them, you need to teach them what you have learned and use concrete business situations as a way to drive home the learning. They usually will react better if they feel a shared, connected purpose in your conversations with them.

It takes two to tango. Some personality styles do not mesh. If you suspect that to be the case with one of your direct reports, ask another executive to take him into her organization for a limited time on a special project. That will enable the person to apply his skills on new tasks while allowing the other executive to try to form a connection. If the special project finishes successfully, hold a three-way conversation and consider making the transfer permanent.

The last resort. Some people may be uncoachable. Others may be unwilling to commit to the standards required for your organization to thrive. Some cannot adapt to your culture. Or they may be in a job that is not right for them. If any of these are the case, document the facts regarding the performance issues and speak with your HR department. With its guidance, you might turn the conversation toward assisting the individual in finding another job or another career. If you have taken all these steps and none have worked, firing the employee may be the only viable option remaining. Although doing so is painful, it is often the best thing for everyone when done in the right way and for the right reasons.

CHAPTER 14

WHAT GETS IN YOUR PEOPLE'S WAY?

Leaders are made, they are not born. They are made by hard effort, which is the price which all of us must pay to achieve any goal that is worthwhile.
—VINCE LOMBARDI

Your people have essential work to do and important goals to achieve. Your ability to assist them in reaching those goals is important to them, to your organization, and to your future. As you develop and motivate them through leadership conversations, your purpose is to have them steadily become more competent in performing their current jobs and, ultimately, to acquire the skills to perform at the next higher level. The tools you can use to remove obstacles from your people's growth path include training, mentoring, and coaching.

ARE YOU AN OBSTACLE?

A business speaker challenged a group of executives: "If you left your organization today, who would lead your business, and how well would they do?" In most cases, there was no clear successor; and even when there was, the executive doubted that person's abilities. For Charles, the CEO of a midsize professional services company, the speaker's question was a jolting wake-up call. He had focused entirely on growing revenue rather than on developing people. He immediately texted his management team to ask, "If I got hit by a truck today, what would concern you most?" Interestingly, helping him recover from the accident was not on their list.

The team compiled their concerns about key customer relationships, financing, succession planning, and other business matters, and Charles worked with them to resolve the concerns. A year later, Charles took a thirty-day sabbatical. When he returned, the team joked that everything ran better in his absence.

Even though that was not true, clearly the organization was stronger because it no longer needed him for routine operations. It may seem paradoxical, but your organization would be stronger if it did not need you to handle day-to-day matters. Instead of being an indispensable cog in the production machine, you need to build your people's skills and knowledge so that you are free to pursue strategic opportunities for your organization. Furthermore, proving your ability to develop others is a big step toward your next promotion—and would open a slot for one of your high potentials. To start working on your next opportunity, ask yourself:

- Why am I in this position?
- What must I learn to get to the next one?
- What opportunities should I be preparing for?
- What will they require of me that is different from my current responsibilities?

Another obstacle to your people's development may be that you are managing at too low a level. Heavy-handed control over operations retards development of high potentials and may cause them to leave. Even in large organizations, a surprising number of executives we coach cite their boss as a factor in performance shortfalls and production disruptions. Their bosses undercommunicate, micromanage, show favoritism, and do work themselves because they feel it would take too long to teach the right person how to do it. As a leader, you control the organizational factors that may adversely affect the performance of high potentials. The most frequently cited factors—other than the boss himself or herself—include

- Faulty organizational structure and overlapping job responsibilities
- Lack of quantitative performance goals and regular feedback

- Inefficient or nonexistent processes, or failure to follow processes consistently
- Outdated technology
- Inadequate support staff

Acknowledge that some things you do or do not do may be impeding development of your high potentials and compromising their ability to deliver top performance. As you grow, you provide room for your people to grow as well.

REMOVING OBSTACLES THAT GET IN YOUR PEOPLE'S WAY

In Chapter 13 we introduced you to Marilyn, a high potential at a law firm who was fired when she failed to meet her boss's performance expectations. The things that blocked Marilyn's success are typical of high potentials whose careers derail. As a leader who is gaining expertise in the four types of conversations, how would you work with Marilyn to improve her performance—and how would you apply similar techniques to assist other high potentials in your organization?

A good place to begin is to explicitly identify the additional tasks you want Marilyn to perform and the performance objectives you expect her to achieve. You might hold a conversation with her about the management and leadership skills required to perform those tasks and achieve those objectives:

"Marilyn, you're a skilled attorney, and that is essential for making partner. We hired you because of your legal acumen and leadership potential. Your legal abilities have proven to be world class—and your clients recognize them. On the other hand, so far we haven't seen the skills needed to convert your abilities into the revenue stream and new clients expected of a partner. Let's discuss what it will take for you to become a partner, and the activities and behaviors that will take you to that goal."

Marilyn's response might be something like: "I'm glad we're having this conversation. I need to know what you expect of me besides meeting revenue goals. I always felt I was given stretch goals. Revenue has increased with all of my clients, yet I'm still not meeting your expectations. What else can I do?"

Marilyn provided key insights into how she has been thinking, which gives you the opening to suggest new activities and behaviors:

"Marilyn, your focus on revenue is admirable, but meeting stretch goals is hard when you do so much of the work yourself instead of delegating it. Besides, revenue is just one criterion for making partner. Your work with clients is superb, but it takes time away from growing your people and growing the firm's client list. As your boss, I'm willing to mentor you in how to simultaneously lead your team, build their expertise, expand our relationship with existing clients, and gain new ones—the full set of skills required to make partner. How would you like me to assist you? Do you need additional resources? Are there any training courses that you would like to take?"

At this point, you and Marilyn might discuss the process for learning the leadership skills expected of partners, and how you could work together to prepare her for that promotion. Then you would want to agree on the improvements she needs to make. If neither of you is sure what is holding her back, you might speak with her colleagues to determine how well they feel she is performing. You could hold face-to-face interviews, use a 360-degree tool (a survey that contrasts Marilyn's perceptions of herself to those of her bosses, peers, and direct reports), or both. When Marilyn receives the results, she can prepare a plan for your approval that outlines a developmental approach and identifies where she will need assistance. When you sign off on her plan, you are committing to provide the resources she needs and giving her responsibility to execute the plan:

"Marilyn, now that you've analyzed the 360 results and I have approved your plan, it's up to you to follow through and ask for assistance when needed. Focus on developing your team as you service our clients. When you are comfortable with how I mentor you, start mentoring the attorneys on your staff in a similar manner. One way to demonstrate your proficiency is to teach your skills to your team and bring out the best in each of them. When you become proficient in developing others and winning work with new clients, you'll also be achieving the revenue targets and be on your way to becoming a partner. I have a vested interest in seeing that you are successful."

Going forward, your responsibility is to balance the assistance you provide directly to Marilyn with the assistance you obtain for her from other sources. Ensure that all of the assistance focuses both on the business opportunities and the development plan to which you and Marilyn have agreed.

Is the Issue One of Skills or Behaviors?

Once you approve Marilyn's development plan, the question is whether she should focus on learning or applying new techniques. She may intellectually know what to do but have difficulty translating knowledge into effective actions and behaviors.

- If the barrier is lack of skills or knowledge, look into training and mentoring to teach Marilyn essential management and leadership techniques.
- If she knows what to do but needs assistance in implementing her skills, explore coaching options to improve her performance.
- If the issue involves both skills and behaviors, combine the two types of assistance.

The main difference between training and mentoring is that most training occurs in a group setting, whereas mentoring is delivered on an individual basis. Training focuses on general issues, whereas mentoring targets an individual's next steps. Conversely, coaching tackles behavioral issues and beliefs that inhibit superior performance and rapid growth.

Training for Your People

When Marilyn began managing her legal staff, she had little prior experience or training in leading and developing others. Her formal education was in practicing law, and she was brilliant at that. Knowing the law—or accounting, engineering, sales, or any other specialty—cannot be equated with knowing how to manage and lead. So the first step in improving performance must be to gain Marilyn's agreement (or your direct reports' agreement) that management and leadership training are necessary. The next step is to identify training courses that might meet Marilyn's needs and fit her schedule. Allowing Marilyn to research and pick her training course(s) will increase her buy-in to the overall process and increase her commitment to learning.

Management and leadership training comes in many forms, including

- Internal training courses on topics uniquely relevant to your organization
- Courses offered by training companies and accredited postsecondary schools
- Seminars given by trade associations in your industry
- Executive education programs at business schools

In addition, there are a wide variety of membership organizations that have regular meetings with instructional presentations by prestigious speakers. Have your high potentials research and find the appropriate course(s) they need.

Mentoring for Your People

A mentor is an acknowledged expert who is able to share experiences, past successes, and failings in a manner that builds trust. Working with a mentor allows high potentials to see that their challenges are solvable. If you determined that Marilyn could benefit from personal attention, ask Marilyn to identify specific mentors who are uniquely proficient in each skill Marilyn needs to develop and would be willing to work with her one-on-one. Mentors would approach conversations as experts to dispense advice and help Marilyn identify options relevant to the situation she faces. Mentors often make such comments as "When I was in your position, I would . . ." or "Based on my knowledge of your industry and your company, I would . . ." or "This is a best practice that you should follow." The mentor(s) would work with Marilyn to implement new approaches and apply new techniques to address her management and leadership challenges.

Your role in the mentoring is to encourage Marilyn to openly share her concerns and problems with the mentor. Ensure that the mentor is thinking not only of what he or she did in the past but about what is likely to work for Marilyn now and in the future. You might mentor Marilyn yourself in some of your strengths if she would accept your inputs. In any case, check periodically to ask how the mentoring is going and what is or is not working for her. Mentoring is an experience, not a destination.

To get mentors to say yes to working with one of your high potentials, specify the skills they have that your high potential needs, and allow them to set boundaries on their availability. You also can increase your chances of getting a yes response by detailing your skills and offering to mentor someone in their organization in return for their assistance with your high potential.

Mentors can be internal or external. Internal mentors are executives in your organization, usually your peers in other departments. External mentors can be recent retirees or executives in companies that are strategic partners. A person qualifies as a mentor because he has held a position that Marilyn aspires to achieve or because he has special expertise in a critical area where she needs to improve.

Marilyn may find an internal person who has the skills to address the issues she faces or, more likely, she will choose to work with multiple mentors, each in an area where he or she excels. Some organizations also provide high potentials with a sponsor within the organization. A sponsor not only offers mentoring but also connects your high potentials with the right people to provide additional assistance. Effective mentors and sponsors will share with you in the pride of seeing Marilyn succeed. Internal mentors have the advantage of knowing the resources and culture of your organization. Their downside is that they are less likely to introduce new ideas.

External mentors generally function like internal ones. They may have worked in your organization, or they understand the operations of organizations in your industry. You might ask an external mentor to provide new skills and perspectives to Marilyn. She can then introduce them into your organization. Asking Marilyn to mentor other people internally as she learns new skills would be a powerful way to reinforce her learning and teach her how to develop others at the same time.

Coaching for Your People

Coaches assist those who possess skills but need to apply them more effectively. There are many things a coach can do for a high potential like Marilyn. A coach generally will

- Provide a safe space for open conversation—an environment free from judgment and risk of negative repercussions from anything she might say.
- Assume that Marilyn knows what to do to be successful in her position (or is willing to learn), and work with her on how to apply her skills.
- Elicit more effective strategies and solutions from Marilyn, but never tell her what course of action to take.
- Guide Marilyn through the process of awareness, reflection, learning, and action by asking questions, listening to answers, and thinking broadly.
- Assist her in identifying and pursuing new methods to achieve her goals.

Although you can certainly coach Marilyn as her boss, providing a professional coach is a valuable employee benefit. Multiple studies have shown it to have positive effects on employee retention as well as individual and team performance. Coaching is meant to be periodic, not endless, so commit to only three to six months initially. If coaching does not appear to be producing progress, have Marilyn discuss this with the coach—that conversation alone can lead to a breakthrough. Coaching and leadership conversations are similar in that they both drive toward action and results.

Today, many executives are trained to use coaching techniques to produce better results. You probably do this naturally when you say, "What are some ways you could reach your goals?" or "How else might you get better results?" instead of directing the action by saying, "The best way to reach your goal is to. . . ." One advantage of internal coaching is that the coach thoroughly understands and supports the culture of the organization. Another is lower costs, as an internal coach is already on the payroll. The downside to an internal coach is that the conversations may not be considered safe. Marilyn may be reluctant to confide her weaknesses to you, her boss, if she feels that the information could jeopardize future promotions and salary increases. Even if the internal coach is a professional from HR, confidentiality still might be an issue if that person is involved in succession planning or compensation discussions. In addition, a coach from HR may not have experience in an operating role or may be lower in the hierarchy than Marilyn, which would render that coach less credible to her.

An external coach is professionally bound to keep confidential everything disclosed by Marilyn, unless maintaining confidentiality would put a person in danger or significant property loss would occur. Coaching conversations with Marilyn would thus touch on not only her hopes and aspirations but also her fears and job concerns. Because coaches work with a variety of organizations, they also bring fresh viewpoints into the coaching conversations. In addition, accredited coaches have met education and experience requirements and have an obligation to obtain continuing education. Visit sites like www .coachfederation.org to view the standards set by the industry and determine whether a coach is accredited. Examine a coach's credentials and check her references.

When you use an external coach, ensure that you and the coach work in tandem to assist your high potential. For example, Jack hired a coach to assist Mason, a new first-line manager with extraordinary capabilities. Once the coaching began, Jack stopped having conversations with Mason. Later, Jack wondered why Mason was falling out of alignment with the results Jack wanted and with a shift in the organization's mission. When he voiced his concern to the coach, Jack said, "I'm not having developmental conversations with Mason. That's your job now, and I don't think it is going well." The coach challenged Jack to see how separating their efforts actually could retard Mason's progress despite Jack's best intentions. The coach sat down with both of them, and they reached an agreement whereby Mason would receive simultaneous coaching by the coach and mentoring by Jack. The integrated result was dramatic. Mason was able to incorporate Jack's mentoring and feedback into his work with the coach, and his performance soared. Jack has since been promoted, and Mason has taken over Jack's position.

YOUR ROLE AS A LEADER

To develop your high potentials, determine the combination of internal and external coaching, mentoring, and training resources (including you) that is appropriate for each individual. Respect the fact that your people will not discuss some topics with you, and find someone in whom they are willing to confide. This also will enable them to discover how to work with you more effectively. Provide appropriate support, and model great leadership and management skills yourself to achieve maximum alignment.

Developing others is about producing top-notch results. Employ tactics that work best for each individual and match her learning style. Classroom training, experiential workshops, and annual reviews are key elements in developing people—if they are conducted properly. Too often, we hear high potentials describe their annual review as "a waste of time. My boss has me write my own review, and he signs it. Then we ignore it until six months or a year later. My boss is just too busy to care about building my skills." In contrast, Jeff Immelt, CEO of General Electric (GE), says that he spends 30 percent of his time on people, and the company spends over a billion dollars annually for training. GE's focus is on cultivating integrity and performance, and encouraging a healthy disrespect for history—figuring out what is most important to change and what should be maintained. Coaching accelerates learning and inspires new behaviors.

COACHING MANAGERS

If you manage new managers, teaching them to coach rather than to direct the actions of their people will be among your challenges. Managers are responsible for getting work done through others, yet they may have been promoted without having developed that skill. In this case, it is more likely that management issues rather than technical issues will get in their way. Watch for the following issues in the managers who work for you:

- **Doing their people's jobs.** First-line managers often exhibit this problematic behavior and get away with it by working long hours. This produces high stress and low performance because the manager becomes a bottleneck and complains about not having competent people or enough time to get the work done. His people complain in turn about being micromanaged.

- **Poor teamwork.** If the team is talented but production rates and quality fall short of expectations, the problem may be that the manager lacks the ability to define and implement efficient processes and then coach people to use the processes effectively. She also may be ignoring feedback from her people.
- **Selecting the wrong people.** Common errors here include promoting people based solely on technical skills without considering their attitude, or picking people who closely resemble, rather than complement, the manager's skills and behaviors.
- **Lack of performance feedback.** When problems are not solved, the real difficulty may be that the manager has not set clear goals or is not providing actionable feedback to his direct reports (or both).

Coach your high potentials on the leadership aspects of their current positions so that they consistently deliver top performance. Coaching high potentials in the requirements of a higher-level position may seem like a good thing to do, but reserve that coaching for those who already perform exceptionally well at their current levels.

Coach your people through successive cycles of building relationships, developing others, making decisions, and taking action. Make sure they use the appropriate blend of management and leadership mindsets for their positions. Listen to their conversations to see if they properly use all three perspectives. If you find that they are reluctant to change, resist being judgmental; ask them to describe their obstacles. Explain how other high potentials have conquered similar obstacles and help them extrapolate those successes to fit their situation. Ask questions and listen more than you talk. The best compliment any coach can receive is one we heard recently: "Just having her there enabled me to figure out how to do a better job and gave me the courage to try new things. Now I know I can conquer any obstacle and make larger contributions to the organization and the people in it."

CHAPTER 15

RECOGNITION—MAKING IT ALL WORTHWHILE

Outstanding leaders go out of their way to boost the self-esteem of their people. When people believe in themselves, it's amazing what they can accomplish.
—SAM WALTON

Some executives feel that work is a necessary evil that only produces a paycheck. They expect people to resent work, so they subconsciously assume the role of oppressor and treat people like victims. Such executives use criticism as a tool to prevent people from repeating unwanted behaviors. Yet criticism actually impedes their ability to lead by blocking conversations that improve performance. In contrast, effective leaders see work as inherently enjoyable and gratifying and seek to place people in positions where they feel rewarded and happy. Your high potentials will benefit from hearing your honest appreciation—even when their results and behaviors are not exactly what you would like at that moment.

People especially enjoy being recognized when they conquer a major challenge. Roger, a recently promoted executive, faced a difficult problem involving the people at a branch in South America. His predecessors tried to encourage them to understand and live by the company's culture of personal responsibility and hard work, but with little success. They used threats, intimidation, and incentives without result. Roger flew to South America and asked the branch manager, Alberto: "What changes can we make to enable you and your people to willingly adopt the company's practices and culture?" Alberto responded, "It's impossible—we're just too different."

Roger kept pushing: "Well, I am glad you are the branch manager because you're the only one I know who can accomplish the impossible." After issuing the challenge, Roger continued: "Call me when you achieve a small victory during the next few weeks, and we'll hold a party to celebrate success. Also, how would you and your people like me to respond when I thank you for succeeding?" This set the time frame, and Alberto knew that he and his people would be rewarded when the cultural change occurred. Six weeks later, major progress had been made in integrating the company's culture into South American operations, and everyone's contribution to that success was recognized.

Effective leaders know that first prize, second prize, and every other prize should be recognizing people for their achievements and contributions. The recognition need not be elaborate or expensive—the appreciation should be commensurate with the level of effort. Creating a culture of appreciation is the first step. Challenge each person to operate at the top of her potential. Let her know that you believe in her and rely on her. Offer assistance when things go awry, and do not chastise the bearer of bad news. During the celebration at the end of a successful project, those moments will be remembered most and become part of the culture of the organization.

MULTIMEDIA RECOGNITION

In our increasingly connected world, the contributions of your high potentials should be recognized through a combination of virtual, voice, and face-to-face communications. Today, positive and negative information is shared instantly online. The challenge for today's leaders is to provide clear direction, usable feedback, and effective recognition with the whole world listening in on your digital conversations. To ensure that your organization thrives in a global economy, you must motivate, coach, and create loyalty even though your people work at remote locations and are from diverse backgrounds. You also will be challenged to facilitate collaboration and knowledge exchanges between older workers and their more "digitally active" younger colleagues.

Recognizing technical expertise is particularly vital in a global economy driven by rapid advances in electronics, energy, health care, manufacturing, and other sectors. If you lead an organization whose success depends on technology, you may worry about keeping abreast of every change. Give it up—there is not enough time in the day to be both an effective leader and a technical guru. Instead you must connect with and motivate the experts who assist you in creating the future of your organization, by

- Acknowledging visionary concepts developed inside and outside your organization
- Building collaborative internal, external, and cross-sector relationships
- Using your people's recommendations in making strategic decisions about projected technological breakthroughs
- Encouraging interorganizational knowledge exchanges

Despite limits on your technical knowledge, you must recognize, motivate, and build trust with experts so that they feed you ideas and offer honest opinions. Even though you may not be the expert, you are still expected to select the right investments, focus the experts on useful outcomes, and arbitrate competing views. By recognizing and guiding the experts, you can harness the creativity and curiosity of your most technically savvy high potentials.

RECOGNITION IS INEXPENSIVE—LACK OF RECOGNITION CAN BE COSTLY

Sophia worked for a nonprofit for three years hoping in vain that her situation would improve. She was a high potential who stayed late and worked weekends on critical projects and grant proposals. Despite being a go-to person, Sophia got little recognition from her boss, received mediocre bonuses, and was not considered for promotion. Instead, her boss continually pointed out trivial errors, ignored her suggestions, and blocked her from working on projects with the nonprofit's top leaders.

One Monday morning after Sophia had worked all day Saturday and Sunday to complete a grant proposal (her boss never came into the office on the weekends), the boss handed her a list of tasks that she had not finished the previous Friday. Sophia quit on the spot, but before the end of the week found a new job at a higher salary. The difference between the old organization and the new one was like night and day. In her second week, Sophia's new boss recognized her at the staff meeting for suggestions she made to streamline the fundraising program. After one year, she became a project manager, and three years later she founded her own nonprofit.

Narrow-minded bosses like Sophia's create costly nightmares when they mismanage high potentials. At a minimum, they destroy productivity and morale. At worst, they cause high potentials to quit. This type of boss is the most common reason employees cite for quitting a job—far more often than salary complaints. And turnover is very expensive. Research by various HR associations shows that the average cost to replace an employee is roughly half his annual salary. And that does not count opportunity costs, which can easily double the cost of replacing high potentials in key technical and sales positions. When you allow knowledge and relationships to exit your organization, you then must fill production gaps, interview candidates, train new employees, and calm customers—all of which take more time and cause more anxiety than recognizing employees. You can reduce turnover by ensuring that your people feel appreciated and rewarded for their contributions.

RECOGNIZE BEHAVIORS AS WELL AS RESULTS

Herman, the procurement director for a Fortune 100 manufacturing firm, coordinated eight procurement managers, who each managed a staff of eight to fifteen people in his or her plant. Earlier in his career, Herman received little recognition and was not seen as a high potential because his priorities were stability at work and time at home with his family. Still, he set high standards for himself and his people and communicated his expectations concisely. Herman was also clear that his top priority was developing others.

The managers whom he supervised relied on him for timely feedback that was fair, specific, and useful.

Herman recognized his people as individuals and adapted his approach to their personal goals and needs. If you asked Herman about his people, you would feel the admiration and passion in his response. Among his most significant contributions was that his high potentials were regularly promoted, and they excelled in new positions. Furthermore, the people promoted into their old positions were fully prepared to become managers. Herman was recognized by top leaders in the company for growing high-performing leaders, even though he was unlikely to advance given his family situation. He was given an award as the most effective manager of managers in the company because of his ability to launch his people into successful leadership careers.

Every high potential wants to be recognized in a way that thanks her for her contributions and salutes her effort. Do not make recognition a complicated process—a spontaneous thank you is often as effective as elaborate recognition later. Recognize three things: (1) the result, (2) the person, and (3) the behaviors that produced the result. You may want to recognize a person and a behavior even if the result was not as good as you expected. Recognizing effective behaviors enables all of your people to see how they can be more successful. In addition, behaviors are lasting, whereas a result is a one-time event. Recognition is important not only to those receiving it—it also motivates and inspires the entire team to achieve more.

CELEBRATE EVEN SMALL SUCCESSES

Whenever you meet with your people individually or collectively, celebrate success by asking what went right. Focusing only on problems stops people from having open conversations. When shortfalls are the only topic, people become reluctant to report bad news. By asking what went right before addressing issues, you give your people a chance to talk about their successes—even if they are small. That approach leads people to prepare for your meeting by thinking about accomplishments they will present as well as the ongoing challenges. Interestingly, when people talk publically about their successes, they give themselves recognition for good work and want to accomplish more so that they have positive results to present at the next meeting.

While briefing the management team, Mitchell, chief operating officer of a growing company, said, "I don't want to be negative, but we should have done better." He was referring to the fact that, although their annual growth goal was 34 percent, revenue had grown by just 12 percent. The management team was crushed. By focusing on the revenue growth shortfall rather than acknowledging the growth that did occur, Mitchell negated a year's worth of hard work in an extraordinarily difficult economy.

Results that one person calls mediocre, others see as outstanding. It all depends on your frame of reference, your viewpoint and assumptions. In this case, Mitchell felt that 12 percent growth was inadequate because it was short of the target, whereas his people saw the same 12 percent growth as excellent performance during a recession. This divergence could have been discussed much earlier in the year and expectations reset or new strategies employed. Then Mitchell might have been able to say at this meeting, "It's amazing to have grown 12 percent during the recession; how can we hit a higher target next year? What resources do you need? How can I be of assistance?"

CELEBRATE PEOPLE

Use group and individual recognition to acknowledge contributions and reinforce effective behaviors. Here are six ways that you can recognize your people, show them how important they are to you, and build a culture of success:

1. **Appreciate routine operations.** Look at what your people do every day. Recognize their contributions and savor the feeling of accomplishment with them when routine activities run smoothly. Give them credit for suggesting process improvements or contributing new ideas, regardless of how well they work.

2. **Tell stories.** Reinforce the behaviors you want with stories of individual and team successes. Post stories of those successes on your organization's website and blog about them for the newsletter and local newspapers.

3. **Listen constructively.** Make it a point to listen to your people. Think of them as expert advisers in their skill areas rather than as employees. Ask questions in a way that leads them to feel as though they contributed the idea that is eventually adopted.

4. **Provide individual attention.** If your organization or industry has recognition programs (such as employee of the year), nominate one of your people every year. Say thank you in a handwritten note or in public while others are listening. Acknowledge anniversaries, graduations, birthdays, and other special events.

5. **Distribute tangible appreciation.** Find out what motivates each of your people, whether it is an afternoon off, a restaurant gift certificate, a spa service, or tickets to a high-profile sporting event. Then distribute these rewards regularly.

6. **Make work fun.** Organize planning events and team exercises that are enjoyable. Hold team-building sessions that are opportunities to celebrate last year's successes as well as plan the coming year.

Actions like these demonstrate that you value people as individuals, which will build loyalty and encourage them to go the extra mile for you. Recognition is an effective way to manage performance, change behaviors, and develop others. It is far more effective than criticizing shortfalls, correcting mistakes, and fixing problems—and more fun too.

TEN WAYS TO PRACTICE GREAT LEADERSHIP IN DEVELOPING OTHERS

1. **Sustain success.** Was your organization's most recent success produced through team participation or the heroic efforts of a few people? If you focus solely on results, you may not notice the long-term costs of not developing people—the hero mode is unsustainable as a growth strategy.

2. **Plan succession.** Are you hiring and developing people for each key position in your organization, including yours? A great personnel choice at a crucial time leads to great success—and effective leadership conversations to develop others provide multiple choices.

3. **Demand more.** Demand more from your high potentials in the five areas that change after every promotion: skills, priorities, measures of success, time frames, and relationships.

4. **Cite specific potentials.** What exactly does each of your high potentials have the potential to become? Can she be a top leader, assume a larger role in her current area, or be an expert in her specialty? Develop each accordingly.

5. **Set expectations.** Eliminate assumptions—ensure that everyone knows what is expected of him. Address the expectations in developmental conversations.

6. **Minimize turnover.** Compare your organization's turnover to industry standards as an indicator of the effectiveness of your leadership conversations.

7. **Promote coaching** as a mission-essential skill in your organization. Recognize the difference between skills and behavior issues, and use training, coaching, and mentoring appropriately to improve performance.

8. **Make feedback a common event.** Plan a piece of feedback for each of your people and deliver it today. Observe their actions and ask them to provide feedback to their direct reports.

9. **Simplify recognition.** A spontaneous thank you is often as effective as more elaborate and expensive recognition later. Recognize three things: (a) the result, (b) the person, and (c) the behaviors that produced the result.

10. **Create an atmosphere of success** by appreciating and supporting your people at all times—even when results fall short of expectations.

PART 4

CONVERSATIONS TO MAKE DECISIONS

Decision making is an intellectual process during which executives select a course of action from among potential alternatives. Managers tend to make decisions based on facts. After all, proven formulas, well-defined rules, and structured logic were instrumental in their past successes. Leaders, in contrast, make decisions based on a vision for the future and conversations with their people to supplement the facts. Managers expect to make the right decision every time. On the contrary, although leaders may be confident that their decisions are best for the organization, they know they will not get every decision right. They miss the mark occasionally, but do not let that possibility paralyze them.

Leaders rarely have the luxury of enough time and information to evaluate every alternative. They ask many questions, especially when they find themselves in a situation with ambiguous circumstances, high stakes, tight deadlines, and no obvious course of action. After gathering multiple inputs, they rely on judgment and experience as much as information to make a decision. Time that a leader spends in effective decision-making conversations with her people is highly valuable. When done well, those conversations ensure that everyone sees the big picture and is inspired to resolve issues and seize opportunities.

Part 4 explores the attributes of great decision-makers and helps you develop those attributes. It looks at how leaders do the right thing at the right time and in the right way, which we call the judgment gene (Chapter 16). You may be surprised to learn that what you know is irrelevant (Chapter 17); what is crucial is what your organization knows and how effectively you tap into that experience and knowledge to make decisions. Furthermore, since you cannot possibly know everything, you must become curious (Chapter 18) and ask questions as you did as a child. Part 4 closes by suggesting ways to make change work for you (Chapter 19)—if you can't handle change, you might as well retire now.

CHAPTER 16

DEVELOP YOUR JUDGMENT GENE

People must be taught how to think, not what to think.
—MARGARET MEAD

Judgment is the ability to consistently make the right decision at the right time in the right way. Good judgment looks like magic to those who do not have it. When a leader takes an unusual and brilliant action that is wildly successful, others wonder where the decision came from. Examples of bad judgment are readily visible because everyone sees their consequences. Good judgment, in contrast, often goes unnoticed because it seems routine. Leaders make decisions every day. Some are easy, but the strategically important ones require judgment and are often complex and risky.

For example, well before the dot-com boom, a government executive challenged his staff: "Let's start a skunkworks to see how we can use that Web stuff." Because building prototype computer systems was not in his budget, he shaved money from other areas to fund the effort. He pushed his people to explore new possibilities, build capabilities incrementally, enroll users in testing, and—most important—not to be afraid to try something that might fail. Two years later during an international crisis, the fledgling system was put to the test, and it passed with flying colors. Easily accessible, it became a trusted source of information for leaders throughout the agency. After another year of prototyping, the executive transferred responsibility for the system to the IT division. How did this executive know that the Internet would become a core resource? Why was he willing to venture beyond his budget to invest in a risky project? Because this executive had spent years developing his judgment gene. You should too.

FIVE REALMS OF JUDGMENT

The decisions that leaders make are more strategic than those made by managers. They define where the organization is going, its mission and vision, its strategic partnerships, and the services and products it will offer. The decisions that managers make determine how well and how fast things get done. Both leaders and managers exercise judgment across five realms when they make decisions:

- **Strategy realm:** What will happen tomorrow? In which direction should I lead my organization? Which actions should have the highest priority?
- **People realm:** Whom should I hire or promote? Whom should I assign to a key role? How should I handle personality differences and conflicts?
- **Resources realm:** Where should I assign my best people? How should I allocate my financial assets? Where should I invest my time?
- **Decisive moments realm:** How will a given change or new technology affect my organization's future? How can I exploit this opportunity?
- **Crisis realm:** How should I resolve this crisis and minimize its adverse impact? How can I transform this problem into an opportunity?

One key use of your judgment gene is to build a team that makes good decisions, so involve your high potentials in decision-making conversations often. As a manager, you may have hired people primarily based on their skills and experience; but as a leader, you will place more weight on their attitudes and their judgment. Judgment depends more on the experiences that people have had and what they learned from them, and less on how many birthdays they have celebrated.

Leaders who have fine-tuned their judgment gene make a high percentage of sound decisions that can be executed effectively. It is not that a great leader never makes a bad decision. Rather, great leaders quickly realize when a decision is wrong. Encourage people to challenge your judgments, and be willing to explain your decisions in terms of the criteria, inputs, information, and experience you used to make them. If subsequent events or new information show that you made a bad decision, you need to admit it, learn from it, and move on. The conversations that occur during the process of making, implementing, and examining the results of decisions will enable you to institutionalize decision-making discipline and develop the judgment gene in your people.

Leadership gurus agree that judgment is learnable, but the lineage of judgment and experience is a hotly contested chicken-and-egg debate. Experience without judgment has little value, but good judgment without experience is still good judgment. At the same time, a person with little experience is unlikely to have good judgment, as experience provides feedback that sharpens judgment. Some people have had long experience but have gained little judgment. They have endured the same one-year experience ten times rather than learning from ten years of progressive experience. Good judgment is born in experience, rooted in emotional intelligence, sharpened by mentoring and coaching, and embedded in the culture of an organization.

JUDGMENT IS A PROCESS, NOT AN EVENT

Great leaders evaluate scenarios and prepare strategies long before it is time to act. Your business plan probably considers the events you expect in the future and is a guide for what you will do in those situations. But when reality throws curve balls at you, as it often does, will you and your people freeze, or will you regain alignment quickly? The judgments you and your people make in decisive moments and crisis situations turn out better when they are supported by planning. Leaders who plan thoroughly are consistent winners in the market, whereas those who do not are left to limp from crisis to crisis.

For example, years before Hurricane Katrina struck in 2005, the Department of Homeland Security issued a four-hundred-page *National Response Plan* that supposedly scripted the government's response to man-made and natural disasters. But when Katrina struck, rescue volunteers and victims were frustrated by the endless planning meetings that were held in the middle of flood zones because the plan did not provide decision-making criteria or describe what actions would be taken by whom. It is dangerous to begin identifying and analyzing potential alternatives in the middle of an emerging crisis.

Most people think good judgment occurs in the instant a decision is made, but it is actually a process that unfolds over time. Good judgment is developed in four steps:

Step 1—Prepare. Preparation takes place long before a decision is needed. It includes defining potential strategies, priorities, and the criteria for success; identifying alternatives; gathering information; and building strategic relationships.

Step 2—Decide. The decision happens when the leader recognizes the need for a new course of action, reviews the situation with colleagues, and makes a judgment call.

Step 3—Implement. Implementation comprises the follow-up actions a leader takes to ensure that the decision is understood and executed in a way that produces the desired result.

Step 4—Assess. Assessments take place after implementation is complete in order to strengthen the plan in preparation for future decisions.

In using this process, hold preparation conversations often in order to prepare everyone for making decisions. During preparation, it is more important to discuss possibilities than to forge the perfect plan. Notice that assessments are really part of preparing to make the next decision; this produces a seamless decision-making process. Highly effective organizations use a process like this to develop high potentials who will make smart decisions and implement them effectively with little hesitation—even in a crisis.

KEYSTONE JUDGMENTS

The effectiveness of decisions that executives make depends as much on the issues they judge to be important as on their ability to address them. Operating in a management mindset, executives sometimes jump into action to solve a problem or exploit an opportunity, whereas experienced leaders consider five keystone judgments before making a decision:

1. **Is a decision necessary?** Ask yourself what would happen if you did nothing and let your people deal with the situation. Executives sometimes are overwhelmed by opportunities and problems that actually belong to somebody else. Effective leaders understand the trade-off between action and inaction, and the probable impact of doing nothing—and make their decisions accordingly.

2. **Is a decision required now?** Decide immediately if you feel you must. But decisions rarely are as urgent as they seem. Great leaders use timing as a key ingredient of their strategy. If the issue is important but not urgent, make a list of information you need, stakeholders to contact, alternatives to consider, and resources to obtain. By delaying a decision until the time is right, you reduce the chances of missing a vital step.

3. **Are you solving the right problem?** Executives make serious judgment errors when they solve the wrong problem. It is easy to think you understand the problem: "Let's downsize," "Let's expand globally," or "Let's implement a new technology." In these cases, the "problem statement" is actually a solution based on assumptions about the underlying challenge. Even though their assumptions might turn out to be accurate, effective leaders rigorously define the problem before solving it.

4. **What is the capacity of your organization?** Most organizations have more opportunities and issues than resources to address them. Nonetheless, we see executives trying to do everything at once—and often end up achieving nothing. Consider the abilities and daily priorities of your people before undertaking a new action. Before deciding which issues to tackle, ask your people which ones they feel are urgent. This is an effective way to assess their willingness and capacity to handle them on top of their everyday workload and other priorities you have set.

5. **Are resources being applied to top priorities?** Every organization must adjust its spending to suit economic conditions. One approach is to increase spending across the board in good times and cut it in bad times.

Unfortunately, that approach inhibits growth and often locks in mediocre results. Instead, start with a baseline budget that covers the expenses and investments essential for core operations. Then apply your judgment to allocate funds to future-looking projects. Those funds must be preserved in good times and bad, even if you have to eliminate some ongoing operations in order to free up resources.

Make these keystone judgments part of your judgment gene so that you and your high potentials will make the right decisions at the right time in the right way—and avoid seeing your name in the news for a bad decision.

HOW DECISIONS ARE MADE

How you make decisions is as important to your success as the decisions themselves. Decision-making conversations add to the potential effectiveness of the organization by

- Enhancing relationships by saying yes to an employee's innovative idea
- Developing others by validating employees' ideas and tapping into their potential
- Creating a sense of ownership for the success of a decision
- Aligning everyone behind the decision and the actions it requires

Leaders unleash enormous energy by using decision-making conversations to help people commit to success. By exploring ideas thoroughly and saying yes, a leader validates his team's value and increases their confidence and commitment.

Making effective decisions is the heart of leadership—it is what leaders are paid to do. Yet business periodicals regularly feature articles about executives who made incredibly poor decisions. Those articles raise the question, "How can an executive with decades of experience and a large support staff make such poor decisions?" It often is because the executives made a decision too fast, too soon, or without using a structured approach. They may have skipped some steps in the decision-making process or not truly listened to the inputs provided by others. In our experience, few organizations have an abundance of effective decision-makers—yours probably does not either. Leaders who consistently make good decisions—in the organizations that make the news because of superior results—teach their people to use a structured and repeatable process to make decisions.

Leaders in those organizations do six things every time—and do them well. Figure 16.1 lists six decision-making elements and describes the viewpoint first-line managers, managers of managers, executive leaders, and CXO leaders generally bring to each element. Ensure that your decision-making conversations cover these six elements.

	First-Line Manager	Manager of Managers	Executive Leader	CXO Leader
ELEMENT 1 *Define the Problem*	May need to be told that a problem exists	Sees problems before they happen	Prevents problems from happening	Considers problems to be opportunities
ELEMENT 2 *Identify the Alternatives*	Based on individual experience	Based on the group's experiences	Based on industry best practices	Based on vision for the future
ELEMENT 3 *Evaluate Pros and Cons*	Primarily uses data in evaluations	Considers data and experience in evaluations	Considers people and experience in evaluations	Evaluates against organization's strategy and vision
ELEMENT 4 *Assess the Risks*	Is primarily concerned with risk to career	Focuses on risks to the team	Considers risks to the organization	Assesses the risk to the industry and the world
ELEMENT 5 *Acquire Resources*	Considers resources as relatively fixed	Looks for ways to secure more resources	Knows resources will be found for a great idea	Does not allow vision to be constrained by resources
ELEMENT 6 *Produce Results*	Asks, What can we achieve this month?	Asks, What can we achieve this quarter?	Asks, Will the organization achieve its annual goals?	Looks ahead three to five years in setting priorities

FIGURE 16.1. Structured Decision Making.

Leaders rarely have enough time or data to evaluate all alternatives, but they still follow a structured decision-making process.

PROBLEM SOLVING VERSUS DECISION MAKING

It is easy to confuse problem solving and decision making—but both are essential. Problem solving is part of the management mindset. In solving problems, the manager evaluates current results against standards and generally sees any adverse deviation as a problem. The problem is solved when root causes that explain all facets of the problem are unambiguously identified. In contrast, decision making is a facet of the leadership mindset. Properly defined objectives are the bridge between the management and leadership mindsets with respect to problem solving and decision making.

Leaders identify and analyze alternative courses of action relative to the time and resources they consume and the risks they entail. One effective approach is to assess the problem and potential solutions in a conversation. Ask your people to challenge the problem definition and assumptions behind that definition because, if you identify the wrong problem, the solution you pick is not likely to succeed. Evaluating alternatives often requires input from multiple sources, such as peer executives, accountants, forecasters, and customer focus groups. For example, finding a solution to declining sales might require you to obtain feedback from the sales force, product performance data, a market analysis, and customer satisfaction surveys. After you have defined potential solutions and collected information about each alternative, you are ready to evaluate the pros and cons.

Quantitative and intuition-based approaches each have a place in the evaluation of pros and cons. Quantitative evaluations look toward the future using new data, whereas intuition is rooted in past experiences. In evaluating alternatives, encourage dissent to ensure that people do not tell you what you want to hear instead of their real thoughts. Do not hesitate to challenge an expert's opinion to confirm how well she understands the problem. Ask other executives to provide input about how your decision might affect their operations. Remember that so-called rules of thumb are often unreliable or irrelevant; and forecasts, though useful at times, may not be accurate.

You may be tempted to jump on the first option that meets an objective. But refrain from shortcutting the process; people need time to form ideas and find the courage to voice them. Make a decision only after its full consequences are considered. If you jump too quickly to a decision, you may cause unintended consequences that force you to repeat the entire decision-making process. Part of your job as a leader is to get others to open up about their concerns and, after the decision is made, to focus their energy on implementing rather than questioning the decision.

MAKE DECISIONS DECISIVELY

Making leadership decisions is like driving in a NASCAR race. When should you take the lead, and when should you maintain your position? If you move into the passing lane too soon, you could waste gas and find yourself further behind. But hesitate too long, and you could miss a golden opportunity to take the lead. So how can you make the right decision at the right time?

Effective decision-makers share three characteristics: experience, confidence, and decisiveness. NASCAR drivers do not have those traits the first time they sit behind the wheel. They develop them over time, often in races they lose. Few fans appreciate the hours that drivers spend practicing and the number of times they have spun out. Winning drivers are confident because they know the limits of their skill and the capabilities of their cars from practice runs and previous races. Similarly, effective leaders have confidence in their decisions once they understand the skills and capacity of people in their organizations, as well as their own limitations.

Decisiveness is different from confidence, however. Decisiveness is the willingness to accept the results of your decisions no matter what they may be. Questioning a decision after you make it can adversely affect results. Many times, initiating action even though you are unsure of its outcome is less risky than not making a decision. But once you make a decision, move on with confidence.

If you feel that making decisions in your organization is as risky as driving in a NASCAR race, you are not alone. Few executives have the experience, confidence, and decisiveness needed to make great decisions on their first day in a new position. However, if you make decisions after appropriate conversations, avoid second-guessing yourself, and learn from your successes and failures, you will soon be winning the races in your industry.

GROWING THE JUDGMENT GENE IN HIGH POTENTIALS

When we meet with senior executives, they often ask how to grow the judgment gene in their high potentials. We respond that the best way to cultivate judgment is to have conversations about recognizing new patterns from just a few pieces of data. Leaders who possess that skill usually are ahead of everyone else in exploiting opportunities. Their decisions meet with uncanny success because they use judgment that is rooted in a curious mind, thorough planning, past experiences (both good and bad), and criteria that differentiate minor risk from major risk.

Data are illuminating for some and mind-numbing for others, depending on how they look at numbers. For example, Pam, a high-potential sales manager, always seemed to recognize emerging trends and make great decisions well before others became aware of a change. When we asked Pam to explain her secret, she responded, "Most people look at numbers to confirm their beliefs, and discount any surprise as an aberration or one-time event. It's as if the numbers are wrong if people don't like them. Even when a problem is obvious, they ignore it and wait for the next month's numbers before making a decision. That gives me an automatic thirty-day head start!"

That made sense, we thought, and asked her what unique techniques and mindset she uses to examine data. Pam reflected for a moment and replied:

> I look at numbers in an open-ended way. I clear my mind and ask what
> they are really telling me instead of hoping they will confirm my
> expectations. I don't accept the numbers at face value—instead I look
> for hidden reasons why. Even if the numbers match projections, I
> wonder why. Should they have been higher or lower? For example,
> sales of our new product line were rising slowly. Some managers felt
> that demonstrated a loyal following and continued with the sales

program. I wondered why they weren't rising faster, and looked for individual products whose sales were higher or lower than average. Those variances may point to new customer preferences. Then I called customers, contacted the marketing group, and talked with the sales team to refine our strategy. Those conversations help us respond faster to new patterns and new opportunities. Our rate of sales increase immediately doubled.

The failure to recognize trends—or refusal to acknowledge and act on them—can undermine the largest organizations. The financial industry is still deluged with ideas to curb the high-risk judgments that were blamed for the near-collapse of the global financial system in 2008–2010. In those years, the world watched respected leaders like the CEO of Lehman Brothers (which declared bankruptcy in September 2008) slide down the slippery slope of bad judgment and destroy organizations and careers. In congressional testimony after the bankruptcy, the Lehman Brothers' CEO maintained that he had exhibited good judgment under the circumstances.

Many executives use that defense when things go wrong; they credit success to their skill and knowledge, yet they attribute failure to factors beyond their control and misjudge the trends. Many employees do not speak up because they assume that the boss has better judgment than anyone else—which is not categorically true. You may have better judgment than your boss in a particular matter, or one or more of your people may exhibit better judgment than you. If this is the case, exercise the superiority of your judgment by having a conversation with your boss or by endorsing your people's decision. It is not a matter of ego—it is about getting the best results.

CHAPTER 17

WHAT YOU KNOW IS IRRELEVANT

Ultimately, a genuine leader is not a searcher for consensus, but a molder of consensus.
—MARTIN LUTHER KING JR.

Well, "irrelevant" may be somewhat harsh, but what you know is less important to the success of your organization than you might think. Several things are more important:

- What the people in the organization collectively know
- The speed at which they (and you) are learning
- How easily and quickly knowledge is shared across your organization
- How effectively knowledge is applied to make and implement decisions

Your knowledge matters only to the extent that you share it in conversations and use it to make decisions. As a leader, you must ensure that opportunities and issues are analyzed thoroughly and dealt with decisively. In most cases, it will not be you who performs the analysis or takes the action—your people will. Because there is a limit to how much you know, conversations with your people that reveal and evaluate possibilities based on everyone's collective knowledge will result in more effective decisions.

Humility requires you to acknowledge that you do not know everything. If you are thinking, "That's politically correct, of course, but I know more than any of my people," consider the leaders in the financial sector who believed they could not possibly make a mistake—until they pushed the world's economy to the edge of oblivion and saw their companies flirt with bankruptcy. The blunt truth is that we are all quite capable of making huge mistakes despite our experience, accomplishments, and education. We individually know less than we need to know to perform at the highest levels of leadership.

Once you accept that you do not know everything and that leadership entails connecting and aligning with people instead of controlling them, it follows that your goal will be to fill key positions with highly qualified people, share your knowledge with them, and tap into their knowledge. As a leader, particularly in far-flung organizations, you will find it hard to stay in touch with all of your high potentials. But you can ensure that they know what you know about the big picture and the kind of developments they should bring to your attention. Trust their ability to get the job done. Whatever they may lack in the way of skill or knowledge is your responsibility as the leader to see that they learn.

Because you know just a sliver of what your organization collectively needs to know to be successful, you must be open to learning. People with technical backgrounds often are uncomfortable until they know most of what can be known. As a leader, you will regularly find yourself making decisions with less information than you would like to have. It is okay if some decisions are off the mark as long as you and your high potentials learn from the mistakes and improve your decision-making skills. If you repeat the same decisions (for example, categorically avoiding risky projects rather than evaluating risk versus reward case by case), you may feel safe, but you are limiting your organization's potential. Allow painful events—declining budgets, relationship conflicts, service complaints, and the like—to teach you and your people how to make better decisions. Be willing to acknowledge a mistake—but do not get stuck there.

ENGAGING YOUR TEAM'S KNOWLEDGE

You may have already found that saying "I don't know" leads to lively conversations in which almost everyone participates. In today's age of real-time information, knowledge changes so fast that knowledge workers quickly become obsolete unless learning is part of the culture. That is true not only in technical fields like health care and information technology but also increasingly in retail, manufacturing, marketing, construction, and other fields. Knowledge-based organizations flourish when everyone understands what his or her colleagues are trying to accomplish. Therefore, ensure that your organization has a culture that encourages learning and teaching. Ask yourself and your people, "What must we learn to stay current?" and "What knowledge can we share so that we all will succeed?" Organizations that regularly examine those two questions are commonly referred to as learning organizations.

The foundation of a learning organization is a belief that the key to growth and the solution to issues lie within the collective knowledge of its members. It is a shift from the Industrial Age workplace where employees had a passive role in decision making to a workplace where people exchange ideas and challenge each other to improve. As a leader, you are building a learning organization when you tap your people's knowledge, encourage critical thinking, and hold conversations to discuss new concepts. In *The Fifth Discipline*, Peter Senge, a pioneer in learning organizations, cites five dimensions that are vital in a learning organization:[1]

- **Systems thinking** is a shift from operating separately to being interconnected, and from blaming something or someone else to taking responsibility to find a solution. The members of a learning organization understand the big picture and recognize patterns in what previously seemed to be unrelated events.
- **Personal mastery** is a commitment to continuous learning on the part of each member of a learning organization. Personal mastery means being realistic about one's abilities and taking action to expand them.
- **Mental models** are instilled in a learning organization to stimulate insights and improve work practices. Mental models require people to evaluate their beliefs and how those beliefs influence the actions they take.
- **Shared visions** blend the personal visions of individuals with the vision for the future of the organization. When achieved, a shared vision produces commitment that is sustainable in good times and bad.
- **Team learning** requires everyone to learn individually and to come together to share his or her knowledge in a way that achieves the organization's goals.

Taken together, these five dimensions fuel the conversations in a learning organization in ways that challenge everyone to apply his or her knowledge to grow the organization and simultaneously respond to the aspirations of individual members.

BENEFITS OF A LEARNING ORGANIZATION

Effective conversations are the core of a learning organization. Today's business world changes so fast that being a learning organization is not a feel-good goal; it is a necessity to meet everyday challenges. In particular, yours is a learning organization if it exhibits the following characteristics and benefits:

- **Responds rapidly to change.** A learning organization naturally responds more easily and quickly to market, workforce, and workplace changes because change is viewed as an opportunity rather than a problem.
- **Adapts to shifting priorities.** When resources are scarce and priorities shift, a learning organization maintains effective alignment among customer needs, organizational goals, available resources, and individual needs.
- **Fills information gaps.** Knowledge flows smoothly from level to level in a learning organization to fill gaps caused by new technologies, retirements, and attrition. In addition, new hires get up to speed more quickly.
- **Facilitates training.** In a learning organization, everyone is responsible for learning, and everyone is a teacher. Even if training budgets are cut, a learning organization integrates training into daily mainstream activities.
- **Builds teams.** A learning organization helps recruit, train, and retain the people who fill knowledge-based positions.

Becoming a learning organization requires commitment from executives at all levels. You must be willing to create and communicate a shared vision for how operations will be conducted. The essential first step is to be transparent in conversations—making virtually all information accessible to everyone—which may be uncomfortable for you. Your people need to feel confident that their views will be considered and that they are empowered to take risks. Of equal importance, the organization must have a strategy for keeping information current, distributing increasing volumes of information quickly and efficiently, and cataloging historical knowledge. You must master the subtleties of moving from a hierarchical to a consensus-driven organization.

GROUP DECISION MAKING

Most people think groups make better decisions than individuals, which may explain why there are so many meetings. Although research shows that groups make fewer bad decisions, the real value of group decisions is that when people participate in decision making, they become more willing to support the implementation of the decisions. The challenge, of course, is that when several people participate in making a decision, you must conduct the decision-making conversation with full consideration for such factors as

- The scope and significance of the decision to be made
- The time available to analyze alternatives and make a decision
- The number and type of people who will be affected by the decision
- The amount of buy-in that is required for successful implementation
- The attitude you want the group to have in regard to the decision

Understanding when it is appropriate to involve others in a decision, whom to involve, and how to handle the decision-making process is an important leadership skill.

It has been said that if three people debate a topic, four viewpoints will emerge: one from each person plus the group consensus. Melding the opinions of a group into an executable decision is challenging. People naturally see things differently because they have different experiences, roles, and needs. For example, you may have operations, sales, financial, HR, and IT people on your staff. Each of them focuses on a specific aspect of a decision—the part he understands and for which he has responsibility. One purpose of engaging multiple people in decision-making conversations is to expose them to diverse viewpoints.

For example, Todd, a new first-line manager, diligently researched two investment opportunities in his area and presented them during his first strategic planning workshop. After opportunities were presented in all areas and return-on-investment analyses were performed, neither of his opportunities was put in the budget for the coming year. When the process finished, he exclaimed: "I had no idea how many good ideas there are for our company. I'm disappointed, but I see why my investments ideas are on the back burner this year. I'll be back next year with new ideas." For Todd, it was a shocking baptism into today's business world, where bigger and bigger decisions must be made with less and less information—and more cooperation. That is why effective decision-making conversations are vital for success.

If a decision must be made quickly, the time required for group decision making can be a liability. Furthermore, when few people have relevant knowledge to contribute, involving a large number of people in a decision-making conversation is inefficient—other than as a learning experience. Your role as the leader is to decide who will participate in the conversation and how the decision will be presented to others.

HOW MUCH CONSENSUS DO YOU REALLY HAVE?

We have seen leaders who, even after conducting a thorough decision-making conversation, begin implementation only to discover that they never really had consensus. To avoid this potentially explosive situation, use a simple polling technique to quickly test the degree of consensus and identify those who may have reservations about the decision. After a decision has been reached, ask members of the group to reflect on how they feel about the course of action that has been adopted. Then ask them to signal their degree of support by raising zero to five fingers to indicate one of the following:

Five fingers: "Yes. I totally support the decision."
Four fingers: "Okay. It's probably the best we can come up with."
Three fingers: "Maybe . . . but I still have questions and concerns."
Two fingers: "I'm uncomfortable. Let's talk about it more."
One finger: "I wish that we would do something else."
Zero fingers: "I'm absolutely against the decision."

Quickly tabulate the responses. Fives and fours signify strong support; if you are a good facilitator (or lucky), everyone will fall into these categories. Threes and twos are not committed, and it would be beneficial to discuss what could be changed to address their doubts. Unfortunately, ones and zeros indicate hard-core objectors—people who may actively resist implementation. The value of this technique is that it allows people to express their doubts without appearing to be hostile or uncooperative. Ask the people who raised fewer than four fingers to say what it would take for them to be able to support the decision. The give-and-take conversations stimulated by that question will improve the decision, gain supporters, and potentially identify new alternatives.

Consensus polling is an iterative technique that can be used to evaluate attitude shifts after each round of conversation. Polling does not guarantee that you will ever reach 100 percent consensus—deadlock is always a possible outcome. A strong negative position taken by even a single person can be enough to block consensus—especially when the conversation did not include discussions in the second and third perspectives. If the group is hopelessly deadlocked, polling should reveal the reasons. Typically, decision-making conversations motivate people to explore alternatives to resolve everyone's concerns. If consensus cannot be reached, you may be forced to make an executive decision. In any case, be sure that your people understand from the start that you will make a decision unilaterally if there is no consensus—take stonewalling off the list of options.

FINDING THE THIRD ALTERNATIVE

Which alternative is best—yours or theirs? You could argue about it for days or weeks without adding value. But what if there were a third alternative that is superior to both? The third alternative, a concept popularized by Stephen Covey in *The 7 Habits of Highly Effective People*, is not a compromise—rather it is an innovative decision that everyone embraces. The key to finding the third alternative is to stop defending your position and start looking for an option that integrates your best ideas with those of others. Figure 17.1 suggests that focusing on *what is best* instead of *who is right* points conversations toward the third alternative.

For example, an upscale community near Washington, D.C., has nine hundred homes worth more than a million dollars on average. During zoning negotiations, the developer was outraged when the county government demanded that he build one low-income house for each luxury house. An

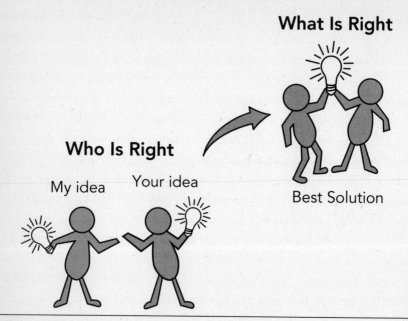

FIGURE 17.1. Aligning Behind a Shared Decision.
The probability of success increases when everyone aligns behind *what is right* rather than *who is right*.

expensive legal battle raged for months until the builder suggested a third alternative. He offered to build all-brick, four-bedroom homes for low-income buyers and subsidize construction with a surcharge on luxury homeowners. Delighted with the new approach, the county willingly agreed to significantly reduce the number of low-income homes that had to be built.

Interest in the new homes among low-income buyers was so great that a lottery was required. One in thirty applicants won the lottery and purchased a house for $75,000. The sales contract included a clause that prohibited low-income homeowners from selling their houses for twenty years. When the twenty-year moratorium expired, the low-income houses sold for nearly $500,000. The county, the developer, and two classes of homeowners achieved their objectives through this third alternative.

To find the third alternative, you must believe that such an alternative exists, commit to looking for it, and be willing to let go of the alternative you have been advocating. You are seeking to combine your objectives with those of the other party. The solution to a problem and the approach to an opportunity exist along a continuum of possibilities. If you force people to pick one of the conflicting options, you may miss other great possibilities.

Are the conversations in your organization characterized by collaboration or confrontation? When they are confrontational, issues can become so emotionally charged that people defend differences without even considering that there could be other possibilities. The third alternative can only be found when people seek to understand the objectives of others—that is, engage in the second conversational perspective. In collaborative conversations, everyone accepts that there are at least three alternatives: one that feels right to you, one that feels right to them, and a better one that you have not discovered yet. When you understand what others want and help them get it, you will achieve your goals as a by-product of the collaboration.

Successful people are generally top-notch collaborators. They know that if they have part of the answer to a daunting challenge, collaboration is the fastest and easiest way to find the missing parts. Collaboration has always been important; but today, going it alone can be fatal in a world where no organization or leader can always be on top of rapidly changing customer needs and emerging technologies. Therefore, your goal as a leader is to build a collaborative team, make collaboration a value, and conduct leadership conversations in a way that encourages the search for the third alternative.

WHAT IF A THIRD ALTERNATIVE DOES NOT EXIST?

If you are thinking that a third alternative does not always exist, you are missing the point: *a third alternative always exists*. It may be hard to find, but your job is to lead the search to find it. The third alternative is the opposite of a win-lose decision. In a win-lose decision, one party gets what she wants (wins) and the other goes home disappointed (loses). In the long run, such decisions do not benefit either side. While the winner celebrates victory, resentments build in the loser, which adversely affect future transactions. The third alternative is not a compromise, because both parties give up something in a compromise; you could make a case that compromises are really lose-lose transactions.

The third alternative synergistically yields a result that is advantageous for both you and your potential adversary. Everyone who joins in a third alternative feels like a winner. Unfortunately, some executives still believe that finding the third alternative is an idealistic objective that wastes time. But great leaders know differently. They look for the third alternative in every negotiation and do not stop until they find an approach that exceeds the expectations that people had when negotiations started.

Stop yourself the next time you become willing to support an alternative that is merely defensible rather than ideal. Refuse to settle for a course of action that is "good enough." Lead people toward the third alternative by announcing at the beginning that the goal is to find an approach that (1) meets everyone's needs and (2) everyone can support unconditionally. Do not end the search until such an alternative is found. Start by asking the group, "If someone offers an option that is better than yours, will you abandon your option and adopt theirs?" Most people will quickly answer yes, and that establishes their willingness to join in the search for an ideal solution. If they say no, a different conversation needs to be held.

After you define the issue and everyone puts his or her ideas on the table, spend an additional ten minutes or so exploring wild and creative options. Use the full ten minutes; otherwise you will find the group thinking for a few seconds and saying, "There aren't any other possibilities." Also, be sure that no one judges any idea to be ridiculous, impossible, or unrealistic. Exploring new ideas can be awkward at times, but do not allow that to end the process prematurely. We challenge you to pursue the third alternative in your next negotiation conversation; we believe that you will produce better results than with any other approach.

PROMOTING TEAMWORK

In most cases, teamwork is essential to achieving objectives. Yet when a diverse group of people works together, team members inevitably have different ideas about how things should be done. The problem with compromise as a decision-making technique is that everyone settles for a solution that is merely acceptable, which produces halfhearted execution and sets the stage for future conflict. Leaders need a strategy to diffuse conflict. Seeking the third alternative is a good one because respect becomes a team value, and everyone is challenged to avoid becoming entrenched in a particular viewpoint. Consider the following practices that also promote teamwork:

- **Prevent conflict.** Nipping conflict in the bud saves time and reduces anxiety. Before interactions begin, review the purpose of the conversation and set ground rules that define acceptable and unacceptable behaviors.
- **Exhibit emotional intelligence.** When people are in conflict, encourage them to acknowledge their feelings and decide what to do with them. Whether or not they feel anger is their choice, but responsibly reducing the tension caused by anger and replacing it with a feeling of challenge will move your team forward.
- **Express needs.** When disagreement emerges, take time to have each party express his needs. This practice allows people to feel heard and helps them understand the needs of others—essential prerequisites to finding an approach that meets everyone's needs.
- **Accept only win-win solutions.** Unchecked, conflict becomes a contest with winners and losers. To ensure a win-win outcome, have each person say how she sees the issue and cite actions (or inactions) on her part that may have contributed to the conflict. Letting go of one position enables people to find a new one.

Disagreements are common when an issue is urgent and the stakes are high. As the leader, you will find these four practices useful in directing the energy of conflict toward finding innovative solutions that everyone supports.

IT'S NOT ABOUT WINNING

The third alternative is a foreign concept to people who feel compelled to win at all costs. Seeking the third alternative is realistic only when people have the courage to express their needs and empathize with the needs of others. Those who push to win no matter what are usually oblivious to the needs of others.

Win-lose transactions breed mistrust, competition, and resentment, and make it nearly impossible to find the third alternative. No matter how competent win-at-all-costs people are, on balance they limit the team's success. Coach them to recognize how damaging their win-lose behaviors are to the team; you may want to replace them if they persist in such behaviors. Similarly, those who always seek to please others can also be a liability to the team. They whine about not having their needs met, even as they consistently abandon those needs to appease others—an ineffective decision-making dynamic.

During your next conversation, look for the following behaviors as indicators that people are genuinely looking for the third alternative in their decision making. If these indicators are not present, step in and change the direction of the conversation:

- **Sincere intent.** The tone shows sincere intent to present viewpoints in a nonthreatening manner, to listen to the views of others, and to seek a solution that meets everyone's needs.
- **Creativity.** The ideas that are presented are entirely new—or are a new angle on existing processes or long-standing challenges.
- **Courage.** Everyone participates in the conversation and offers his or her views with clarity, conviction, transparency, and respect.
- **Openness.** People are willing to hear and suggest new ideas, even if those ideas are controversial, risky, unproven, or incomplete.
- **Desire to understand.** People ask insightful questions at appropriate times and listen carefully to the responses.

When your team cannot find the third alternative, be willing to end the conversation and walk away. You might have a difficult time walking away from a workable solution when it only fails to meet a few people's needs. If a creative third alternative eludes your team, then walking away becomes the third alternative. The ground rule is that there must be a win-win decision for everyone or no deal. In our experience, leaders who walk away make a clear statement: "The third alternative is the only decision we accept in this organization." You will be amazed at how well the next decision-making conversation will go after you have walked away from the previous one.

CHAPTER 18

BE CURIOUS—ASK GREAT QUESTIONS

Millions saw the apple fall, but Newton was the one who asked why.
—BERNARD BARUCH

Would you characterize yourself as a curious person? Most people think of themselves that way, considering that the opposite traits—close-mindedness, apathy, and the like—are not flattering. Curiosity pushes people to explore and learn. To be curious is a choice that humans make from the day they are born until the day they die—although you had more time to be curious as a child than you do as a harried executive. Even still, leaders are innately curious about how the world works—and that curiosity propels business, technological, and social progress.

The program manager of a billion-dollar government program proudly proclaimed that open-mindedness and innovation were core values in his program. He encouraged his staff to be open and blunt with him, with each other, and with other organizations. One day he asked his coach, "My people don't suggest as many ideas as they once did. Sometimes I feel like they aren't telling me the whole story. Why?"

The coach provided feedback: "Do you recall last week's staff meeting when you said the new approach that Ian suggested was the dumbest thing you had ever heard?"

The program manager responded, "Yes, I said that—but even you thought it wasn't a viable option."

The coach continued. "As presented, his idea did seem unworkable. But judgments like that derail creativity. I was actually curious why an experienced engineer like Ian would think it was a good idea. If you had asked him, you might have uncovered the golden nugget behind his idea. Your more outspoken staff members aren't affected by judgments, but mild-mannered ones like Ian become reluctant to suggest controversial ideas."

That reluctance had turned the program manager's conversations into one-sided rituals instead of the vigorous discussions of bold strategies that he wanted to encourage.

Great leaders are curious about curiosity itself. They wonder how they can be more curious themselves and promote curiosity in their organizations. Paradoxically, what you already know is an obstacle to curiosity. Experts make decisions instantly because unconsciously they believe they know everything they need to know. Effective leaders see the fallacy in that thinking and escape from the "knowing trap" by keeping an open mind and asking questions to learn more.

CURIOSITY PUSHES THE BOUNDARIES

Throughout history, curious leaders have expanded horizons, accelerated economic growth, and increased living standards. The curious, risk-taking spirit of the Vikings and Marco Polo and other Renaissance explorers is common in much of today's global workforce. To lead that workforce, you need different skills than your grandfather used in the Industrial Age. Industrial Age workers sold their skills to one employer at a time. Today's workers market knowledge-based services around the world. A growing number of workers are free agents who contribute their knowledge to projects on an ad hoc basis and move on when the project is completed. In this dynamic environment, you will be challenged to build a workplace that attracts and retains the best and brightest decision-makers. Likewise, the high potentials you hire will be challenged to refresh their knowledge continuously because the useful life span of knowledge is shrinking. Curiosity is the key to meeting both of these challenges.

Knowledge workers are vital in identifying alternatives, solving problems, developing new products, and delivering services. Being curious and up to speed on new technologies, they contribute insights that will influence your decisions, priorities, and strategies. Because the pace of change has been quickened by social media, you need to give the knowledge workers who work for you freedom to participate in peer-to-peer networks that share new ideas across organizational and international boundaries. Those networks, in turn, will help you build strategic alliances, exchange knowledge freely, and make better decisions.

Driven by the rapid expansion of Internet-based relationships, the demand for knowledge workers has skyrocketed. Knowledge workers will contribute to your decision-making conversations by

- Creating or adapting strategies to implement new technologies
- Promoting collaborative relationships inside and outside the organization
- Analyzing massive amounts of information in order to uncover and understand trends
- Developing and deploying new products and services quickly
- Brainstorming creative solutions in their field of interest

These contributions contrast with management-mindset activities related to production work and repetitive tasks that knowledge workers rarely perform. Knowledge workers are exceedingly valuable in solving information-rich customer service tasks, such as providing technical support, resolving sticky issues, and responding to open-ended inquiries. In addition, they can increase the value of your organization by developing products and services that are patentable or copyrightable.

CURIOSITY CREATES OPPORTUNITIES

In the hands of a capable leader, curiosity converts problems into opportunities. Managers tend to focus on solving the problem at hand, whereas curious leaders explore options before deciding what to do next. Brainstorming is a technique that curious leaders use to assemble a list of possibilities that improve decision making. By being genuinely curious and asking open-ended questions, you can stimulate ideas, reduce inhibitions in your high potentials, and maximize your group's creativity. Because the quality of your decisions ultimately depends on the quality of the solutions you consider, you may want to use one of the following techniques in your next decision-making conversation to generate better alternatives:

- **Idea pyramids.** Write the issue on a whiteboard and discuss its importance with the group. Next, have each group member write an approach to the issue on paper and then pass the paper to the next person. The second person adds thoughts to expand the first idea, then passes the paper to the third person. The process continues until everyone receives his original paper back. Finish the divergent portion of the conversation by having each person read his idea aloud along with the additions that others have made. This approach takes time, but you will be astonished by the in-depth thinking and collaborative solutions it produces.
- **Idea linking.** Initiate the process by explicitly defining the issue and giving the group a few minutes to exchange ideas. When the time limit expires, merge ideas in a fishbone-style idea map. Start by having the first person write her ideas on the map. The second person continues by connecting his ideas to the first person's ideas on the map. Do not reject any idea and accept ones that start a stand-alone thread. During the mapping process, group members will develop a deeper understanding of the potential solutions as they consider how their ideas link with the ideas of others. It is not unusual for entirely new threads to emerge during the linking process.
- **Digital collaboration.** Digital technologies enable geographically disbursed groups to collaborate in decision making. Virtual brainstorming is popular these days and could be supported by your meeting software or readily available, free digital services. It also can be done via simple emails. In either case, colleagues develop ideas independently and share them over the Internet. Ideas are visible to everyone, although they can be presented anonymously to encourage openness. The ideas can be compiled with the virtual equivalent of the idea pyramid or idea linking techniques just described. This approach also permits participation over an extended

period. A digital collaboration conversation lasting several weeks is not unusual if the topic is strategically important but not urgent.

The four common principles that make these brainstorming techniques effective as decision-making tools are (1) produce as many ideas as possible, (2) welcome off-the-wall ideas with enthusiasm, (3) suspend judgment during idea generation, and (4) integrate ideas to form even better ones. Techniques like these generally lead to clear decisions that everyone understands and accepts.

Stimulate curiosity in your high potentials and allow time for new ideas to emerge. How many decisions you make—or even how many decisions you get right—does not matter. Rather, it is how many of the strategic calls you get right, and how solidly your people embrace those decisions. Good leaders make better decisions; but, more important, they know which of the decisions are most important and get a higher percentage of those decisions right. They are adept at the entire decision-making process, from recognizing the need for a decision to framing the issue, developing alternatives, choosing one, and motivating people to implement it effectively.

FOCUS ON OPPORTUNITIES

If your decisions focus on fixing what is wrong in your organization and ignore things that are going well—stop. Focusing on problems is like being stuck in a rut. Even when you succeed in getting out, all you have done is get back to where you were. Instead, have conversations about opportunities—the possibilities that lie ahead. In doing so, you will channel your people's creative energies toward pursuing tomorrow's success rather than merely fixing old problems. Along with yielding better results, you create optimism, instill confidence, and inject a sense of accomplishment in your team.

Be especially careful how you present the need for continuous improvement. If taken to an extreme, it can imply that nothing your team does will ever be good enough and that no matter what objectives the organization achieves or how well it performs, the results will still be inadequate—and the people will feel that way as well. In the leadership mindset, problem solving is a creative activity that produces growth, better customer service, and improved quality. Avoid being one of those executives who is out of touch with people and scratches her head wondering why morale is low when the business is doing well. The key to making decisions that unleash top performance lies in asking questions that stimulate curiosity, innovation, and commitment in the pursuit of new opportunities.

EVEN GREAT LEADERS DON'T HAVE ALL THE ANSWERS

Many people think that leaders simply have a knack for knowing the right answers because they were born with superior intuition, aptitude, and magnetism. Charismatic leaders are seen as being in an exclusive class of people who are immune to uncertainty and doubt and have an uncanny ability to avoid major failures. In short, they conclude that leaders are not like the rest of us. Although this image may appeal to high potentials who seek to become great leaders, the reality of leadership is more complex.

In our experience, virtually every leader undergoes periods when she is confused, discouraged, pessimistic, or unsure of the future. She feels alone searching for answers and wondering why other leaders seem to have an easier time—even as she maintains an outward façade of confidence. Your success as a leader will depend in large part on how you deal with your periods of self-doubt. The key is to acknowledge those feelings and, more important, involve trusted relationship partners and your high potentials in the decision-making process. Take time to ask questions and search for answers that define the objectives, diagnose the problems, and develop action plans for you and your organization. Being open, exhibiting curiosity, and asking questions will enable you to focus on the future rather than on an unrealistic standard for how great leaders are supposed to feel.

Have you made significant business decisions with minimal discussion with your team about alternatives and consequences? When you believe you know the answer and do not ask questions, they may think you are not listening—or worse, that you do not care about what they have to say. Unless you ask questions, you are settling for the best of what you know rather than the best of what your team collectively knows. At each higher step on the leadership ladder, you will know a smaller part of what you need to know to make decisions. Examine the questions you ask in your conversations. Do they uncover opportunities for tomorrow (leadership mindset), or do they focus on getting today's job done as quickly as possible (management mindset)? Do they stimulate growth (leadership mindset) or put boundaries on the options (management mindset)?

Antonio's main job as a director in an aerospace company was business development, so when the Air Force issued a Request for Proposals (RFP) to develop an enterprise computer system, he managed the proposal team. Phase I of the multiyear project was design. In total, the government estimated that all three phases would cost $350 million. The RFP's first line read, "The government intends to award two fixed-price contracts not to exceed a total of $15 million for Phase I." To win, Antonio and his team concluded that the Phase I bid had to be $7.5 million or less. The team worked day and night for weeks to prepare the proposal and cut costs to a bare-bones $8.1 million. Antonio flew to headquarters to present the proposal to the CEO and obtain his approval for investing $600,000 of company funds in Phase I of the project in order for them to reach the target fixed-price bid.

During Antonio's presentation, the CEO listened carefully but did not ask questions. When it ended, the CEO said abruptly, "If the government wants us, they'll find the extra money" and walked out. The proposal was submitted at $8.1 million and lost. Two other companies won contracts at $7.5 million each. Antonio and his proposal team were angry after working so hard on the proposal. Because the CEO did not ask questions, they felt that their proposal lost because of a capricious decision, and every one of them left the company within a year.

Possibly the most effective technique a C-suite leader can use in conversations is to ask insightful questions. Questions imply professional respect for the person to whom they are directed. Asking questions may seem weak to some; but, in reality, a leader who asks questions is directing the flow of the decision-making conversation. Asking questions is an effective way to discover what issues your people are concerned about and what resources they need to succeed. Use the third conversational perspective ("What else is possible?") to ask great questions that lead to possibilities that no one had recognized before the questions were asked.

MANAGERS ANSWER QUESTIONS— LEADERS ASK THEM

Remember when your mom complained, "Everything I tell you goes in one ear and out the other." Well, in a neurological sense she was correct. If she had asked questions instead, you would have retained more of her messages. That is because the brain functions with the obstinacy of a child: tell it what to do, and it starts analyzing the implications; if instead you ask the brain a question, it will treat it as a problem to be solved—a game to be played. People like solving problems because doing so gives them a rush when the brain releases neurotransmitters that act like adrenaline.

The leadership lesson is that you need to ask your people questions and let them decide the course of action, rather than telling them what to do, how to do it, and when it should be done. Leaders use questions liberally in their conversations, whereas managers spend much of their time answering how-to questions for their people. For a leader, questions are more than a source of information. They are an efficient and effective way to gather feedback, uncover new ideas, establish priorities, and clarify goals.

If you ask your people the right questions, you generally will not have to tell them what to do—they will figure it out themselves. Asking questions in a curious manner encourages high potentials to think in new ways. Asking the right questions is more complex than it seems. For example, consider the following types of questions you might ask:

- **Open-ended questions** do not have a specific answer. Instead they solicit new viewpoints and open new topics. "What trends are you seeing in the market, and how can we accommodate them in our strategy?" Open-ended questions promote reflection and cause the conversation to diverge.

- **Closed-ended questions** seek specific information and can be answered with a yes or no response, a quantitative answer, or a brief description. They also can be used to confirm your understanding of a situation. "Do those numbers show a decline in customer satisfaction?" or "Are you asking that we allocate more resources to the product launch?" Notice that the learning from closed-ended questions is narrow. If the answer is no, you will have to follow up with an open-ended question to discover the reason for that answer. Ask closed-ended, convergent questions when you are driving for closure.

- **Explorative questions** elicit information about a particular person, event, or subject and are useful in assessing status. "When the new project begins next month, what staffing changes are you considering?" Explorative questions are like open-ended questions, except that they set boundaries on the topic being discussed.

- **Follow-on questions** are designed to obtain additional information relative to a previous question or answer, or to solicit an opinion on what was said earlier. "If we implement that plan, how will people react to the extra workload?" Follow-on questions deepen understanding of a topic, but usually keep the conversation moving in the same direction.

- **Socratic questions** foster critical thinking by challenging the completeness or accuracy of an idea. "What if . . . ?" and "What haven't we considered . . . ?" are typical beginnings for a Socratic question. Socratic questions are effective at expanding the boundaries of a conversation when that is your objective.

- **Coaching questions** cause the responder to think deeply, reflect for a period of time, and respond candidly in ways that may be new and uncomfortable. "What is the biggest career mistake you have made, and what would you do differently today?" Be prepared for an unexpected answer when you ask a coaching question.

At appropriate intervals in decision-making conversations, share your viewpoints and ideas in the first perspective so that others will know what you are thinking and why. In the second conversational perspective, ask questions that are expansive and nonjudgmental. Use close-ended and follow-on questions when your objective is to drive the conversation to a conclusion—but use them carefully, as they can be seen as an attempt to take control of or dictate the outcome. Finally, use the third perspective to explore options that still may not have been identified.

Ask Questions to Diffuse Explosive Situations

When you are being challenged, asking questions instead of making statements is an effective way to diffuse everyone's frustrations. Great questions will provide you with useful information about the concerns of others and demonstrate that you will listen before making a decision. Questions unlock the door to collaboration, if you know what to ask and when. First ask yourself, "What information am I missing?" and then form your questions to collect that information. Use open-ended questions that invite a free response. Avoid questions that challenge the veracity of someone's idea or push the conversation into an "I'm right and you're wrong" rut. For example, do not ask, "Weren't our results terrible the last time we did that?" Instead you might ask, "As we discussed, we both want better results this time, so what can we do differently?"

Ask questions with a respectful tone and be especially careful not to second-guess. If you are not satisfied with the answer, tread softly when asking for clarification. Be sensitive if you see that a responder is uncomfortable and possibly in a situation that is over his head. Unless you are questioning in a professional capacity, as a lawyer or reporter would, confrontations do not benefit anyone. Consider following up later in private. Remember, it is easier to diffuse an explosive situation when you have built a relationship with your people before the difficult situation occurs. Take time to meet with them regularly to understand their motivations and their personal challenges. The more you know about each other, the better equipped you will be to make effective decisions and lead them through a crisis.

Ask Questions to Build Loyalty

Imagine that your star salesman, Bill, walks into your office and says he has taken a job with a top competitor. When you ask why he is leaving, Bill only replies, "It's time to move on." You are shocked—and concerned that he may take customers with him. What signals did you miss? Where did you go wrong? A few days later, Jan, an HR rep, visits your office to hold the exit interview. Her first question to Bill is, "What suggestions can you offer to make this a better place to work?" In that moment you realize that you rarely had conversations with Bill to solicit his views on market changes and your sales decisions. You failed to nurture his loyalty to you, your methods, or your company.

HR surveys consistently show that many employees resign because they feel unappreciated. Exit interviews are standard in most organizations. They are a good practice; however, they are useful only in making changes after the employee has left. By contrast, asking your people for inputs on key decisions amounts to conducting "stay interviews," because they build loyalty. Consider these stay-interview questions that you might ask during a decision-making conversation:

- Are your objectives in coming to work here being fulfilled?
- Are your strengths being used effectively?
- What was your biggest success last year, and how can we repeat it here?
- How could this process be changed to expand your success?
- Where could we make best use of your knowledge and experience?

Focus these questions on areas that are important to your people; listen curiously to their responses. Make stay interviews a regular part of your decision-making conversations—everyone benefits when your organization is a place where people want to stay.

Ask One More Question

Simple questions can make a huge difference. For example, Lee was the CEO of a company whose typical contracts were complex, multimillion-dollar projects. The business was profitable and growing, yet Lee was frustrated by the executives he assigned to manage the projects. They sometimes struggled to resolve issues, missed deadlines, and lost money on contracts. Lee's modus operandi was to get angry when he found a wayward project. He would jump in, fix the problem, and then return responsibilities to an embarrassed and discouraged executive. Lee hired a consultant to eliminate the recurring project problems. Over a year, the consultant assisted Lee in implementing quality control procedures, holding project reviews, and developing a staff training program. Those changes improved performance, but occasionally projects would still blow up because the project manager missed something. Lee would blow up too, and his frustration and anger were evident to everyone in the building.

One day, the consultant overheard an exchange between Lee and an executive about a troubled project. Lee told the executive that the client had complained about a late deliverable that was delaying the project's schedule and increasing costs. Lee asked if the deliverable was late, and when the executive said yes, Lee reassigned two people from other projects to finish it. Later, the consultant suggested that Lee might have instead asked the project manager why the deliverable was late and how he planned to fix the problem. Lee ignored the suggestion and changed the subject. At the end of the meeting, the consultant was putting papers in his briefcase and offhandedly said, "Lee, have you considered how your senior people feel when you make decisions without asking them what is happening on their project?" Lee said nothing, and the consultant left feeling as though he had done little to address the underlying issues.

The consultant arrived for their meeting the following week not expecting much change. But Lee was animated. He exclaimed, "I've been doing what you suggested, and it's fantastic!" The consultant did not recall suggesting anything. Lee continued, "I've been asking one more question before I make a decision, and it's unbelievable how much more I am discovering." When the consultant asked him to explain, Lee said that when he discussed status with a project manager and thought he knew what was happening, he would find one more question to ask. Each time, that was when the real conversation began. Of course, Lee still had to regain his executives' trust, but his asking one more question was a breakthrough.

When you feel that you have learned all you can, there is always at least one more question to ask. Try "What question were you expecting that I didn't ask?" which often elicits key information on which to base your decisions.

QUESTIONS GO BOTH WAYS

Decisions—even yours—get better when they are questioned by cynics. Uncontested leadership often produces mediocre results, so welcome with an open mind others' questions about your decisions. You have no doubt participated in discussions where the ideal solution was found only after someone was skeptical about the outcome of a decision. We have also seen extraordinary results achieved because a sincere naysayer challenged a group by saying, "I think we can do better." Political analysts say, arguably, that the most effective presidencies of the last fifty years were those of Presidents Reagan and Clinton because they dealt with an opposition party that challenged every idea before any decision was made. These presidents were forced to think more broadly and deeply about the issue. The leadership lesson for you: build a culture that welcomes questions and debate.

You might be tempted to squelch dissent and open-ended discussions because they delay action. Dissenters are often annoying. You probably have dealt with an office pest who drives people crazy by objecting to everything. But resist the temptation to ignore questions from that person—or anyone else. Whether you are leading a small team or a global enterprise, recognize and reward the best ideas no matter where they come from or the manner in which they are delivered. Make heroes out of people who are willing to offer unpopular views, and endure dissenters long enough to understand their concerns. After all, challenges to the status quo are a sign that people care about the organization and are loyal to you as its leader. When they challenge your ideas, they are helping you make better decisions.

CHAPTER 19

IF YOU CAN'T CHANGE, RETIRE

The man who views the world at fifty the same as he did at
twenty has wasted thirty years of his life.
—MUHAMMAD ALI

After making a big decision, most executives tend unconsciously to gather information that justifies their decision and then to make other decisions that support the first: "Let's stick with this approach until it has had a chance to work," or the classic "We've always done it that way." Sticking with the status quo may feel safe; yet in a rapidly changing world, "safe" potentially means missed opportunities, lost market share, and stagnation. Your challenge as a leader is to avoid defaulting to safe decisions.

You might consider change to be complex and risky—something to be undertaken only in desperate circumstances. This attitude ignores change … until it is too late. Instead, understand that change is inevitable and that the pace of change is accelerating. Although change for change's sake is disruptive, sustained success is possible only when you and your team are willing to embrace new ideas, new technologies, and new ways of doing business in your decisions.

Making a major change is challenging under any circumstances, but it is virtually impossible when business is going well. The more successful an organization, the larger the faction that resists change. Paradoxically, that phenomenon makes successful organizations especially vulnerable to decline in times of rapid change—like the foreseeable future. Success makes it easy to deny that the world is changing. If you feel that your organization is humming along and does not need to change, consider retiring to a tropical island.

(But even there, global warming may change the environment and affect your decisions.)

STAYING AHEAD OF CHANGE

Jack Welch, the former CEO of General Electric, challenged his executives to "change before you have to." For example, imagine you were a forty-year-old executive with a manufacturing company in 1996 when 6.5 percent of the U.S. population (17.5 million people) worked in manufacturing to produce 16 percent of the U.S. GDP ($1.2 trillion). In 2007, you still were not old enough to retire (just fifty-one years old) when only 4.5 percent of the U.S. population (13.5 million people) was employed in manufacturing to produce 12 percent of the U.S. GDP ($1.7 trillion). Some of you may be among the four million workers, managers, and leaders who were forced to change careers because of massive changes in the manufacturing sector. If you feel safe because your expertise is outside the manufacturing sector, beware. It is just a matter of time before game-changing transformations affect your industry, your career, and your people's lives. Are you and your organization making decisions that put you in the position of leading change, or are you at risk of suffering through the consequences and stress of forced change?

A tsunami of acquisitions, reorganizations, new technologies, process improvements, offshorings, and outsourcings is accelerating change in today's global economy. Social scientists forecast that the rate of technological and cultural change that we have been experiencing could double. One reaction is to resist change by making decisions that maintain the old "normal." Yet change is not going away, and it will not slow down. Whether you choose to ignore change, resist it, or integrate it into decisions about your future and the future of your organization, the world will continue to change.

Many executives treat events that do not fit their expectations as anomalies. But change happens incrementally, sometimes in ways that are hard to recognize. If you are not looking for change, you may not see it until it is too late to react. Ask the following questions regularly in your decision-making conversations:

- What changes will occur in the next quarter, the next year, the next two years?
- Are we focusing on those new possibilities, or are we consumed by today's priorities?
- What mechanisms are in place to warn us that customer needs, demographics, or technologies are shifting?
- How well are we using feedback from those mechanisms in our strategic plans?
- How certain are we that our vision of the future is realistic?

Train your people to anticipate and respond to change in their everyday decisions. Even when a change does not affect you directly, evaluate what might happen next. You can ride the upside of change by making decisions that use change to your advantage. If you are not already making those decisions, this chapter will assist you in exploiting change to expand your success and that of your organization.

WHAT IS DRIVING CHANGE?

We hope that you are among the few leaders who recognize the early signs of changing markets. Yet that knowledge is essentially worthless unless you are willing to adapt to the new environment through decisions that unlock the treasure chest of opportunities. The following four factors drive rapid and dramatic changes in today's business world:

- **Ubiquitous communications.** Today's world is powered by the Internet, smartphones, iPads, and other devices that enable people to communicate with anyone, anytime, virtually anywhere, on any subject. Instead of the weeks or months it used to take, a decision can be implemented today in hours or days over the Internet. Furthermore, mobile applications and cloud computing have eliminated time and location constraints on the collection, analysis, and redistribution of massive amounts of data.

- **Global relationships.** Organizations and people in every corner of the globe and every sector of the economy are working together more creatively than ever before. This seismic change promises to deliver worldwide prosperity—and success and wealth to those who make it happen. Strategic relationships are becoming increasingly vital in decision-making processes.

- **Intense competition.** International organizations are competing for market share in first-, second-, and third-world countries. For example, Mercedes, BMW, and Toyota make decisions not only on the basis of the market share of General Motors, Ford, and Fiat-Chrysler in Europe and the United States; they also must worry about autos that Tata and Hyundai are marketing in Africa.

- **Large investors.** The concentration of capital in mutual funds, pension funds, and venture capital funds has reshaped investment markets and influenced CEOs and government executives alike. The funds hold investment positions in companies that give them power to force executives to bend—or lose their jobs. Armed with up-to-the-minute data about markets and competitors, institutional investors raise the performance bar by monitoring the daily decisions of executives and shrinking the time allowed to produce results.

The Industrial Age was linear. Decisions that changed the organizational structure, processes, or tools produced proportional increases in output. By contrast, the levers in the hands of today's decision-makers work geometrically. They can multiply success overnight through innovative decisions that couple a relatively small idea with creative new relationships. Change will never stop. Once you grasp that simple reality, you instantly add change to your repertoire of decision-making strategies. You begin to anticipate and exploit tomorrow's changes, instead of chasing the status quo.

TO CHANGE OR NOT TO CHANGE

Whether to change or not is a tough leadership decision. Multiple studies show that half of all organizational change initiatives fail to produce the target results despite backing from top leaders and a large investment of effort and resources. High potentials facing a need for change are justifiably scared, because a failed change makes the situation worse. After a failed change, the time to respond is reduced, the range of options shrinks, considerable resources have been spent, and people are skeptical about what will come next. Although this may be an overly pessimistic picture of change, the equally important truth is that leaders must decide to initiate change—the sooner the better.

Human reactions to change are complex. In large part, resistance grows at an emotional level: change stimulates confusion, anxiety, and fear. Decisions are relegated to "later." As one would expect, people who struggle with those emotions will try to avoid change. Others find excitement in uncertainty and view change as an adventure. So a decision to change will excite some of your people and feel like a crisis to others. Most people, however, are between the two extremes. As the change leader, expect your people to relate to change in diverse ways.

Despite the diversity in responses to change, surveys show that a wide majority of people claim they are open or very open to changes in the workplace. If that is true, why do more than half of all change initiatives fail to achieve their stated objectives? In our experience, it is because some executives do not know how to lead their people—particularly high potentials—through the complicated layers of decision making inherent in the change process. They do not hold conversations that consider strategy and people to be equally important components of change. People are essential to the success of any change because they ultimately must embrace and implement it.

Some executives react too slowly, ignore change, or want to avoid risk in their decision making. They spend more time perfecting existing products and services than bringing new ones to market. Yet coming up with innovative services and products is how an organization maintains preeminence in changing markets. For example, Xerox's innovative research group PARC invented an exceptional set of new products that became massive best sellers—for someone else. Unfortunately for Xerox, the products included the computer mouse and graphical user interface (GUI) that Steve Jobs introduced in the Apple Macintosh. Xerox's versions languished in the lab for lack of support from its marketing department because they were used in computers rather than copiers.

Innovation is inherent in a leadership mindset. Leaders strive to uncover innovation in the high potentials and the environment around them. Xerox held management conversations about improving its copiers, while Steve Jobs held effective leadership conversations at Apple and decided to champion products that Xerox had invented but ignored. And as successful as Apple has been, the company missed web-based innovations that propelled start-ups like Google and Facebook to success. A leader's most effective decisions are those that concurrently improve current performance and stretch for tomorrow's greatness. Complacency in decision making is a consistent loser.

Given the hazards, why would any high potential risk championing a major change? The answer is survival. Entire industries are in turmoil. Some government agencies (the U.S. Postal Service, for example) are searching for a mission that is relevant and sustainable in today's business world. Typically, organizations struggle because their decision-making conversations fail to anticipate and respond to technological advances, emerging global relationships, massive market implosions, or new competitors. Organizations that were state-of-the-art a decade ago are in decline today. Others have downsized, failed to innovate, or simply faded away. The fundamental decision you must make as a leader is not whether to change—it is how, how much, and how fast to change.

WORKING WITH DIFFERENT CHANGE STYLES

People in your organization, including yourself, have different attitudes toward change and different ways of participating in decisions about change. If you recognize and accommodate different styles when you lead a change, you increase the likelihood that you will face less resistance, have fewer misunderstandings, and implement the change successfully. For purposes of this discussion only, we divide people into three categories to describe the change styles you are likely to encounter:

- **Trailblazers** are always willing to consider new and unusual ideas. They are comfortable with uncertainty and risk, and do not hesitate to challenge the status quo. You would think that as sources of breakthrough ideas, they would be a change leader's best friends—but beware. Trailblazers can be impulsive in making decisions. Entrepreneurs often are trailblazers with respect to change.

- **Traditionalists** are basically okay with how things are today, and they seek only incremental improvements. They honor past successes and operate under proven assumptions. When facing change, traditionalists are cautious and predictable. Actually, they can be assets to a change leader because they offer thoughtful advice when everyone else gets caught up in the passion of possibilities and the speculation about tomorrow.

- **Fence-sitters** can go either way, which makes them a good barometer of the effectiveness of a proposed change. They are outcome oriented and want practical decisions. When facing change, fence-sitters are flexible and can seem indecisive at times. They are catalysts for productive conversations because they will consider both sides before making a decision. As the change leader, you will do well to allow them to steer the conversation if you feel that a middle-of-the-road solution might be best. They are the ones most likely to sway the decision.

All three styles play a useful role in making decisions and implementing change. The key to having them work together is to understand how you are likely to interact with people whose style is different from yours. For example, if you are a trailblazer and are having a conversation with traditionalists, you may see them as inflexible and cautious; they worry about your impulsive and half-baked ideas. If one of your key assistants is a fence-sitter, you might see him or her as indecisive.

There is a tendency in decision-making conversations about change to view trailblazers as allies and traditionalists as enemies of progress. Besides jeopardizing relationships, that outlook is often entirely wrong. Sometimes, for example, trailblazers might be leading the organization toward a disaster, while traditionalists point out valid reasons why the proposed change is a bad idea. This situation would be a great time to seek the third alternative (discussed in Chapter 17). Bottom line: when it comes to change, do not confuse any of the styles with competence. All three play an important role in the to-change-or-not-to-change conversation.

When you became a leader, strategic change jumped to the top of your things-to-consider list—equal in importance to developing people. But change does not need managing as much as the high potentials who are participating need leadership. Some executives who are extraordinarily effective during day-to-day operations crash and burn when challenged to lead people through the uncertainty of change.

Regardless of the size of a change, be aware of how your style in regard to change—trailblazer, traditionalist, or fence-sitter—biases your decisions and affects the way others perceive you. In an ideal world, everyone would understand how his style affects his attitude toward change, his openness to new ideas, and his willingness to find the third alternative. Leading your high potentials toward that ideal by making change a regular part of your leadership conversations will separate your organization from those that are struggling to deal with yesterday's change. It will enable you and your people to make decisive decisions relative to change and put them into action effectively.

TEN WAYS TO PRACTICE GREAT LEADERSHIP IN MAKING DECISIONS

1. **Cultivate judgment.** Discuss scenarios and plan responses prior to the need to act. Address emerging trends with your high potentials by asking, "What happened recently that surprised you?" Not what was good or bad—rather, what was unexpected?
2. **Use a repeatable process.** What process do you use to make decisions? Leaders who consistently make good decisions teach people to use a repeatable process. Do you follow your own process?
3. **Say "I don't know."** What you know is less important than what your people know, how fast they learn, and how effectively knowledge is used in decisions. Saying "I don't know; what do you think?" opens the door to lively conversations. Endorse your people's ideas and enjoy the commitment to success that the endorsement creates.
4. **Find the third alternative.** Are your decisions usually based on consensus or compromise—or are they innovative alternatives that everyone embraces?

Find the third alternative by looking for an option that integrates your best ideas with those of others.

5. **Escape the "knowing trap."** Are you curious? Experts make decisions under the assumption that they know everything they need to know. Effective leaders escape the knowing trap by being curious no matter how much they already know.

6. **Be willing to change your mind.** Encourage people to challenge your decisions, and be prepared to cite the information, experiences, and criteria you considered. When results show that you made a poor decision, admit it, learn from it, and move on.

7. **Ask one more question.** When you feel that you have learned all you can, ask at least one more question, such as "What questions were you expecting that I haven't asked yet?" This question often elicits new information and new alternatives.

8. **Encourage innovation.** Take five creative people who are currently very busy managing. Have them leave the office and walk in the park with only a pad and a pencil—no cell phone or iPad. When they return, discuss the ideas they generated.

9. **Recognize change drivers.** What drives change in your industry? Four drivers are prevalent: ubiquitous communications, global relationships, intense competition, and concentration of capital. Recognize and use those drivers to unlock opportunities.

10. **Accommodate change attitudes.** Are you a trailblazer, traditionalist, or fence-sitter relative to change? By accommodating these styles in leading change, you are likely to face less resistance and achieve greater success during implementation.

PART 5

CONVERSATIONS TO TAKE ACTION

The purpose of building relationships, developing others, and making decisions is to set the stage for effective action, because at the end of the day, only action produces results. The management mindset of executing the plan, using resources efficiently, and focusing on results takes center stage when action begins—the priority being to get things done. But the leadership mindset of doing the right things, acquiring resources, and focusing on people is still vital in order to respond to changing circumstances and keep the vision of the future clear in everyone's eyes.

Some executives use ridicule and threats to motivate action, which leaves their people reluctant to take risks. Great leaders inspire teamwork by showing their people a better future and how they can be part of it. As a result, people enjoy what they do, work diligently to achieve goals they believe in, and know they will share in the rewards. As the leader, you must ensure that everyone supports the plan, understands her role, and knows what is expected of her. You also must determine what motivates each of your high potentials to do his best. Some are motivated by encouragement, some respond to enticements, some are driven by competition, and others need more direct motivation.

Part 5 discusses several aspects of leading action, starting with a smooth transition from talking to action (Chapter 20). However, if you take action before planning, you are likely to deploy people and resources inefficiently and produce inferior results (Chapter 21). One of the most challenging actions you can undertake is to initiate a strategic change (Chapter 22). Effective leaders hold conversations to evaluate both successful and unsuccessful actions in ways that improve current results and lay the foundation for future actions (Chapter 23). Part 5 closes by discussing techniques you can use to motivate and inspire people in turbulent times (Chapter 24). Each chapter makes key distinctions between leadership and management mindsets in terms of how they empower and direct people to take effective action.

CHAPTER 20

MOVING SMOOTHLY INTO ACTION

Even if you're on the right track, you'll get run over if you just sit there.
—WILL ROGERS

Leaders take decisive and effective action themselves, and cultivate that ability in their people.

Bruce, the CEO of a government services firm, tendered his resignation when a charge (which was later dropped) was leveled against his $800 million company by a federal agency. This intense crisis could have forced the company into bankruptcy within weeks, and employees easily could have blamed Bruce. He chose to settle the matter by offering his resignation in order to save the company. Many companies turn on their CEOs amid scandal. However, because of the atmosphere of teamwork Bruce created and the results they had produced together, employees chose to praise Bruce in hundreds of unsolicited letters and emails:

"You have the incredible ability to spend short bursts of time with individuals, reach inside them, and attach yourself to their hearts. You spend just enough time on personal conversations to seamlessly weave a professional message of work hard, be accountable, and hit the numbers!"

"Your qualities of integrity, caring about people, and leading by example inspired me to work hard and make this company succeed. Your willingness to listen and understand that people drive a company is what has made us successful. I'll miss your handshakes and your smiles."

"I'm sending you a farewell message to thank you for all you have done for the company as well as for me. Since the shocking news last week, I have

reflected back to when you first came to our company and faced a different culture than you were used to. You have extraordinary skill at one of
the most difficult things on the planet: getting people to leave their
comfort zone and take action."

Bruce's leadership counted for more than just the success the company had
achieved. More important, he left a bias for action as his legacy to the company.

Three themes occur repeatedly in these emails: the connection people felt
with Bruce, how that connection motivated their actions, and how they link
their success to his leadership. After you have built effective relationships,
developed your people, and made great decisions, there is no limit to the
power of the actions you and your people take. If you left your organization
today under difficult circumstances, what feedback would you receive from
your people? What actions would they take in your absence?

WHAT MOTIVATES LEADERS?

When Bruce stared into the abyss of losing his position as CEO, his sense of
responsibility for those he led, not money, was a motivator. In this pivotal
moment, he chose to take decisive action to save the company. He resigned to
preserve his people's jobs and deferred the clearing of his name to a later time.
He explained to us, "For me, leaving was not even a choice. We hadn't done
anything wrong, yet they insisted on having a sacrificial lamb. I was sad to
leave; but it was an action I had to take, so I took it without hesitation. I knew
that I'd get past this event professionally; but if the company had closed,
thousands of people would not have fared as well, and that would have
weighed heavily on me. Now I'm the CEO of an exciting new venture, so
taking the right action has been rewarded."

In your career, you probably have seen that leaders who are motivated by
power, wealth, and perks produce stress in their people. In contrast, leaders
who have a selfless vision of the future motivate their people to action and
usually produce superior results. Bruce is one of those leaders whose vision was
to achieve great things with his people. He created a special place for them to

work and grow while they produced results for the company. As a result, they worked harder and longer than they would have if he had pushed them to meet purely financial goals—and they attained high levels of personal satisfaction too. They stayed when the going got tough. Respecting people as individuals and building relationships based on that attitude create connections that motivate effective actions and achieve personal and organizational goals.

ACTION OR INACTION—IT'S A CHOICE

Actions take place every day in your organization. How well do your people perform? What is your role in their actions? Do you set direction as a leader or get things done as a manager? Each action you take—or do not take—is a choice. Action and inaction are two sides of the same coin, and both are appropriate at times. You can take action to move your people ahead rapidly, or let the latent energy build while you wait to see which idea will triumph. Some actions are proactive; others are just a reaction to what your competitors, your customers, or your stakeholders have done. Your actions may deal with accomplishing objectives (management mindset) or pondering what else is possible (leadership mindset), or you may toggle between the two frequently.

Conversations about opportunities and issues usually focus on what, if any, action to take—the underlying assumption being that the action will be initiated as soon as possible. But it is equally important to take action at the optimal time. When you discuss start dates, ask your high potentials what they expect to achieve by their choice of date and why they favor that timing. Ask them to consider what other actions their people will be taking during that period, what timing would work best for their customers and their personal schedule, and how timing will affect the odds of a successful outcome—balancing all three is critical. Ensure that each new action will build rather than disrupt momentum. Bottom line: timing is equally as important for success as the technical feasibility and financial impacts of any new actions you consider.

No matter whether you are in planning mode or action mode, getting people to act in alignment and with passion and commitment is the essence of leadership. Motivating people to achieve seemingly impossible things time after time is what separates great leaders from also-rans. Organizations cannot accomplish the impossible—but people can and do. The ability of your organization to act will depend on the people you select, the relationships you build with and among them, how well you develop their skills and attitudes, and the decisions you make in concert with them. The effectiveness of all four of those leadership activities depends on the quality of your conversations.

THE CONTEXT FOR ACTION

Figure 20.1 shows the different contexts within which managers and leaders operate relative to their roles in taking action. In general, managers deal with

	First-Line Manager	Manager of Managers	Executive Leader	CXO Leader
Vision	Is still learning the vision	Provides input to the vision	Converts vision into strategy	Creates future through vision
Objectivess	Is assigned discrete goals	Defines goals and schedules	Defines strategy and objectives	Charts the direction of the organization
Planning Role	Focuses on current projects	Focuses on current and future projects	Builds organizational capabilities	Pursues strategic acquisitions and partnerships
Resources	Consumes resources	Allocates existing resources	Finds new resources	Creates sources of resources
Nature of Actions	Directs people to complete tasks	Directs teams to achieve goals	Empowers the organization	Stretches the organization
Measure of Success	Completing a quality job on time	Meeting goals efficiently	Surpassing projections	Defining new possibilities

FIGURE 20.1. The Context for Action.

Managers and leaders have different contexts for the goals they set, the actions they take, and the results they seek to produce.

the known and tangible, whereas leaders deal with the future, create the vision and strategy, and provide the resources to implement the strategy. Efficient managers measure results quantitatively; transformational leaders look at qualitative measures.

Organizations are operating in a management mindset when they (1) incrementally improve yesterday's actions; (2) work substantially within existing markets, boundaries, and resources; (3) focus on tasks and numbers; and (4) are satisfied with their current level of success. Conversely, organizations are in a leadership mindset when they (1) enter new markets, (2) create and market innovative products and services, (3) engage in transformational thinking, and (4) unleash their people's strengths by providing coaching and mentoring. Obviously, both mindsets are needed to produce both short- and long-term success. By holding conversations that stretch boundaries and tap new resources, the leadership mindset creates the new rather than incrementally improving the old. Then the management mindset efficiently implements the plan that supports the short- and long-term strategy.

AN ALL-STAR TEAM ISN'T ENOUGH

Among Major League Baseball's thirty teams, the New York Yankees annually have the highest payroll. It generally exceeds $200 million for the twenty-five-man roster—most starters earn over $10 million a year. There is a current or former all-star at almost every position and several on the bench as reserves. Yet in the ten-year period from 2002 to 2011, the Yankees won the World Series only in 2009. Even high-potential all-stars must perform as a team to realize their full potential. Aligned actions are as critical to success as the skills that each high potential possesses. Hiring the most talented people does not guarantee teamwork or success—leadership and aligned actions do.

Many executives use precise metrics to measure individual and team performance. When it falls below targets, they try to upgrade the team by focusing on the weakest department or weakest people. They try to improve their performance or replace them with superstars. The underlying assumption is that if you hire experts, the results will take care of themselves. As the Yankees' record demonstrates, that assumption is false. A team needs leadership and vision in addition to talent, especially when it must face fierce competition, market shifts, and new technologies. Two core measures of a championship team are (1) how well the team members align with the team's goals and each other and (2) how much they believe and trust in each other. How often does someone on your team act independently despite your best effort to create alignment? How could you harness that independence to support the team's success and achieve its goals?

Teamwork is essential for success. When you hear complaints that executives feel as though they are "herding cats," that agreement is difficult to forge, that communications are muddled, or that high potentials are stagnating, you are hearing telltale signs that teamwork is missing. Leaders work in concert with each other and with their high potentials to align everyone's actions with the mission. When teamwork is missing, then silos compete for resources, and consensus takes a backseat to the struggle for power and control. Conversely, when all segments of an organization are aligned, then healthy conversations help everyone produce extraordinary results.

THE PLAN-RESULTS GAP

Late one afternoon, we met with a government executive, George, in his corner office. He looked tired when he confessed, "I'm frustrated. It's been a year since we held that strategic planning off-site, and there is still a huge gap between our target and actual results."

The off-site was held in an ideal setting and had included stakeholders from all divisions of the enterprise. The meeting's agenda clearly addressed the agency's core challenge: to cut costs and invest in the future. George was at a loss to explain why the strategic initiative had stalled. Everyone understood the urgent need for change and embraced the strategic plan. He lamented, "Our top leaders were there—our best and brightest. They were empowered to take action. We aligned our incentives and resources with change. Commitment was high. But a year has gone by, and we aren't even close to our goals." His question was, "What did I miss?"

Unfortunately, we have heard similar frustrations from other capable, experienced, and committed leaders who understand the difficulty of change and seemingly have done all the right things. Even with a superb staff and a clear vision of the future, they fail to achieve the desired results. When the shortfall becomes common knowledge, their credibility inside and outside the organization evaporates, and people become cynical about change. Of course, what they are missing is effective conversations about converting decisions into action.

The business world is littered with programs that failed despite huge investments. They are launched with optimism and fanfare—then fall to the wayside. The bottom line is that, without effective conversations, the organization wastes time, money, and focus. It would have been further ahead if it had not attempted the change in the first place. Leaders must own these initiatives, ensure that they are designed properly, and hold regular conversations about them to inspire others to take action.

Executives often spend too much time developing a brilliant strategy and too little time planning how they will implement it and measure progress. These executives participate in well-planned strategic workshops and leave in agreement on the steps to be taken. Yet fundamental change rarely takes place. Lack of committed action is the root cause of this pattern every time. Action is more than a plan, a schedule, and accountability and control mechanisms—although those elements are essential. Action is a discipline embedded in the culture that aligns and drives people to do what is required to achieve specific, agreed-on goals.

CHAPTER 21

PLANNING SUCCESSFUL ACTIONS

Alice came to a fork in the road and saw a Cheshire cat in a tree.
"Which road should I take?" she asked. "Where are you going?" he replied.
"I don't know." Alice answered. "Then," said the cat, "it doesn't matter."
—LEWIS CARROLL, *ALICE IN WONDERLAND*

Virtually every executive says he has a plan for success—yet for many the plan is in their heads and not on paper. The reasons for not writing the plan range from a belief that others would not understand it, to not having sufficient time to write it, to being afraid that a plan will limit his options. Some ask, "Which is more important, taking action or spending time to plan?" Our response is that action by high potentials in the absence of a written-out, thoroughly understood plan yields inferior results and wastes resources.

The planning process is often more valuable than the plan itself. Conversations in all three perspectives—listening to each other, questioning each other, and considering what else is possible—are vital in preparing people to take action, aligning their actions, and enabling them to adjust when unexpected events occur. No organization-wide conversations are more vital than those that build a strategic plan. Yes, it takes valuable time to create or update a strategic plan and the tactical plans that support it. Yet high-performing leaders value the learning and alignment that occur during the planning process and use those conversations to drive unified action.

Some executives voice their aversion to planning by asking, "I don't have time to be good. How can I skip to being great instead?" The challenge with these clients is that they truly want us to answer this question, and they would prefer a root canal to the effort required to build a plan. They want the secret sauce, the silver bullet, the easy way to create a vision and alignment. Their let's-get-it-done management mindset pushes them to skip planning.

These executives feel overloaded, yet they themselves are creating that feeling. Their actions are driven by a reactive sense of urgency rather than a set of widely understood and accepted priorities. They remain stuck until they realize that a thorough plan that addresses transformational possibilities will produce a higher return on their time investment than a single-minded focus on efficiency. They get unstuck when they begin to view the world through the eyes of stakeholders, customers, and employees. Then they willingly invest the time to develop a great strategy, build a comprehensive plan, create alignment, and initiate great actions. In a complex world, you need a simple but powerful plan to ensure that everyone's actions are aligned.

Planning requires you to identify alternatives, discuss them, and select the best approach. So gather your team virtually or physically to discuss the changes everyone is seeing, examine the options, and plan your response. As we have noted previously, the time you spend in up-front planning conversations will invariably be less than the time you would otherwise spend correcting the unintended and potentially costly consequences of poorly planned and misaligned actions. The plan must be in writing so that people who did not participate directly in the planning process can understand the plan, know the assumptions and alternatives considered, and rally behind its implementation.

PLANNING IS AN ESSENTIAL CONVERSATION

In our experience, people who think strategically, hold planning conversations, and write plans to codify their decisions achieve most of their goals. A plan that exists only in your head cannot drive unified action throughout your organization. If you are extremely busy doing your job, thinking strategically to create a plan will produce a net savings of time. It will ensure that you and the high potentials who work for you are focusing on strategically important actions.

So why is a formal planning process not standard practice in all organizations? As high potentials, you and other senior executives are capable of effective individual action without a written plan because of your experience and skills. But your actions cannot be replicated by others if they have no plan to follow. Your excuses for not writing a plan may seem plausible to you only because the benefits of a written plan will not be visible until you have written one and seen the improved actions that it causes to take place.

In consumer product companies, the marketing group spends months each year in extended brand reviews and market planning sessions. Tim, a freshly minted MBA, at first felt that the conversations were a colossal waste of time. Yet after the first cycle, he saw that planning was a catalyst for effective action. During the planning cycle, daily routines were set aside to meet with customers, market analysts, salespeople, manufacturing specialists, and others. With everyone contributing ideas, the conversations brought freshness and ultimately alignment to the diverse group. The plan also empowered Tim's brand group to take action and expend resources for the rest of the year without further permission as long as the actions were consistent with the approved plan and budget.

Planning conversations are an opportunity for stakeholders to discuss the difficult, the unknown, the improbable, and the impossible. Because conversations create value only when action is taken, the planning discussions must end to allow the plan to be put into action. Leaders must ensure that high potentials complete their plans and put them into action in a timely manner to harvest the fruits of planning:

"Jenny, where do you stand on implementing that new program? As we discussed, your plan is strategically sound, your team and other stakeholders are aligned, and the resources are available."

"I hear you, Jack. Thanks for your inputs. But I want to take a close look at what we might do if we encounter significant problems or supplier delays."

"That's the beauty of the conversations you held. Since you and your colleagues were directly involved in the decisions, they will be able to recognize early signs of an issue and call it to your attention for resolution. I'm here to help too, of course, and I'll check in with you periodically."

"Okay, we'll launch in the morning, and I'll keep you up-to-date on our progress."

Strategic plans should be insightful, yet simple enough to be easily implemented. At the end of each planning conversation, shift the focus from what is possible to ironing out execution techniques and defining measures of success.

GUIDING PEOPLE TO DELIVER VALUE

Some of the best conversations we have seen during strategic planning workshops were focused on envisioning what the marketplace and customers will look like in three to five years. These conversations enable you to define changes to your products and services and how to make the changes in a way that maximizes value. The concept of a customer is clear in private industry, yet it often is a second-tier consideration in other sectors. However, the core mission of every organization is to satisfy the needs of an external group—and that must be the purpose of your strategic plan. Because resources are finite, tactical operating plans in such areas as personnel, marketing, manufacturing, logistics, and finance may be needed to support the strategy. A sound strategy identifies key customers today and in the future and focuses on developing the capabilities required to satisfy their needs.

Ideas never grow to full bloom in a comment box. They come from people who care enough to imagine a better solution or a smoother process— people who feel compelled to accomplish great things. They think outside your box because they draw on different experiences. Their contributions are vital in developing the strategy because no one knows everything, and one of your jobs is to be a learner. Great ideas often begin with one person's idea and mature into breakthroughs during conversations that add other views. The key is to cultivate ideas at their inception. Find and nurture the kernel of creativity and guide it through the conversations necessary to incorporate it into the strategic plan and put it into action.

IN THEORY, GOALS ARE FIXED— IN REALITY, THEY EVOLVE

Great plans integrate inputs from multiple sources and evolve to replace assumptions with facts. In some organizations, planning seems to be either a top-down or bottom-up process. The most effective planning process is both. Yet responsibility to initiate the planning process, set goals, facilitate conversations, and push the plan to completion remains with top leaders.

Every strategic plan starts at the current point in the organization's history, projects where the organization wants to go, and defines a strategy to get there. The plan becomes the best guess at that moment in time. But plans need to evolve continually. Having a plan is critical, but the conversations and process that created the plan are also useful once the action begins. A thorough planning process improves the information available, the decision-making skills of participants, and the ability to adjust to evolving circumstances and move decisively to new actions in the heat of battle.

Actions create learning. As you and your high potentials learn, goals will evolve and the strategies to reach them may shift. Your organization's position relative to the marketplace and competitors will change constantly. The key to successful execution of your plan is to look for indicators that confirm or contradict the assumptions on which it was based. If necessary, modify the plan and ensure that the entire organization aligns with and implements the new actions.

TELL EVERYONE WHAT THE PLAN SAYS

Plans are not secrets to be guarded. In the 1980s, when strategic planning was in its infancy as a discipline, companies held strategic plans closely. At one consumer products company, the early strategic plans were numbered and given only to division presidents, who were told not to make copies even for their direct reports. Division presidents cooperated to implement the plan, but could not (in theory) disclose information from the plan to managers in their division—even though those managers helped write it. Would you be surprised to hear that the company went through a multiyear period of declining earnings? If you are hesitant to share some elements of your plan—say, the pricing algorithm or the formula for your secret sauce—then redact those portions, but share the rest of the plan as widely as possible.

All members of your organization should be aware of salient parts of the plan if you expect them to put it into action. Once a plan is written, follow it unless and until it is changed. It should be a guide for every decision and every action. Because high-potential executives do what they say they will do, by signing off on the plan they are committing to follow its direction and lead its implementation. They also are committing to help others put the plan into action. That is why you wrote a strategic plan in the first place: to ensure that everyone pursues the same goals using an aligned strategy.

The focus of a strategic plan may also be biased based on the functional group that prepares it. When written by finance, it naturally emphasizes capital requirements and budgeting. When it is written by marketing, the focus usually will be new products, improved sales processes, and expanded distribution. When written by a stand-alone strategic planning department, it might be more elegantly written yet be somewhat disconnected from the organization's true capabilities. The solution: align silos during the planning conversations, the writing, and the implementation of the plan.

MAKING MIDCOURSE CORRECTIONS

A Navy midshipman's initial assignment on an aircraft carrier was to work with the navigator to plan the voyage from Norfolk, Virginia, to Naples, Italy, in hour-by-hour detail. When the ship left Norfolk, he was reassigned to the Engineering Department, yet he visited the navigator's shack every morning to check the ship's position. He was shocked to find that it was off course every day compared to the plan. Unexpected events like engine failures and circumnavigating a fishing fleet occurred while crossing the Atlantic and disrupted the plan. However, by knowing the ship's current position, its destination, and the target time of arrival, the navigator calmly calculated course and speed corrections for the captain. Six days later, the ship cruised through the Straits of Gibraltar and entered the Mediterranean Sea on schedule despite having been off-course every day.

Your career plan and your strategic plan are similar in two respects to that ocean crossing. First, unexpected events will delay or disrupt every plan you make, and how well you handle those disruptions will be a major factor in your success. Second, you must hold regular conversations to measure interim results and uncover deviations from the plan. Determine what caused them and make corrections to get back on course. Strategy is an important start, yet your ability to adapt effectively to unexpected developments will largely determine your success.

CHAPTER 22

WHEN THINGS CHANGE

In preparing for battle, I have found that plans are useless,
but planning is indispensable.
—GENERAL DWIGHT D. EISENHOWER

Effective leaders use an open-door policy to obtain early notice of emerging changes and help their people escape from tight spots. They tell high potentials, "My door isn't open so that you can dump problems on me—I have a desk full of my own. Rather, bring me a set of solutions, and I'll help you look at trade-offs and get the resources you need. Then we'll decide what actions to take together."

Of course, open-door conversations are effective only when your people trust you. They need to know that when they take reasonable risks and circumstances change, you will support their actions no matter what the outcome. And they expect you to recognize and reward them when they anticipate change and take risks that succeed.

Unfortunately, organizational change has become synonymous with downsizing, outsourcing, and layoffs. Yet a strong case can be made that more jobs have been lost when organizations did not take the necessary actions to address change than when they do. Polaroid, Blockbuster, Kodak, and the U.S. Postal Service were once innovative organizations that ultimately fell into difficult times by ignoring or resisting change. Their business models, once fabulously successful, no longer worked when they did not anticipate or fully understand the importance of market changes.

That lack of vision generally exists in organizations that are obsessed with conversations about profits and costs while neglecting conversations about innovation and change. Yet organizations can rebound from trying times by embracing change. One company, IBM, was on the verge of being broken apart when the computer market shifted to distributed processing; but it reinvented itself in the technology services sector by changing its mindset, and has since thrived. Many organizations experience nonstop success by evolving continuously to suit a new world. Yours can too.

This chapter is about mindsets and conversations that are effective in leading the actions that produce change. Some organizations initiate change by hiring consultants who move across the organization, interview executives, and deliver a plan to the top leaders. The consultants usually understand world-class systems and processes and are well grounded in finance, IT, and systems design. Yet too often they recommend sweeping organizational and technological changes, assuming that employees will adapt. But employees are the pivotal ingredient in change. Strong leadership is essential to maintain trust during times of extensive and uncertain change.

CHANGE IS THE NATURAL ORDER

You and your organization can change proactively or reactively. Either way, eventually you must change because the world is changing. As a leader, you must stay in front of change, or jobs will be lost—possibly yours. The better your current performance, the more conversations you should hold to find the next breakthrough. It is hard to catch the next wave when you are contentedly riding high on the current one. The management mindset extracts maximum benefit from the current wave, while the leadership mindset looks for the next wave.

People are generally more afraid of uncertainty than of change. Yet every time you try a new strategy, undertake a new venture, implement a new system, or switch to a new supplier, you are introducing uncertainty. People become concerned if they do not know how a change will affect them or if the change process is not honest and transparent. To align them behind the actions required to change, ensure they believe that

- The change is necessary for sustained success.
- Their concerns and ideas have been heard and considered.
- The process of defining the approach to change has been fair.
- They will receive help to overcome adverse effects of the change.

During periods of change, it is important to define the actions that will be taken, who will be impacted by the change—and how—and steps that will mitigate any adverse impacts.

What people fear most are the effects of a hidden, poorly designed, or improperly implemented change. The perceived unfairness of such changes undermines trust and disrupts the organization. People assume that if a change was designed secretly, there must be something to hide. Their actions will be halfhearted and less effective than when pursued with passion. In poorly implemented changes, valuable employees can be left wondering why their old jobs are gone when mediocre performers kept theirs. That is a question worth considering. For example, eliminating a function and sacking everyone, even those who could be productive elsewhere in the organization, may be easy to implement, but it is not smart.

Tackling sensitive issues up front in a transparent manner is not easy. One top executive who filled politically appointed positions in two federal agencies under two presidents said that he thinks in terms of a four-year action plan for a major change. It takes that long to define the change, develop the implementation plan, deal with the resistance, execute the plan, and perfect and institutionalize the change. Directing people to work diligently while their jobs are changing or when they might lose their jobs is operating in a management mindset. Investing as much thought in eliminating disruptions to employees as in designing the change is operating in a leadership mindset.

Tell your people precisely why the change is necessary. Describe the core problem it addresses or the opportunity it creates. When you are up front with people about change, you can deal with their concerns in an atmosphere of trust and respect. Conversations about concerns are easier and more effective than ones about fear: fear evokes emotional responses, whereas concerns can be addressed logically.

LEADERSHIP: THE ESSENCE OF CHANGE

Organizations do not change; people do. When people change their viewpoints, their behaviors, and their actions, they change the way an organization performs and the results it achieves. But for people to change, they must be open to doing so. Change begins by recognizing trends in customers, technologies, and the marketplace that potentially create a new future for the organization and its people. Design and explain changes in a way that your people can rally behind. Spend as much time creating the people strategy for change as you do designing new processes and systems.

Historically, change initiatives are only partially successful because they

- Did not get people to change their actions and priorities
- Produced adverse unintended consequences
- Were abandoned before completion or replaced by a subsequent change

It is irrelevant whether the cause of failure was the strategy, the execution, or both. The important issue is that failure, especially in a culture of blame, drives high potentials to avoid change in order to minimize career risk. External factors are rarely the cause of failures. Leaders must engage with people in a way that connects and aligns them; change, like any core leadership activity, cannot be delegated.

For example, those who use LEAN manufacturing strategies know that the CEO and other top leaders make the process work by personally participating in Kaizen sessions side-by-side with people from the factory floor. These dynamic exchanges energize everyone. Leaders must believe in the change wholeheartedly and hold frank conversations with the people who will be affected. A small change that has wide support will produce better results in the long run than a more elegant change that does not align people.

FORCED CHANGE DOESN'T WORK

We assisted a U.S. government agency in an A-76 initiative that required employees to compete for their jobs against private contractors. The purpose of the initiative was to increase efficiency and reduce costs by awarding the work to the party that offered the most attractive business case. The initiative was so controversial that agency executives worried about the potential for violence and sabotage in the workplace. Employees were justifiably afraid of losing their jobs after working in the agency for an average of twenty-two years—or the equally bad alternative of keeping their jobs at a lower pay grade. They knew that a contractor—if it won the competition—would fill their positions with lower-skilled workers who would accept reduced salaries and benefits and have less experience in performing the agency's technical projects. Government employees won the competition and implemented the changes they proposed, but the scars of the forced competition took years to heal.

Agency executives struggled with conversations during the competition because they could not defend it with integrity to their people. Instead, they took action to ensure that as few employees as possible lost their jobs and to help those who were laid off to find a suitable position elsewhere. After the competition, those who remained continued to apply their talents and experience in a productive way, and the agency's capability to perform its mission remained intact. At top levels, the A-76 competition was seen as a success because it appeared to cut costs and make better use of taxpayer funds. But what was not taken into account were the thousands of man-hours consumed by the competition, the productivity loss by a demoralized workforce after it was completed, and collateral damage to the agency's customers. Many thought that these added costs exceeded the savings. As a leader, you are responsible to hold conversations which ensure that a change is the right change, for the right reasons, for quantifiable results, and for the benefit of all of the organization's stakeholders.

Whether or not you personally have felt the sting of a difficult change initiative, we hope that you have learned critical lessons that enable you to plan and implement changes effectively. In any change, minimize the impacts on your people and make trade-offs that leave the largest number of people in the best possible situation when the actions are completed. The management mindset pushes to finish a change initiative as quickly as possible to realize bottom-line benefits. The leadership mindset ensures that the change offers opportunities for everyone.

Compassionate leaders help those who lose their jobs as the result of change to find a new position in the organization, or provide outplacement assistance. Even jobs that are saved may be so radically modified that people feel as though they lost their old job. Ironically, those who leave often find great jobs and are better off than those who remain, especially if subsequent layoffs occur. What few executives consider is that those who remain are under great stress, especially if they must do the work once done by those who are no longer there. Often they feel what is called "survivor's guilt" for having kept their jobs while others were laid off. They also are afraid of what may come next. Anxiety lingers long after a change initiative is over, and it can cause productivity to drop unless you conduct leadership conversations with skill and empathy.

CONVERSATIONS ABOUT SPECIFIC ACTIONS

In a meeting to set goals and establish budgets for the coming year, Cynthia, the quality assurance director, told Andy, the vice president of manufacturing, that she planned to eliminate the backlog of quality deficiency reports (QDRs) and reduce the time to process new ones by half. Several of Cynthia's peers nodded their heads in approval and agreed that timely QDR processing would improve their operations. Andy, also excited by her ambitious goals but concerned about how they would be achieved, said, "Cynthia, the goals are super. How will you achieve them? What resources will you need to change the process and support the new one?"

Cynthia anticipated those questions from Andy and provided well-reasoned answers, but Andy pressed further: "Are your people behind the changes? How long will it take to change the process? What intermediate milestones can we use to measure progress?" Andy did not just accept Cynthia's goals and approve her budget request. Instead, he pushed her to present details, encouraged her peers to contribute their viewpoints, and used the conversation to build a shared commitment to the new QDR process.

Effective implementation of a change requires leaders to get to the heart of the actions through constructive and persistent conversations. Because most conversations begin in partial ignorance, the following guidelines are useful:

- Set the tone of the conversation in opening statements: be challenging or helpful, whichever is more likely to produce the result you want.
- Ask questions to gain a full understanding: "What do you mean by ... ?"
- Do not argue—neither side ever wins an argument.
- Remember that people take action to satisfy their needs, not yours.

Use these guidelines in conversations about goals, the strategies to achieve them, the measures of success, and the resources that will be required. Ultimately the agenda for change must be shared to be successful.

DON'T ASSUME—DISCOVER

Executives risk drawing faulty or incomplete conclusions and taking ineffective actions when they make assumptions, especially about people. Assumptions about the priorities and needs of others seem accurate only because executives rarely inquire to find out what those others really are thinking. Many executives regularly assume that

- Everyone is using the same information to analyze the situation.
- Given the same information, everyone will take the same actions.
- Past actions are an accurate forecast of future actions.

All three of these assumptions are often wrong. Avoid making them and instead have conversations to discover what information others have, what actions they intend to take, and what they might do differently in the future.

Have you noticed that when you make an assumption, you normally make several and link them? Every time you do that, your probability of being right falls. For example, if you have a 50-50 chance of being right (two choices) and string three assumptions together, then you would have one chance in eight of being right on all three. If you have a 25 percent chance of being correct (four choices) and again string together three assumptions, you will be right one time in sixty-four. Why gamble your career on those odds when you can have a conversation that lifts the percentage into the 90 percent range?

What draws executives into making assumptions instead of asking questions? The primitive part of our brains instinctively works that way. The "Ladder of Inference" developed by Chris Argyris and his colleagues at Harvard over a fifty-year period provides insights into this human behavior. Drawing on the observations you make, you select data that fit your worldview and then attach your own meanings to the data. Then you fill any information gaps with assumptions, draw conclusions, make decisions, and take action. You go through this cycle in the blink of an eye. It is an instinctive behavior developed long ago when humans were in imminent danger of being eaten by saber-toothed tigers. Today, we have the time and the tools to fill information gaps, engage our logical brains, and ask questions to connect and align with others. Use them.

Terry, a brilliant but disruptive student in an executive education program, said to the class, "My assumptions about people are always right." His fellow executive students were stunned—but this was an insight into why he behaved the way he did. Terry was always right in his own mind, but was unable to connect with others to align perspectives and coordinate actions. The assumptions he made, combined with his unswerving conviction in their accuracy, disrupted the class. Frustration grew rapidly until the students systematically ignored Terry and avoided being on his team during group exercises. It is likely that Terry experienced the same reactions from people in his organization—and the same isolation from his colleagues.

Assumptions send negative messages and stifle conversations. When you make assumptions, high potentials feel that you expect them to think as you think and do things the way you do them—which is far from empowering. They also think that you are saying they are wrong because their perceptions of reality are different from yours or their actions do not conform to your expectations. Furthermore, they presume that you are convinced you are right because you did not ask for their ideas or opinions.

Executives claim that they make assumptions to save time and avoid confrontation. They would rather not look someone in the eye and ask what she is thinking. Maybe so, but they also are missing potential opportunities and avoiding useful feedback. The desire to avoid conflict is understandable, yet holding conversations that address conflict is a leader's job. When done effectively, handling small differences in a timely way is always preferable to allowing a conflict to grow to the point where it becomes a hurricane. Put on your leadership hat and hold those uncomfortable conversations where conflicting viewpoints are voiced and reconciled. To reduce conflict, eliminate assumptions.

CHAPTER 23

LESSONS FROM SUCCESS AND FAILURE

Checking results of a decision against its expectations shows executives where their strengths are, where they need to improve, and where they lack knowledge.
—PETER DRUCKER

Chad, a bright and dedicated F-16 squadron commander, served his country with commitment and distinction. Yet he initially washed out of the pilot training he began a week after getting married. First-stage training was so easy that he finished second in his class with little effort. The lesson he took from that success—that he did not have to work hard to get by—nearly ended his career before it began. Predictably, he paid even less attention during second-stage training and failed. In his words: "I went from an air of invincibility to being knocked on my tail."

He asked for a meeting with the squadron's commanding officer (CO) to explain his poor performance and seek permission to continue the training. He realized that his entire career—everything he had dreamed of—depended on his being able to convince the CO that he was worthy of another chance and that he had the determination and ability to regain his place at the top of the class. "Sir, I've given you ample reason to wash me out of flight school. I apologize for letting you and the service down. After finishing second in the first-stage class, I didn't realize how much more difficult this stage would be, and I didn't ramp up my effort. I take full responsibility for my failure. If you see fit to grant me a second chance, I'm determined not only to pass but also to regain my position at the top of the class and serve my country in excellence."

Despite seeing sincerity in Chad's eyes, the CO continued to test his commitment: "Are you really up to the challenge of being the best in the squadron? After your failure, merely passing won't be enough because it would mean that you'll never be a top-notch pilot. In the past you have shown that you can excel, but how can I trust that you will do so again? What will you do differently?"

Chad responded, "I have always wanted to be a pilot—it is my dream and my passion. I know I can handle the training, and I've already adjusted my attitude to deliver the effort required to be number one. I learned that I must give the training and you 100 percent of my effort. If I'm not at the top of the class, I will resign rather than making you wash me out of training—and I assure you that will not happen."

The CO let Chad repeat the training. He finished first in stage-two training, learned that focus and hard work produce sustainable success, and went on to excel in third-stage training and as a combat pilot. Chad was among the few leaders we interviewed who explained his current success in the business world in terms of both the failures and the successes he had experienced earlier in his career.

Executives universally say that they learn more from their failures than from their successes, mostly because they seldom examine success as a source of learning. Mistakes are an accepted part of growth and a powerful learning tool—but so is success. Learning from successes as well as failures enables you to accomplish more in each successive action. When you set stretch goals that require innovation and intense effort, your organization's capabilities will expand—whether the effort is successful or not.

THE COMFORT ZONE VERSUS THE LEARNING ZONE

Everyone has a comfort zone—you, your high potentials, and your boss. The zone expands over time as you face challenges and embrace the lessons they provide. The zone feels comfortable because you know what to do—you have been in similar situations before. Minimal learning occurs in the comfort zone because the status quo is the performance standard. Chad operated in his comfort zone during stage-one training.

When you push yourself and your high potentials to achieve more than you ever have before, you leave the comfort zone and enter the learning zone. The heightened emotional state feels uncomfortable, yet the learning that occurs in this zone expands your comfort zone. In his second try at stage-two training, Chad embraced the learning zone and excelled. There is also a panic zone where people become afraid that things could go catastrophically wrong. That state is so jarring that learning is severely inhibited. Fortunately, Chad remained in his learning zone when he washed out of stage-two training and focused on repeating the training. Had he been in the panic zone, he likely would have failed the second time and been washed out of the program.

Effective leaders operate in the learning zone to expand boundaries and optimize performance. Regularly ask your people whether good was good enough or whether you could have done better. Evaluate results that meet or exceed expectations with the same intensity with which you evaluate those that failed. Expectations are not the Holy Grail—they are merely targets that you select prior to taking action. How much more could you accomplish if you leveraged successes with the same effort that you expend to avoid failures? Inspire your people to focus the same attention on expanding success as they apply to correcting what went wrong. By all means celebrate a good quarter or a good year; but, at the same time, have conversations about what more might have been achieved.

CONVERSATIONS ABOUT SUCCESS AND FAILURE

If you want your high potentials to do their best, do not make them fear failure. Avoid beginning conversations with "Let's analyze what went wrong with . . . ," which raises the unspoken "Was I to blame?" fear in everyone's mind. When you chastise failure, people become reluctant to take bold actions, and the door to transformational actions closes. Incubate innovation by asking, "What went right with … ? What can we learn that would enable us to be even more successful next time?"

The unfortunate reality is that most organizations take success more or less for granted and punish failure. Why not eliminate the concept of success and failure and replace it with the goal of learning from every action you and your people take? That attitude encourages people from diverse disciplines to unite to support the common cause. It also breaks down silos and institutionalizes teamwork.

No organization systematically examines past actions more effectively than the U.S. military. After each training exercise or fire-for-effect engagement, military units dissect the action step-by-step to determine what worked, what can be learned, and what could be done better next time. They perform after-action reviews (AARs) even for missions that are unqualified successes. They look for ways to achieve victory more quickly, save more lives, and use fewer resources. Even in situations where lives are not at stake, this best practice pays generous dividends by uncovering opportunities that might otherwise go unnoticed. Having worked with hundreds of organizations as employees, consultants, and coaches, we can count on one hand the number of times that successful operations (outside the uniformed military) were evaluated to see what could have been done better.

Chad told us how important pre-mission briefings to quantify expectations and post-mission debriefings were to improving future actions. During pre-mission briefings, the objective and strategy were explained, mission goals were prioritized, and parameters—sometimes as many as 250—were established to measure success. The briefings pushed everyone to look past obvious goals like bringing everyone home and to ask hard questions about what that goal would really mean if things went wrong. In briefings and debriefings, there was no rank. Whoever had the floor owned it until he or she finished. Everyone got to speak, everyone listened, and everyone's input was valued. In discussing the mission, aircraft call signs were used instead of the pilot's name to focus attention on actions and results rather than individuals. During debriefings, even when everything had gone perfectly, they analyzed what might have gone wrong, how they would have reacted, and how those lessons could be applied to future missions.

AFTER-ACTION REVIEWS IN THE COMMERCIAL SECTOR

Today, Chad is the president of a multibranch bank that undertook a major technology conversion. When the bank last upgraded its systems fifteen years ago, there were ugly service disruptions, schedule slippages, and cost overruns. Borrowing techniques from his military service, he started the project by briefing everyone on the bank's objectives: "We are expanding rapidly and cannot meet our customers' needs without a technology upgrade." To set expectations, he added: "Mistakes are a normal part of complex projects like this, so let's hold conversations to correct them before they become customer-service issues. We will own this project as a team—that means no one will point fingers or assess blame."

They set the completion date, divided work into phases, evaluated contingencies, defined success criteria for each department, and acknowledged that the path of progress would zigzag rather than follow a straight line. At the conclusion of each phase, they held a debrief to ask, "What did we learn from what went well and what didn't go as well, and what changes can we make so that the next phase will go even better?" The conversations aligned the entire bank behind the initiative and resolved problems as they went along. Chad also insisted that everything be written down so that "next time we attempt a bankwide initiative, it will be even easier."

Peter Senge, a recognized expert in the concept of the learning organization, said, "After Action Reviews are arguably one of the most successful organizational learning methods yet devised. Yet, most corporate efforts to graft this innovative practice into their culture fail because, again and again, people reduce the living practice of AARs to a sterile technique." Done well, the AAR evaluates options in a way that enables them to be easily adopted in future initiatives. The more options you have and the more distinctions you make in planning, the greater your ability to take powerful actions in implementation. There are three clear benefits of letting your people know that an AAR (or similar process) will be used for all major actions:

- **Transparency.** The reviews encourage everyone to participate actively. People become observers as well as doers during the action because their feedback will be solicited during the review. They look for options that were not seen when the action was planned, they are less defensive and more open to feedback, and they consider events from all three conversational perspectives.

- **Ability to leverage strengths.** After-action conversations leverage strengths in addition to eliminating weaknesses. They focus on boosting future performance to higher levels by identifying and considering a wide range of potential actions.

- **Culture of success.** They create a culture of success by eliminating the word "failure" from the vocabulary. Failure need never be an end state: you have not failed when you learn from the results, especially when that learning creates the ability to achieve the goals next time.

The most valuable aspect of an action can be the learning it provides, regardless of whether the short-term goal was reached. Further, the process of evaluating actions as a team builds relationships, promotes growth, and facilitates better decisions and more effective future actions.

LET GO OF PERFECTION

Vance, an avionics company's COO and a PhD engineer, had a reputation for brilliant system designs and manufacturing innovations. During the early stages of directing preparation of a multibillion-dollar proposal, Vance made valuable contributions to the win strategy, proposal themes, and system design. Everything went according to schedule until two days before the proposal due date, when Vance came up with several innovations. He insisted that the ideas be included in the five-volume proposal, even though doing so would necessitate a major rewrite. The already exhausted proposal team worked forty-eight straight hours to include Vance's changes, and then hand-carried the proposal cross-country in the CEO's corporate jet to meet the proposal deadline. The proposal won, but not because of Vance's remarkable innovations. In fact, the customer's evaluators were concerned by inconsistencies in the proposal between the original design and the modified design—the last-minute proposal changes nearly caused the company to lose the contract.

Recognize the appropriate situations in which to operate in the management mindset and the leadership mindset. Nothing deflates high potentials faster than the perfect-solutions quagmire that grabs some otherwise brilliant executives. They acknowledge the need for action, yet they delay the start to gather more data and analyze more alternatives. Executives with extensive academic credentials—doctors, scientists, accountants, lawyers, and the like— are particularly susceptible to these excesses of the management mindset. We understand that perfect answers with near-zero risk have a place. Would you volunteer for a trip to the moon on a rocket that had a 90 percent chance of a safe return? We would not. We would insist that every executive be at least 99.99 percent certain that every item on the rocket would perform flawlessly. When human life is at stake, high levels of certainty are necessary, and everything should be double-checked.

However, most leadership decisions are made at substantially lower confidence levels. The opportunity cost of gaining near certainty is generally too high compared to the benefits (when lives are not at stake). Ask your team what would be an adequate confidence level, have conversations about the completeness and reliability of the information you have, and then make the decision and take action. Operating in the leadership mindset, let your people figure out the details as they move forward with the actions. Toggling between a leadership mindset and a management mindset in making decisions and trusting people is difficult for some technically minded executives. Yet they must do so to inspire their high potentials into action.

CHAPTER 24

INSPIRING PEOPLE IN TURBULENT TIMES

In any moment of decision, the best thing you can do is the right thing and the next best thing is the wrong thing—the worst thing you can do is nothing.
—THEODORE ROOSEVELT

Today's global economy is characterized by rapid and unpredictable change. The challenge of such turbulent times can only be met by employing an appropriate blend of the leadership and management mindsets. You must sense and adapt to change. Sometimes adapting will require innovation, and other times it may mean renewing an old best practice. Because change is unpredictable, it follows that your actions may be different too—at least from the viewpoint that actions that worked yesterday may not work as well today. Conduct leadership conversations in ways that challenge habitual, comfortable actions to be sure that they still work. When a new action is required, hold conversations so that people understand the what, when, why, and how of the change.

Barry, the CEO, took the podium in front of his executive team after they had heard the CFO report that, for the fourth consecutive quarter, sales had declined and the bottom line was red. The company was proud of its multi-decade record of success, but recently it had lost market share in virtually every division. The room was funereally silent as Barry began to speak:

> Our challenge is to determine across each customer segment what we
> need to keep and what we must abandon and replace with innovative
> new products and services and industry best practices. There's a fine
> line between losing sight of what makes our company great and

changing to serve our customers' evolving needs. It's as if we are walking on the crest of a hill where on one side we see the successes of the past and, on the other, possibilities for the future. We must think strategically and act decisively to regain customer loyalty by combining the best of our heritage with the best of the new world.

Kashur, the VP of marketing, waved his hand vigorously and was recognized by Barry. Kashur said, "I feel like that's what we've being doing for the past year—and it's not working. We have been changing too quickly and in too many areas to coordinate process changes, R&D, and expensive investments across the divisions. We aren't sharing market intelligence the way we used to, and in some areas, divisions are actually selling against each other. We need to take a breather, compare notes, unify our strategy, and focus on mutual areas of success."

The room was restless as Barry thought for a moment before responding:

I agree, Kashur. Let's adjourn and invest the rest of today in small groups sharing across divisions what you are seeing in today's markets—the good and the bad. Over the next two weeks, I'd like each division to hold conversations to identify what is working, what isn't, new things you want to try, and resources you will need. When we reassemble at the off-site, each division will share its findings, and we'll merge them in a cohesive strategy. In addition, each division should bring to the off-site several high potentials who deserve recognition for special achievements in these challenging times. I want everyone to hear stories where our actions super-pleased a customer or scooped a competitor. And don't be afraid to recognize a valiant attempt even if it fell short. We will weave their stories into our strategy so that people visualize success in times of rapid change.

When Barry finished, the room fell silent again as the executives pondered what he had said and which high potentials they would recognize at the coming off-site. But that silence was different from the silence that preceded his message—it was silence rooted in a groundswell of innovative thinking and optimism that stiffened the resolve of the executives to restore the company to its former greatness.

THE MEANING OF SILENCE

Silence is an integral part of conversations, so learn to use it effectively. It can be simply silence, or it can be the prologue to decisive action. Silence can be a time where nothing—or everything—is happening. It may be a pause without conscious thought or the prelude to something big. Instinctively, people lean into silence wondering what will come next. Silence also allows people to clear clutter from their heads and prepare for action. It is frequently the time when insights sprout and the next set of actions is imagined.

During periods of silence, people process information, consider alternatives, and think about the potential reactions of others. When people become quiet, let the silence run its course and give them time to reflect, consider alternatives, and make a decision. Some of the most powerful answers we have received during coaching interactions have come after thirty seconds or more of silence. When people respond after having that much time to think, they often come up with revealing insights. Silence can connect and align people behind a new action.

The average two-hour movie contains roughly thirty minutes of dialogue and ninety minutes of silence, during which you interpret the action using nonverbal cues. These periods often are the most evocative segments of a movie because they allow people to inject personal thoughts and feelings into the scene. In the context of action, silence is where you ask one last question—the one that knocks down the last barrier. It is the moment when people commit to take action. Let silence work for you. Do not fill the void mindlessly. Silence can drive the actions you want.

REQUESTING ACTION VERSUS DEMANDING ACTION

How many times have you left a meeting that ended in silence thinking that there was agreement, only to hear people voicing concerns in the hallway about the supposedly agreed-on actions? For example, a ski goggle company tested a material that would allow its goggles to remain soft and comfortable at skiing temperatures. Unfortunately, once formed into goggles, the material melted at 95 degrees into a distorted blob. Despite that issue, the division president told Brennan, the product manager, to order full production quantities of the material and hang a tag on the product warning customers to keep the goggles away from heat. Brennan said nothing.

At the end of the meeting, Brennan merely acknowledged the president's directive and drove back to his office, using the time alone to think. Later that day, he signed an order to purchase just 10 percent of the production quantity. The manufacturing vice president called him to question the reduced order. Brennan confirmed that it was correct, and said that he would rather be fired than take an action that could damage the company's reputation. The conversation necessary to persuade and inspire Brennan to take aligned action had not occurred during the meeting—there had been only the president's demand for action.

Agreement is real only when both parties (1) acknowledge what has been agreed to, (2) know the actions that will be taken, and (3) concur on the expected outcomes. As a leader, be sure your requests are stated as requests and that your demands—the few times you must make them—are clearly stated as demands. To clarify the difference, normally the only acceptable response to a demand is "Yes." In contrast, there are multiple acceptable responses to a request, including "Yes," "No," "Let me get back to you [later today]," or continuing negotiations until the two parties agree on whether the answer will be yes or no. Requests show respect for others; demands do not. Requests lead to conversations that produce better decisions and inspire aligned action. At best, demands elicit compliance.

PUTTING LEADERSHIP INFLUENCE INTO ACTION

Leaders have significant influence—and the responsibility to use it wisely. For example, Habib, a division manager in a public company, also was a leader in the U.S. Persian community. As a group, they worked to safeguard their interests in the post-9/11 era. Fellow Persians in his company told him that a well-known job-search website, because of its interpretation of the Patriot Act, was not distributing resumes for anyone who had the word "Iran" in his or her profile. They needed to use the website because of pending layoffs, and asked Habib to speak to a newspaper reporter about the situation. He did so, but the reporter insisted on citing the Habib's name and company in the article. He called his company's public relations director to get permission, but his request was denied. This was a seminal moment—how should he respond? How should he show up as leader? How much did he owe to his community and the people in his company who were facing layoffs?

Habib called the PR director again, asked about the origin of her French accent, and reminded her of the backlash against the French because they refused to join President Bush's coalition after 9/11. In light of looming layoffs, he asked, "How would you feel if the website extended its policy to exclude French people?" That question converted her from a roadblock to a supporter. She obtained approval, and he completed the interview with the reporter. Facing public scrutiny, the website instantly reversed its policy. Habib's action positively impacted not only employees of his company but also thousands of others who may have been affected by the website's discriminatory policy.

Consider the power you have as a leader to influence and assist thousands—maybe millions—of colleagues, customers, suppliers, and stakeholders based on the actions you take or do not take. You will reach your goals more quickly and easily by connecting and aligning with them. What better way is there to direct the actions you want people to take and the results you want to achieve than to build a high-performing team? Connect individually with each member of your team, develop her potential, respect her contributions, and take action to meet her needs and satisfy the needs of your organization at the same time.

WHEN YOUR TEAM IS EFFECTIVE, YOU BECOME PROMOTABLE

We have coached scores of high potentials whose goal was to be promoted to partner, SES, flag officer, or CXO. Many of them believed that their next promotion depended on the effectiveness of their personal actions. They were surprised to learn that how well they built their team's capabilities and how effectively that team performed were more important than their direct contributions. The better the results their teams produced—without their direct involvement—the more promotable they became. Consider the following tactics to expand your opportunity to move up the leadership ladder:

Tactic 1—Train your replacement. Make yourself replaceable. Ensure that your boss recognizes that your team would perform well even without you. Building your team will help you get your next promotion. You owe it to yourself, your people, and your organization to build a team that can excel without you, not simply carry on. Identify people who could fill your position, and have conversations with them to ensure that they know their jobs and learn yours too.

Tactic 2—Get yourself ready. Being great at your current job is not usually enough to be promoted. The higher you are in an organization, the greater the risk of failure after your next promotion. Minimize the risks by learning the actions and displaying the blend of management and leadership mindsets required to be successful at the next rung on the ladder.

Tactic 3—Make it about them. Make it clear that you can build a team, implement efficient processes, and connect with and align people. It is essential to demonstrate that you can motivate a team to deliver great results—not just get people to do what you tell them. Furthermore, motivating other leaders is a different and often more challenging job than inspiring individual contributors and managers—you must cultivate their use of leadership competencies. Demonstrate your ability to create great leaders as well as build effective managers.

Tactic 4—Manage the fit. What are your personal strengths and skills, and how well do they fit the position you want? How is the new position different in terms of the actions you will take and the actions you must motivate others to take? Growing to fit the new position requires honest self-assessment, asking great questions, being open to feedback, and using that feedback effectively.

Tactic 5—Get the most from your team. A legendary NCAA basketball coach says that he defines success less in terms of getting his team into the final-four round of the tournament, than by how well he was able to develop and blend the talents of that year's players. Each person is unique, so as a leader you must identify and apply each person's strengths to produce the most he can as part of a team.

Tactic 6—Act as a team. In competitive rowing, rowers willingly carry the weight of a coxswain because that position unifies their actions and steers the boat on the winning course. As the leader, you are the coxswain who sets the team's direction and rhythm. Ensure that your people see your value as part of the team.

LEADING IN STRESSFUL TIMES

Leaders in all sectors—industry, government, the military, academia, and non-profits—are being challenged to do more with less to better utilize their people's time, physical assets, and budget. Your first response to a shrinking budget might be to do more yourself. An alternative is to delegate more to team members either proportionally or by getting your high potentials to take on extra work. In the first case, you are likely to burn out and have insufficient time to lead. In the latter two cases, you burn out either everyone or just the best people on your team. There is a better way: eliminate low-value tasks.

Stefan, an associate director in a government agency, received a constant stream of Freedom of Information Act (FOIA) requests, which by law must be addressed promptly. He lamented that answering the requests was making it virtually impossible for his people to perform their core mission; his thinking was rooted in ways that worked well for him in the past. Doing everything that was asked was one of Stefan's core values and a source of pride for him. We asked him to consider other approaches he could use to process the FOIA requests. Stefan met with his boss and asked her to assign some of them to her staff. A few hours later, she agreed that her staff would handle the more controversial requests because they involved policy issues. The impossible became possible, and his team continued to excel at their core mission.

Budget limitations are often less of a barrier than executives make them out to be. One private sector client, Adrienne, desperately needed additional funds to finish a priority project by the year's end. We encouraged her to contact her peers to see if any of them had funds remaining in the current budget year that could be transferred. It turned out one of them had just cancelled a project, and funds were indeed available. After brief negotiations with the CFO's office, the budget authority was transferred, and a vital project was completed on time—within the existing overall budget.

The core lesson in these two stories is to think broadly in your definition of your team—it is more than just you and your direct reports. It includes everyone who has a stake in your success. Look for alliances that can dramatically expand the capabilities, resources, and reach of your team. A second lesson to understand is that when you do not ask a question, you are really the one who is saying no. When you ask questions, you tap into others' knowledge so as to create new possibilities. The boundaries of your possible actions are no longer what you know, but rather what the organization and community know and can do.

Downsizing is becoming a major challenge for leaders. The best advice we have heard about leading during a downsizing is, "Don't waste time at the watercooler listening to rumors. Instead, get your work done and encourage your high potentials and direct reports to do the same."

If the evolving global economy or budget cutbacks mean that a downsizing is coming in your organization, guard against your team's becoming distracted and inefficient—ensure that they continue to take effective actions. The threat of layoffs can easily turn cooperation into competition and debilitate a team. Get your people to focus on outcomes and to make every action count. If you and your team maintain a positive attitude and produce results, you increase your chances of emerging with your job and the team intact.

Even if you are downsized, if you and your team continue to perform well, you are likely be the ones who receive the most formal and informal assistance in finding new positions. Ask the highest-ranking person surviving the cutback to provide proactive referrals on behalf of you and your people. During the 2008 downturn, many high potentials—especially in financial companies—were laid off, even though they were top performers. There was just nothing for them to perform. Those whose bosses called their networks to recommend them as valuable hires got better jobs—and faster too. Be a leader who helps everyone survive the crisis.

At the end of the day, only action produces results. Building relationships, developing others, and making decisions lead to more effective actions; but it is the actions of you and your team along with the outcomes they produce that will build your reputation as a great leader.

TEN WAYS TO PRACTICE GREAT LEADERSHIP IN TAKING ACTION

1. **Choose action or inaction wisely.** Deciding when to take action is a basic leadership choice. You can lead your people into action quickly or let the energy build while they prepare for what must be done. Both approaches are appropriate at times.
2. **Make teamwork a priority.** Even high potentials must perform as a team to be successful. Conflicting actions or complaints about difficulties in getting agreement are symptoms of poor teamwork. Fix the teamwork issues first, and other challenges will be easier.
3. **Hold planning conversations.** The time you spend in up-front conversations will be less than the time you otherwise would spend correcting the unintended and costly consequences of poorly planned and misaligned actions.
4. **Ensure that the plan is understood.** Ask high potentials, especially those who did not participate in planning, to describe your organization's goals and strategies. If their answers are accurate, congratulate yourself. If they are not, improve the methods you use to communicate the strategic plan to your people.
5. **Plan obsolescence.** Look at the products and services you offer today. Which will be irrelevant three years from now? Are you developing the next generation of offerings? Whether you are or not, someone else is.
6. **Create a people strategy.** Invest as much in creating the people strategy for your next major change as in developing new processes and systems. People will accept change when they feel it is necessary, when their inputs are heard, and when they believe that the process of change is fair.
7. **Learn from success.** Looking back, would you say you learned more from your failures than from your successes? If you said yes, spend more time examining your recent successes to determine how you can repeat and expand them.

8. **Stretch the comfort zone.** Think about your team's biggest achievement last year. What have you learned since then that could have made it bigger? Push your people into the uncomfortable learning zone and coach them to higher levels of success.

9. **Confirm alignment.** Next time you finish a key meeting, ask each person what he or she plans to do—especially to support each other. Agreement is real only if all parties share the agreements, the actions to be taken, and the expected results.

10. **Get comfortable with silence.** Silence can be the prelude to a big decision or decisive action. Use silence in your conversations as thinking and reflecting time.

PART 6

YOUR LEADERSHIP CONVERSATIONS

Part 6 examines how the point of view, span of control, and time horizon of your conversations evolve each time you are promoted to a new level. In particular, Chapters 26 through 29 look at how you—as either a CXO leader, executive leader, manager of managers, or first-line manager—hold leadership conversations with

- Your boss
- Your peers
- Your high-potential direct reports

Those chapters show how the content and mindset of your conversations shift to fit the role and priorities at each rung on the leadership ladder.

Chapter 29 closes Part 6 by providing instructions for taking the online assessment to determine the current level of your leadership conversations. But wait to take the assessment until you have reviewed the leadership conversations that are appropriate for your current position and the next level up. That way, the assessment will accurately measure your current leadership competencies and motivate you to prepare and implement a customized personal action plan to assist you in reaching the next level.

CHAPTER 25

CONVERSATIONS AT THE TOP

*The final test of a leader is that he leaves behind him in other men
the conviction and the will to carry on.*
—WALTER LIPPMANN

In many organizations, the leader at the top is called the chief executive officer (CEO), and his or her primary colleagues are also called chiefs: chief operating officer (COO) and chief financial officer (CFO), for example. In the last decade or so, the practice has spilled into the federal government, where—by act of Congress—large agencies must have a chief technology officer (CTO), a chief human capital officer (CHCO), and a CFO. The practice is less common, but not unusual, in the military and nonprofit organizations. Collectively, we refer to these individuals as CXO leaders. You may be in this group even if the word "chief" is not in your title. If you have broad responsibilities for a critical business function across the organization and report directly to the CEO—even if you do not call him or her by that title— then you are a CXO leader.

THE CXO LEADER'S ROLE

CXO leaders have positions that wield considerable leverage. They set policy, establish objectives, and define practices for the organization. Although they direct a vital function and are the CEO's primary adviser in their areas, these leaders focus—or at least should—on the success of the entire organization today and in the future. CXO leaders spend virtually all their time on such leadership activities as strategic planning, organizational alignment, and growth initiatives, and little time on management tasks. Does this fit with how you spend your time?

Because your influence is nearly as broad as the CEO's, the consequences of your actions are wide ranging. You must share goals and find common threads with leaders in other functional areas to build synergy and alignment across the enterprise. Everyone is watching and will align with what you do—regardless of what you say. As a model for the leadership mindset, you need to conduct your conversations in an atmosphere of trust and respect that produces alignment with the organization's vision and mission.

CONVERSATIONS BY CXO LEADERS WITH THEIR BOSS

The CEO and board have given you an opportunity with wide responsibility. If you are not sure what the CEO expects, if an issue arises, or if a breakthrough occurs, have a conversation as quickly and openly as possible to build a relationship where ideas and information flow freely. Your discussions with the CEO will address all four conversation types:

- **Building relationships.** Hold baseline and feedback conversations at the trusted level that enable you to fully understand each other's needs and concerns. Be the honest broker by delivering the essential facts—be they positive or negative—succinctly, directly, and in a timely manner.
- **Developing others.** Although it is not your job to develop the CEO, help your boss see how his actions (or inaction) impact the ability of you and your team to produce results. These are tough conversations, yet they are vital to ensure that you, the CEO, and the organization consistently perform at high levels.
- **Making decisions.** If you are not fully on board with any decision made by the CEO or other CXO leaders, speak up to seek alignment. Use your voice to lead everyone toward the third alternative—a better decision that

everyone can endorse. Use constructive conflict to sharpen the decision-making process.

- **Taking action.** Have the CEO mentor you. Ask for his views on the subtle nuances of your job and his job. Proactively ask for the resources required to accomplish the objectives that have been allocated to you and your team.

CONVERSATIONS BY CXO LEADERS WITH THEIR PEERS

When CXO leaders do not work together closely, the organization under-performs. Each of you has risen to a power position because of your skill, knowledge, and performance record. Respect what your fellow CXOs have accomplished and tap into their expertise.

- **Building relationships.** To build trusted relationships and coordinate actions, schedule regular one-on-one conversations with the other CXOs individually and as a team. Focus on conversations that assist each other and the CEO in achieving the organization's goals and mission.
- **Developing others.** You are not responsible for developing other CXOs, yet you can offer to mentor them in leadership areas where you have special skills. Accept their mentoring (if offered) in your shadow areas.
- **Making decisions.** Perhaps the most important conversations you will have with other CXOs will involve working together to make difficult strategic decisions. Each of you brings a unique point of view and set of experiences to decision making. Listen to the other CXOs and consistently seek the third alternative. Consider giving the CXO who is most affected by a decision an extra vote in that decision.
- **Taking action.** Once you agree to a plan with other CXOs, meet your part of the bargain every time unless and until everyone agrees to modify the plan. Success expands rapidly when coordinated actions take place across all functional areas of an organization.

CONVERSATIONS BY CXO LEADERS WITH THEIR HIGH POTENTIALS

CXOs usually have more conversations with their direct reports than with the CEO and CXOs combined. Who would replace you if you left your position? What is your continuity-of-operations plan? How well would your people execute it? How often do you hold conversations to ensure that high potentials are acquiring the skills to do their jobs and yours? What are their career aspirations? Would you be surprised or angry if one of them left to work with a major competitor? Hold leadership conversations in a trusted-adviser mode with your high potentials to discuss these topics.

- **Building relationships.** Be proud of your high potentials, tout their abilities, and build trust and respect with them, and they will be loyal to you. If they are brilliant but lack people skills, coach them. Let them participate in some of your relationship conversations to observe your techniques. Introduce them to others with whom they might form productive transactional relationships.

- **Developing others.** Succession planning is among your most important leadership responsibilities—make it part of your ongoing conversations. Are you grooming replacements for the key jobs of the future? Does your team know exactly what is expected of them today and what will be expected with their next increase in responsibilities? Mentor them and teach them how to coach others. Challenge them to both grow personally and build the capabilities of their staffs.

- **Making decisions.** If you are like most CXOs, you worry about the ability of your high potentials—especially in remote offices—to make decisions consistent with the organization's strategy. What repeatable decision-making process do you use? Are you teaching them to use that process and to develop their judgment gene?

- **Taking action.** If you were traveling or on vacation where there was no email or cell phone coverage, could your people do their jobs and yours without you? Try it sometime. Then hold a conversation to address any topic they felt compelled to contact you about to clarify expectations and strategies. Have the same conversation with remote offices if you find that they regularly do not take actions that are in alignment with the agreed-on plan.

Your responses to the challenges posed and questions asked in these conversations with your boss, your peers, and your high potentials will be evaluated when you take the online leadership assessment. We expect those who feel they are ready to become the CEO to achieve a near-perfect score. Do not let that intimidate you—take the assessment anyway. A word of caution: the personal action plan you will prepare after doing so will not be about what you will have others do; rather, it will be about *who you are* and *what you will do* to become a great leader.

CHAPTER 26

CONVERSATIONS FOR EXECUTIVE LEADERS

Great communicators have an appreciation for positioning. They understand the people they're trying to reach and what they can and cannot hear. They send their message in through an open door rather than trying to push it through a wall.
—JOHN KOTTER

As an executive leader, you have crossed the chasm from management to leadership. At this level, you may not be the top person in your area, yet you are responsible for achieving crucial strategic objectives. You either report to the CEO or one of the CXOs. Your office may not be in the headquarters building with the CEO and CXOs, so you must be effective at communicating remotely. More than likely, you are the senior executive directing operations for a region, a product or service, or a group of customers. As a high potential, you definitely are in the hunt for your boss's position.

So how can you earn that promotion? To start, spend most of your time on such leadership activities as creating a vision for the future, forming strategic partnerships, and developing your people. Reduce the time you spend focusing on achieving short-term goals and schedules. You lead a diverse team of managers; tap into their skills and experience. You will not get to the next level by micromanaging; instead, leverage your conversations to produce results that exceed forecasts.

THE EXECUTIVE LEADER'S ROLE

Your role as an executive leader is operational and multidiscipline rather than functional. If you work in a corporation, you probably have bottom-line responsibilities and certainly have revenue goals or production quotas. In a government agency or nonprofit, you are responsible for delivering vital services or producing complex products for a category of people. In the military, you lead a multicapability fighting force or logistics unit with thousands of men and women under your command.

You are the primary strategist for your operation; and, in a strategy rollout, you are the one who allocates objectives and resources to your high potentials. Because you are the primary interface between the top leaders above you and the high-potential managers below, you must integrate the needs and concerns both of headquarters and of your people. Your power derives not from your position but from your people believing in you as a leader.

CONVERSATIONS BY EXECUTIVE LEADERS WITH THEIR BOSS

Your boss, the CEO or a CXO, counts on you to make your operation run smoothly. You not only support her strategic goals but also must provide a high return on investment for the resources you control. In conversations with your boss, you will be expected to report succinctly how things are proceeding relative to plan, how resources are holding up, and new trends and issues that are developing in your area of responsibility.

- **Building relationships.** Do not hesitate to ask your boss to introduce you to stakeholders and to assist you in building trusted relationships. Become adept at multimedia communications, especially if you work in a different region than your boss. At times, you may find yourself caught between your boss and other leaders. Develop a long-term view of relationships that also satisfies short-term requirements.
- **Developing others.** Many of the conversations with your boss will focus on succession planning—your development as a leader and development of your high potentials. Be prepared to discuss those topics in terms of strategies for the future, the current performance of your staff, and changing market conditions.

- **Making decisions.** Provide timely recommendations to your boss to support strategic planning, and be prepared to implement decisions made at the boss's level. Familiarize yourself with the process and criteria your boss uses to make decisions, and provide feedback that is valuable relative to strategic decisions.

- **Taking action.** Know what your boss expects of you and deliver results that meet or exceed those expectations. Any shortfalls at your level will have wide impact and be highly visible. Have conversations with your boss to ensure that your actions are in alignment with her expectations and with actions in other segments of the organization.

CONVERSATIONS BY EXECUTIVE LEADERS WITH THEIR PEERS

In your role as an executive leader, your resources are not limited to those under your control. Look for opportunities to work with your peers as well. At this level, your conversations with peers should be about ways for all of you to be successful concurrently.

- **Building relationships.** We will be blunt: if you do not work effectively with your peers at this level, it is unlikely that you will be promoted to the next. The CEO and CXO leaders are assessing your ability and willingness to work with others to achieve the organization's strategic goals—in all areas, not just yours. Think horizontally in building relationships and act vertically in producing results.

- **Developing others.** You have no authority over peers, yet their performance may affect your results. Your incentives may be split between how well you do and how well the organization performs, so you have a vested interest in your peers' success. If a peer needs coaching, offer it if he has given you permission and you are genuinely concerned about his success. If your relationship is competitive, you might start with a conversation about why the competition exists and how to align your mutual efforts against your outside competitors.

- **Making decisions.** Be mindful that the decisions you make are likely to impact your peers. Avoid conflicts by meeting with your peers to find a third alternative when a decision you might make in your best interests seems contrary to theirs. Incorporate their inputs to make more powerful decisions.
- **Taking action.** In planning, look for situations where your actions can be leveraged with the actions of your peers. Discuss the extent to which you might share resources to produce superior results. After an action is completed, meet with your peers to determine how the teamwork and results could be improved.

CONVERSATIONS BY EXECUTIVE LEADERS WITH THEIR HIGH POTENTIALS

In conversations with your high potentials, you will find that their views are likely to be more management oriented than yours. After all, your job is weighted toward leadership, whereas theirs is still a blend of leadership and management. Assist the high potentials who work for you in achieving the right blend and realize that they may be reluctant to let go of skills that made them successful in the past. Toggle between a leadership and a management mindset during your conversations with them.

- **Building relationships.** Coach your high potentials to be proficient at building the transactional relationships required to surpass their goals. Encourage them to find mentors and to build trusted relationships to help them achieve future success. You should not be their sole source of mentoring and coaching.
- **Developing others.** You have three goals relative to developing your high potentials. First, develop their leadership and management mindsets, ensuring that the blend of the two is appropriate for their roles. Second, show them how to coach their direct reports. Third, include them in strategic conversations to grow their strategic thinking ability and their understanding of and commitment to the organization's strategy.

- **Making decisions.** As an executive leader, you are—or should be—removed from most operating decisions and issues. Therefore, teach your people to use a structured decision-making process. Mentor and coach them through high-impact decisions and problem resolutions. Show them how to engage their people's knowledge and experience in the decision-making process.
- **Taking action.** To reach their objectives, high potentials must get their direct reports to act in alignment. Help them allocate resources efficiently and urge them to ask for additional resources when necessary. Ask them to provide inputs to the strategy, and ensure that they understand the strategy and can implement it.

Your ability to conduct effective conversations with your boss, peers, and high potentials will be evaluated when you take the leadership assessment. As an executive leader, you should score high. After you complete the assessment, you will receive feedback that identifies areas where you are performing above, at, or below the executive-leader level. When you prepare your personal action plan using the online tools, you will use the results from the assessment to identify areas where you may want to boost your abilities. The personal action plan will focus on developing your leadership brand, taking the actions necessary to be more effective as an executive leader, and preparing you for a CXO position.

CHAPTER 27

CONVERSATIONS FOR MANAGERS OF MANAGERS

I have yet to find the man, however exalted his station, who did not do better work and put forth greater effort under a spirit of approval than under a spirit of criticism.
—CHARLES SCHWAB

If you are a midlevel manager, you manage other managers rather than production work. You may have succeeded in earlier positions without engaging the leadership mindset and growing your leadership capabilities, but that will no longer work. Manage your people through delegation and assist them in growing as well. You may also be managing high potentials who work at remote sites, which is an additional challenge. Furthermore, you now report to an executive leader who has broad responsibilities and expects you to meet your goals and resolve issues with minimal assistance.

THE MANAGER OF MANAGER'S ROLE

Your job as a manager of managers is a fairly equal split of management (getting things done on time and on budget) and leadership (motivating people to produce and grow). Your span of control may be larger, but now you have only indirect influence over operations. In addition, for the first time you will be immersed in strategic planning, and your decisions must be guided by the strategic plan. In fact, you may be assigned specific strategic goals to achieve. One unique challenge you will face is getting first-line managers to put aside their technical skills and produce results by operating in a management, not a technical, mindset. Mentor first-line managers to ensure that their high potentials also realize their full potential.

CONVERSATIONS BY MANAGERS OF MANAGERS WITH THEIR BOSS

As a manager of managers, you will spend much of your time in conversations with your boss and other executive leaders; anticipate the questions they might ask. The conversations will be broader and of higher impact than in any previous position you have held. Demonstrate that you can apply your leadership skills to motivate managers to perform at their peak. Sharpen your leadership mindset and begin to define a leadership brand that will carry you to success at higher levels.

- **Building relationships.** The broad scope of your responsibilities and your role in strategic planning will place you in conversations with executive leaders other than your boss. Use those conversations to develop transactional relationships. It is also possible that one of them could become a mentor. Because your boss will have the biggest say in your next promotion, you must not only produce results but also prove that you have the leadership and management skills required to succeed at that level. Your relationships with multiple executive leaders will be essential for your future success; make them a priority.
- **Developing others.** Conversations with executive leaders will push you to develop your leadership mindset as well as sharpen your management mindset. Speak up when you have a strategic idea that will help the organization. To grow as a leader, identify areas in which you will ask your boss for mentoring. You also may want to seek external sources of coaching. Share with your boss the steps you are taking to develop your people and discuss how well they are responding. Tout your people's capabilities and accomplishments whenever possible and appropriate.
- **Making decisions.** Ask your boss to teach you the process she uses to make decisions. Determine the extent to which she wants to participate

in pivotal decisions you will make. Be careful in presenting definitive decisions to your boss, as her preference may be to discuss strategic issues in general early in the planning process. Show that you understand the strategic context and have considered the people side in your decisions. Make timely decisions; do not let issues fester while you ponder what to do.

- **Taking action.** Ensure that your actions align with your boss's priorities and with the strategic plan. Share with your boss how you assign your team members to strategic tasks, how you allocate resources, and how you measure results. Be prepared to describe how your first-line managers work together to achieve their goals. Provide succinct and timely reports about the results you are achieving, the issues you are addressing, and where you may need assistance.

CONVERSATIONS BY MANAGERS OF MANAGERS WITH THEIR PEERS

In all likelihood, you and your peers are reaching for the same thing: your boss's job or one like it. So the challenge is to cooperate and compete at the same time. If your boss asked your peers to rate you on your readiness to be an executive leader, would the peers praise your leadership strengths or your management strengths? Conversations with peers are an excellent opportunity to develop your leadership mindset.

- **Building relationships.** Meet regularly with your peers to exchange ideas and discuss possibilities—not just when one of you needs something. Be open to sharing resources with your peers to ensure that everyone succeeds. Do not let your competitive spirit cloud your relationships; find ways to unite with your peers to make your organization the best in your industry.
- **Developing others.** To what extent are you willing to share people and training resources with your peers in order to achieve peak overall performance? If they asked for help, would you loan them your best, your average, or your lowest performers? Do you and your peers mentor and

coach each other, or does everyone hide quietly on the sidelines when one of you has an issue? Start to demonstrate your leadership mindset horizontally.

- **Making decisions.** You and your peers have an opportunity to assist each other in making important decisions. Do you regularly tap into your peers' experience as a decision-making resource? Are you open to similar requests from them? Do you have conversations about the issues you face and what you might do differently if additional resources were to become available?

- **Taking action.** Do you routinely coordinate actions with your peers? When you agree to assist a peer, do exactly what you have committed to do—every time. After you finish a joint action, have a conversation with your peers to determine how you can work together even more effectively next time.

CONVERSATIONS BY MANAGERS OF MANAGERS WITH THEIR HIGH POTENTIALS

The first-line managers who work for you reach their goals through others. For some, especially those who possessed extraordinary skills as individual contributors, directing others will be more challenging than doing the work themselves. You are familiar with this challenge because you have faced it. When you guide first-line managers through this major transition, shift their perspective from a technical to a management mindset. Their jobs entail mostly management tasks, such as organizing, scheduling, and evaluating work, with a sprinkling of leadership tasks. Coach them to balance the two. Notice that personally performing production work is not on either of your priority lists.

- **Building relationships.** Some first-line managers who work for you may have been your peers in the past. Have you held a baseline conversation with them to explain your expectations and hear their concerns? Coach them to reinvent and strengthen their relationships with you and to cooperate with other managers. Expect to spend a lot of time mentoring them to recognize differences between management and leadership mindsets and to develop both.

- **Developing others.** Developing the managers who report to you is essential for your next promotion; it deserves priority attention. New first-line managers are likely to need assistance in dividing projects into tasks, defining completion criteria, and providing useful feedback. Cultivate their management mindset by challenging them to resist the temptation to do production work. Also show them how to motivate and train their people—the leadership portion of their job.
- **Making decisions.** Resist the temptation to participate in day-to-day production decisions. Instead of answering the questions first-line managers ask, ask them what they recommend and why. Unless you are absolutely certain their ideas will not work, let them implement them to ensure that they learn from both successes and failures. Encourage them to engage their people's knowledge and experience in the decision-making process. Allowing first-line managers to make decisions and learn from the results is an effective way to develop their judgment gene and enhance their decision-making skills.
- **Taking action.** To reach your objectives, get your first-line managers to work together effectively. Coach them to share resources and to ask for more when necessary. Encourage them to continuously look for ways to streamline their business processes and to use new tools and technologies in creative ways.

Your ability to meet the challenges and answer the questions we have posed in conversations with your boss, peers, and high potentials will be evaluated when you take the online leadership assessment. As a manager of managers, you are not expected to know everything there is to know about leadership or management. After you take the assessment, you will receive feedback that identifies areas where you are performing at or above the manager-of-managers level, and areas you may want to improve. Using the results, you will be able to prepare an online personal action plan that will accelerate your future success.

CHAPTER 28

CONVERSATIONS FOR FIRST-LINE MANAGERS

Never tell people how to do things. Tell them what to do
and they will surprise you with their ingenuity.
—GENERAL GEORGE S. PATTON

Welcome to management! You have achieved a significant career milestone. You may have been promoted because you were the most skilled or most productive independent contributor among the candidates or perhaps because you demonstrated management and leadership potential. Ideally, you were promoted for both reasons. What you do with this opportunity will set the stage for your future success. Now is the time to show that you are a high-potential executive with an aptitude for leadership. Start by waving good-bye to your independent contributor mindset. As a first-line manager, most of your time will be spent mastering the management mindset. Your performance will be measured by how well your people perform—not by the results of your direct efforts. Your past accomplishments as an individual contributor, no matter how many accolades you received or how big your bonuses were, are not relevant to your future success.

THE FIRST-LINE MANAGER'S ROLE

Your role is to manage a team of independent contributors to perform specified tasks on schedule and according to budget while meeting quality standards. You probably know how to do the tasks well, which is one reason why you were promoted. Your performance will be graded on what your team produces (the management side) and how well you engage and inspire your people to become top performers (the leadership side). The third determinant of your success is how efficiently your team works together. Some leaders intuitively balance the management and leadership mindsets—but most high potentials have to figure it out as they go along.

Your first challenge is to avoid thinking that your people will mimic what you did in their position. They are not you, so they naturally will not do things the way you did them—nor should they. They each have unique strengths to leverage. The second challenge is to clearly communicate what must be done, who will do it, by when, and how they will be evaluated and rewarded. The third challenge is to form relationships that motivate your high potentials to perform. There is a good chance that some of your direct reports wanted your promotion and were disappointed when they did not get it. Demonstrate by your leadership conversations that you were the right choice.

CONVERSATIONS BY FIRST-LINE MANAGERS WITH THEIR BOSS

You have the opportunity to excel in a new position and adapt to change. You have not been anointed as the master of a kingdom. You are one of the king's knights—but just a step above the laborers. Save the celebration until after your first review. In most organizations, your boss will offer training and coaching to you—avail yourself of those resources. Conversations with your boss will be vital in helping you learn, perhaps for the first time, how to produce results through others.

- **Building relationships.** Ask for frequent baseline and feedback conversations with your boss, and demonstrate a thirst for learning during those conversations. Also accept coaching from other people, and pass the lessons on to your high potentials. Seek to understand and emulate the effective relationship behaviors that are used among senior executives in your organization.

- **Developing others.** Show your boss that you are willing to learn and to lead your team's growth. Ask what strengths led to your promotion and probe for areas to improve. Request ongoing feedback from your boss. Be flexible, but do not allow your boss to skip those feedback sessions. Show your boss that you can resist the urge to be a hero: delegate work to your people and coach them.

- **Making decisions.** Learn and apply the process your boss uses to make decisions and engage your people in your decision making. Ask for an explanation when your boss makes a decision that does not seem to fit the facts as you see them. Do not challenge the decision; rather, try to understand it. In fact, do not rebut your boss's decisions unless you have vital new information. But when you do, speak up. Use the same practice in dealing with your people: invite them to ask you to explain your decisions and encourage them to offer their viewpoints.

- **Taking action.** Ensure that there is agreement with your boss on (1) your team's goals, (2) external people with whom you must coordinate, (3) resources you control, and (4) the boundaries of actions you may take on your own. Plan before you act, and review the plan with your boss. Tell your boss when a major change occurs or there are sizeable deviations—either positive or negative—from the expected results. After completing a major initiative, review with your boss the actions you took to determine how even better results can be achieved next time.

CONVERSATIONS BY FIRST-LINE MANAGERS WITH THEIR PEERS

Experienced first-line managers are your new best friends. They know the ropes and can teach you the secrets. This is a two-way street: you are expected to assist them as well. You will find that you have strengths that other first-line managers are missing, and they have capabilities that they could teach you. Peer coaching and mentoring can propel everyone to higher levels of success.

- **Building relationships.** Respect and trust others, and learn how to earn their trust and respect. It may seem as though you are competing with them, but you cannot win the high-potential lottery by operating independently. They will be your peers for years to come, so be a resource to each other. Everyone wins when you all exceed your goals. Develop best practices together, find ways to assist each other, and celebrate your successes.
- **Developing others.** You are learning the mechanics of leading and managing—share your experiences, discuss them, and learn from them. Coach each other to offer and accept feedback as part of these conversations. Focus on what, not who, is right. Collaborate to identify and develop your high potentials.
- **Making decisions.** Ask your peers what decisions they would make given the facts you have. They often will offer views that you did not see. Base your decisions on the organization's goals, not just your goals. At times, it may feel as though you have to give up something to endorse a mutually beneficial decision, but in the long run you will find that everyone succeeds at a higher level when decisions are made in that context.
- **Taking action.** Joint actions generally turn out better because more people are vested in their success. Discuss the industry and organizational changes you are seeing. Any change that affects you probably affects them too. Consciously try to transform changes and problems into opportunities. Be frank with each other about actions that worked and did not work; let your learning benefit everyone.

CONVERSATIONS BY FIRST-LINE MANAGERS WITH THEIR HIGH POTENTIALS

Some who now work for you were your peers before your promotion. Hold baseline conversations to discuss mutual expectations and have regular feedback conversations to make sure each of them is reaching his goals. Observe how your boss and other executives treat you and how their actions make you feel. Develop your unique management and leadership persona by emulating the best practices you have seen, consciously avoiding bad practices, and developing new ways to manage and lead.

- **Building relationships.** Recall bosses who inspired your growth: bring that inspiration to your team by borrowing techniques from them. Recognize high potentials who offer fresh ideas. Demonstrate the importance of relationships and how to build them by forming transactional relationships to help your high potentials reach their goals. Remember that your mood affects your people's performance; if you are having a bad day, do not let it ruin everyone else's day.
- **Developing others.** You are responsible not only for your own development but also for developing the technical and management skills of your people and for modeling good leadership. Learn to mentor and coach your staff. Take a genuine interest in their growth, celebrate their successes, and recognize their contributions. After all, you liked it when you were treated that way.
- **Making decisions.** Become curious and infect your people with curiosity. Ask your high potentials for their ideas and views on key decisions. See what they have to offer by asking insightful questions to assist them in making effective decisions. This approach will make it clear who the high potentials are on your team.
- **Taking action.** Involve everyone in developing plans and defining measures of success. Do not make assumptions—instead dig for the facts and the underlying reasons for what is happening. Caution your people that the best-laid plans often change; thus feedback and flexibility are essential as they take action.

We have posed sizable challenges for conversations with your boss, peers, and high potentials—but assistance is on the way. The next chapter will guide you through the assessment that measures your skills in each of the four types of leadership conversation. The good news is that as a first-line manager, you are not expected to have a perfect score. When you complete the assessment, you will receive feedback that identifies areas where in your leadership conversations you are performing at and below your current position. Using your assessment results, you will prepare a personal action plan using tools at myleadershipconversations.com. The website will also be a resource to answer your specific leadership and management questions.

CHAPTER 29

YOUR PERSONAL ACTION PLAN

When you have exhausted all possibilities, remember this: you haven't.
—THOMAS EDISON

The next step in your journey to great leadership will take place after reading this chapter, when you take the leadership assessment and develop your personal action plan online. Up to this point, we have discussed management and leadership as they apply to high potentials in general. Some concepts aligned with your specific needs, some you had already mastered, and some were not relevant to your current situation. Some concepts may have resonated with you more than others because, consciously or unconsciously, you know which parts of your leadership and management mindsets you would like to enhance and which are serving you well.

The four types of leadership conversations may have felt familiar because you participate in them regularly—or hear them happening at levels above you. You may feel effective in holding some of the four conversations and uncomfortable with others. The intent of the assessment is to measure your management and leadership aptitude in each of the four conversations as the basis for preparing a personal action plan—your personal strategic plan as a high potential.

One common business maxim is, "If it's not in writing, it doesn't exist." So we ask that you capture your thoughts, strategies, actions, and measures of success in writing. We understand that you are busy, so we designed the Internet-based leadership assessment and online tools to help you build your personal action plan efficiently. Your plan will contain actions that are unique to your industry, your position, and your concerns. and will include possibilities that you ordinarily would not have considered. Based on results of the assessment, your plan will be tailored to the leadership and management requirements of your current position and the next higher position.

In general, the assessment applies the following guidelines:

- **First-line manager:** shows basic understanding of effective management practices and awareness of the need for leadership competencies
- **Manager of managers:** is proficient in using best management practices to improve performance; consciously uses leadership conversations to motivate people to high performance; coaches and mentors high potentials effectively
- **Executive leader:** is results driven—management effectiveness is an unconscious competency; is proficient at visioning to create the future and inspiring people to achieve it; consistently demonstrates emotional intelligence
- **CXO leader:** has established effective management practices and leadership standards across the enterprise in his or her area of responsibility; holds effective leadership conversations across all levels and all topics
- **CEO:** has a clear vision for the future and a strategy for getting there, and articulates both to stakeholders; consciously builds an organizational culture that embraces high performance standards, ethics, and a leadership mindset

Your leadership assessment will provide guidance on where to focus to become great in your current position and to prepare for the next level. You have a responsibility to everyone in your organization to be the best leader you can be—and should expect the same from others. If you are reading this book with your colleagues or an external group, consider sharing your action plans and mentoring each other. Whom would you trust to mentor or coach you?

GUIDE TO TAKING THE LEADERSHIP ASSESSMENT

The leadership assessment will evaluate the degree to which you possess the management and leadership mindsets and skills discussed in this book as appropriate to your current position. In areas where you have mastered the skills needed for your current level, your personal action plan will guide you to develop proficiencies for the next level. If you are not yet fully competent in your current role, we suggest you focus on the skills to reach competence there first. After a few months, retake the assessment and refine the plan for earning your next promotion. Your personal action plan will point you toward areas that will provide high value for you.

Your personal action plan will have two distinct yet interrelated sections that are designed to be developed and implemented concurrently. After you have taken the assessment, the online plan development tool will guide you through preparation of

- **Your personal management plan.** This is the "doing" plan—what you will do to fulfill your high potential. It focuses on actions you will complete during the next six months or so to leverage your strengths, make improvements in shadow areas, and mitigate your weaknesses. The plan will help you develop the skills, competencies, and techniques you need to be effective as a manager and leader.
- **Your personal leadership plan.** This is the "being" plan—who you will be in order to fulfill your high potential. It focuses on who you are as a person, a manager, and a leader, and builds your personal brand based on your strengths. In building your brand, you will become clear about yourself, your stakeholders, and the unique value you deliver. This plan zeroes in on what you can do to show up as a powerful leader who connects with, aligns, and inspires followers.

Now that you have a feeling for the value your personal action plan will provide, take the assessment and develop your action plan by following these four steps:

1. **Take the leadership assessment.** Log into www.myleadershipconversations.com, register your name and email address, and take the assessment. Consider retaking this assessment every three to six months (or in preparation for your next promotion) in order to monitor your progress in translating learning into action.
2. **Review assessment results.** The assessment feedback will be returned automatically to your email address. It will identify leadership

conversations where you scored at, below, and above your current position, and pinpoint areas that need attention. The feedback will help you choose high-value actions to insert in your action plan. You also can add actions based on unique requirements of your industry and organization, as well as specific areas where you want to brand yourself as having a unique competency.

3. **Create your action plan.** The website will guide you through preparation of the management and leadership sections of your personal action plan. Each section will address all four types of leadership conversations. The actions you put in the plan should be executable within a six-month window. By reviewing the actions and updating the status in your personal action plan regularly (we recommend weekly), you will accelerate performance improvements that will make you a great leader. Only you will have access to your online plan. However, you may want to print portions of the plan to use in a study group or to review with your boss, coach, or mentor.

4. **Tap into additional resources.** The action plan will reference sections of this book that you may want to review if assessment results show there is learning to be done. The website provides additional digital tools and identifies resources, such as education and training courses and other periodicals and books, that offer leadership insights.

We invite you to communicate with leadership experts, other readers, and us on the website. When you interact with others who face similar leadership challenges, you will be working toward common goals using the same methodology and tools on your quest to become a great leader.

WHAT COMES NEXT?

You can take your next steps in the journey to becoming a great leader on an individual basis, as part of a group in your organization, in a public forum at myleadershipconversations.com, or in a combination of all three. As you climb the leadership ladder and lead larger and more complex groups of people, you will benefit from these additional resources.

This book enables you to participate in Internet-based leadership conversations with your peers, leadership experts, and us about the challenges and opportunities you face. These conversations will be enhanced because everyone shares a common language. New features, content, and digital tools will be added regularly. As of this writing, the following resources are available on the website:

- **Keep the conversations going (public forum).** Participation in this forum is structured by topic under the four types of leadership conversation. You can initiate a conversation by asking a question or submitting an article on a topic. You are also encouraged to contribute your knowledge and viewpoints about ongoing topics. Both of these are powerful ways to continue to learn, because people learn by teaching and being open to new ideas. We encourage you to apply the three perspectives of conversation (what matters to you, asking questions of others, and what else is possible) as you participate in the forum.

- **Special-interest conversations.** Access to the special-interest forum is open to any reader who shares the challenges of the following groups (other groups can be created upon request):
  - Being the chief executive officer (CEO)
  - Leading a government agency
  - Leading a military unit
  - Leading a nonprofit organization
  - Leading an educational institution

- **Conversations with experts.** In this forum, readers may submit a question to engage a top business strategist, coach, or author. If the expert or other author has not yet participated in a previous strategic question, we will do our best to entice him or her into joining the conversation and discussing his or her views.

- **Peer coaching and cross-mentoring (private forum).** This forum is a community of high performers working together to ensure that everyone realizes his or her potential. At the time of this writing, this feature is a unique resource. There is a tutorial on how to peer-coach and cross-mentor, and a mechanism to find those who are willing to cross-mentor and peer-coach you on a no-fee basis in a private conversation. You may convene a group of like-minded people or limit the conversation to two people—entry into each group is permission based. You also can offer your expertise to peer-coach or cross-mentor other high potentials.

- **Supplemental information.** The supplemental information, which is open to all readers, is organized by subtopic within each of the four leadership conversations. It contains materials that augment discussions in the book and enables you to push learning to deeper levels.

We are always open to recommendations to expand the value of the website by adding content or starting new forums. Let us know via email or the website how we can make this resource more valuable and user-friendly for you.

LEADERSHIP COACHES AND SURVEY INSTRUMENTS

In addition to forums, peer coaching, and supplementary materials, the website also identifies professional coaches—many of whom we have worked with personally—who have experience working with the methodologies and concepts in this book. They all have appropriate certifications and first-rate professional reputations. You may want to engage a coach for individual coaching or to facilitate a workshop based on *Leadership Conversations*.

The website also catalogs leadership survey instruments, 360-degree assessments, and other tools from world-class training organizations. One of the most valuable services that a coach can offer to you and your organization is to conduct a leadership survey or a 360-degree assessment. The results will fuel conversations that are critical to your future. Four words of advice: listen, reflect, learn, and act. Be open to feedback because this openness indicates that you are a learner and have high potential for growth.

A professional coach can assist you in performing better in the short term and reaching your high potential faster than you would otherwise. A coach does not need to know the fine points of your industry—that is the role of a mentor. Instead, a coach's job is to assist you in becoming aware of your shadows, defining your leadership brand, and acquiring the competencies required to become a great leader.

Notes

Chapter 7

1. Grant, A. M., Gino, F., and Hofmann, D. A. "Reversing the Extraverted Leadership Advantage: The Role of Employee Proactivity." *Academy of Management Journal,* 2011, *54*(3), 528–550.

2. The exact origin of this model is unknown. Partial attributions have been found: Joan Flemming (1953); R. A. Hogan (1964); and an interview with Lewis W. Robinson, *Personnel Journal,* July 1974, *53*(7), citing the four categories. Gordon Training International originated its version of this model in the early 1970s.

Chapter 17

1. Senge, P. M. *The Fifth Discipline.* New York: Doubleday Business, 1994.

Bibliography

Leadership in General

Blanchard, K., and Hodges, P. *Servant Leader*. Nashville, TN: Thomas Nelson, 2003.

Boyatzis, R., and McKee, A. *Resonant Leadership*. Boston: Harvard School Business Press, 2005.

Covey, S. R. *The 7 Habits of Highly Effective People*. New York: Free Press, 2004.

Kouzes, J. M., and Posner, B. Z. *The Leadership Challenge*. San Francisco: Jossey-Bass, 2007.

Conversations in General

DuPree, M. *Leadership Is an Art*. New York: Crown Business, 2004.

Goulston, M. *Just Listen: Discover the Secret to Getting Through to Absolutely Everyone*. New York: AMACOM, 2010.

Patterson, K., Grenny, J., McMillan, R., and Switzler, A. *Crucial Conversations: Tools for Talking When Stakes Are High*. New York: McGraw-Hill, 2002.

Stone, D., Patton, B., and Heen, S. *Difficult Conversations: How to Discuss What Matters Most*. New York: Penguin Books, 2000.

Building Relationships

Ferrazzi, K. *Never Eat Alone: And Other Secrets to Success, One Relationship at a Time*. New York: Currency Doubleday, 2005.

Goleman, D., Boyatzis, R., and McKee, A. *Primal Leadership: Realizing the Power of Emotional Intelligence*. Boston: Harvard Business School Press, 2002.

Kotter, J. P., and Cohen, D. S. *The Heart of Change: Real-Life Stories of How People Change Their Organizations*. Boston: Harvard Business School Press, 2002.

Roberto, M. A. *Why Great Leaders Don't Take Yes for an Answer: Managing for Conflict and Consensus*. Upper Saddle River, NJ: Pearson Prentice Hall, 2005.

Shell, R. G., and Moussa, M. *The Art of WOO: Using Strategic Persuasion to Sell Your Ideas*. New York: Portfolio, 2007.

Tannen, D. *That's Not What I Meant: How Conversational Style Makes or Breaks Relationships*. New York: Harper Perennial, 2011.

Developing Others

Charan, R., Drotter, S., and Noel, J. *The Leadership Pipeline: How to Build the Leadership Powered Company* (2nd ed.). San Francisco: Jossey-Bass, 2011.

Cooperrider, D. L. *Appreciative Inquiry: A Positive Revolution in Change*. San Francisco: Berrett-Koehler, 2005.

Davenport, T. H. *Thinking for a Living: How to Get Better Performances and Results from Knowledge Workers*. Boston: Harvard Business School Press, 2005.

Kouzes, J. M., and Posner, B. Z. *Encouraging the Heart: A Leader's Guide to Rewarding and Recognizing Others*. San Francisco: Jossey-Bass, 1999.

Making Decisions

Kouzes, J. M., and Posner, B. Z. *Credibility: How Leaders Gain and Lose It, Why People Demand It* (2nd ed.). San Francisco: Jossey-Bass, 2011.

Marquardt, M. *Leading with Questions*. San Francisco: Jossey-Bass, 2005.

Senge, P. *The Fifth Discipline: The Art and Practice of the Learning Organization*. New York: Doubleday, 2006.

Tichy, N. M., and Bennis, W. G. *Judgment: How Winning Leaders Make Great Calls*. New York: Portfolio Trade, 2009.

Taking Action

Blanchard, K., and Miller, M. *The Secret: What Great Leaders Know—and Do*. San Francisco: Berrett-Koehler, 2009.

Ciampa, D., and Watkins, M. *Right from the Start: Taking Charge in a New Leadership Role*. Boston: Harvard Business School Press, 1999.

Goldsmith, M. *What Got You Here Won't Get You There: A Round Table Comic: How Successful People Become Even More Successful.* New York: Hyperion, 2007.

Horwath, R. *Deep Dive: The Proven Method for Building Strategy, Focusing Your Resources, and Taking Smart Action.* Austin, TX: Greenleaf Book Group Press, 2009.

Joiner, B., and Josephs, S. *Leadership Agility: Five Levels of Mastery for Anticipating and Initiating Change.* San Francisco: Jossey-Bass, 2006.

Kundtz, D. *Stopping: How to Be Still When You Have to Keep Going.* Berkeley, CA: Conari Press, 1998.

Acknowledgments

We thank the people who played an essential role in publishing this book. First, Carole Sargent in the Office of Scholarly Publications at Georgetown University, who got us started in the right direction by introducing us to our incredible agent, John Willig. John in turn connected us to our editor, Karen Murphy, at Jossey-Bass, who added immeasurably to the book with valuable suggestions and insights. These caring people saw promise in the book and challenged us to demonstrate our potential in writing it.

Equally important is Gordon Swartz, who gave Alan the opportunity to be a professor at the McDonough School of Business at Georgetown, where many of the ideas in this book were formed and tested. Gordon also read every word of the drafts and provided helpful feedback. We also thank Tyler Schaeffer for his counsel in brand marketing and social media strategies. Others who played an important role in challenging us to improve this work were Jim Schleckser, Bob Busch, Kristin Haffert, Bernard Bailey, Mark Bowers, John Bukartek, and Carol Roche Austin. In addition, we acknowledge James Li for contributing conceptual artwork. We thank these people for sharing their time and creativity, both of which are precious indeed.

Alan S. Berson
I thank my parents for their unwavering belief in the contributions I would someday make. I wish my mom were here to see the book on the shelves, and

am thrilled that my dad is able—at ninety-four—to walk into the bookstore and show it to his friends. I also thank my daughters, Caroline and Julie, for teaching me much about relationships, each in her own way. As my wife and trusted adviser, Leslie helped keep me sane and gave me the space and support during the process of writing this book. Finally, a thank you to Dick; our leadership conversations resulted in a much more powerful book than I initially envisioned.

Richard G. Stieglitz

From the bottom of my heart, I thank my wife, Mary Ellen, my best friend and biggest teacher, who has been supportive and understanding during the thousands of hours of writing and meetings with Alan. And a special thank you to my perceptive daughters, April and Tracy: a teacher learns a lot from his students. And also a warm thank you to all my associates and clients before, during, and after my twenty-two years at RGS Associates; I treasure the lessons I learned and the memories of our work together.

About the Authors

Alan S. Berson, MBA, CLC, PCC

Alan Berson's leadership experience and stories were collected over thirty years during eleven different careers in leadership, marketing, finance, and strategic planning at Fortune 500 firms, including Gillette, Bausch & Lomb, Lincoln First Bank, Marriott (as a contractor); a VC-funded firm; and start-up companies. Berson has been an executive coach for twelve years and a leadership professor for the past four years.

Berson earned his BS and MBA from Wharton, received his Certificate in Leadership Coaching (CLC) from Georgetown University, achieved the PCC certification from the International Coaching Federation, and is certified to deliver assessments of the CCL, PDI, and StrengthsFinder. He has done team and individual coaching at dozens of organizations, including NASA, NCI, KPMG, LexisNexis, Children's Hospital Foundation, and Bearing Point.

At the McDonough School of Business at Georgetown University, Berson taught and coached in the Executive Masters in Leadership and in the Georgetown/ESADE Global Executive MBA programs; he also taught change management to second-year MBAs and in Booz Allen Hamilton's Change Management Advanced Practitioner Program (CMAP). He is a learning director at Wharton Executive Education. Berson also speaks at corporate and industry events.

Richard G. Stieglitz, PhD

Stieglitz's leadership skills were acquired during forty years of practical experience, mentoring by trusted advisers, and service in the U.S. Navy. He built and later sold a consulting company that helped executives in federal agencies lead change. His company grew rapidly because of his ability to guide high-potential employees through two industry-shaking events—the fall of the Berlin Wall and the rise of the Internet—and recurring economic peaks and valleys.

Stieglitz earned a PhD in nuclear engineering from Rensselaer Polytechnic Institute, and received extensive leadership training and experience as a U.S. naval officer refueling nuclear submarines. After leaving the Navy, he became vice president of a software company and director of defense consulting for an aerospace firm. In 1984, Stieglitz founded his company and in 2006 sold it to devote time to writing, executive coaching, and consulting. He has written three previous books on the subjects of personal change, change in business, and mergers and acquisitions. Stieglitz also publishes monthly e-letters titled *My Leadership Conversations* to business contacts and speaks frequently at industry and government forums on the subjects of leadership, change, relationships, and growing privately held companies.

The authors invite you to visit www.myleadershipconversations.com—use it as a source of learning and building relationships. Tell us about your successes and which portions of the book were useful in your leadership journey and your promotions. In addition, we welcome your feedback and recommendations and will do our best to reply promptly and personally—we want to continue the leadership conversation with you.

Index

Page references followed by *fig* indicate an illustrated figure.

B

Baby boomers, 16

Baruch, Bernard, 173

Baseline conversations: about priorities, 119–120; about relationships, 119; description of, 115, 117–118; on performance standards, 118–119; suggestions when the usual routines do not work, 125–126

Behaviors: indicating a sincere search for the third alternative, 172; "Ladder of Inference" on, 222; reinforced through stories of success, 145

Blockbuster, 215

Brainstorming: description of, 175–176; techniques used for better, 176–177

Building relationships: benefits of, 35; creating resources by, 47–48; CXO leadership conversations on, 246, 247, 248; embracing differences for, 83–88; getting started on the right foot for, 59–60; progression of, 51fig–54; ten ways to practice great leadership for, 88. *See also* Conversations to build relationships; Relationships

C

C-suite. *See* CXO leaders

Calendar: how organization position impacts your, 120; setting priorities items on your, 119–120

Capital investment, 190

Caring standard, 28

Carroll, Lewis, 207

Celebrating: both small and big successes, 143–144; making work fun through, 145; people, 144–145

Centers for Disease Control and Prevention, 14

Change: attitudes toward, 192–194, 195; being willing to change your mind about, 195; challenges related to making a, 187–188; compassionate leaders helping employees to adjust with, 220; drivers of, 189–190, 195; effective implementation of, 220–221; failure of forced, 218–220; innovation for, 191–192, 195, 234, 235, 242; leadership as the essence of, 218; leadership decision to make a, 190–192; open-door policy to identify emerging, 215; organizational ability to response to, 164; recognized as the natural order, 216–217; staying ahead of, 188–189. *See also* Conversations to make decisions; Conversations to take action

Change attitudes/styles: being willing to change your, 195; fence-sitters, 193, 194, 195; traditionalists, 193, 194, 195; trailblazers, 192–194, 195

Change drivers: global relationships, 190; intense competition, 190; large investors, 190; learn to recognize, 195; ubiquitous communication, 189

Chief executive officers (CEOs): as the leader at the top, 245; mistake of not mentoring their CXO leaders, 93–94; personal action plan guidelines for, 270; planning for CXO to succeed, 101–102; realizing that they don't have all the answers, 178–180

Chief financial officer (CFO), 245

Chief human capital officer (CHCO), 245

Chief operating officer (COO), 245